Book Cover by Jim Olen.

UNDERSTAND YOUR RIGHTS

TENANT POWER

NEW YORK

A Renter's Plain-English Guide

NGOZI E. BOLIN, ESQ.

Contents

Legal Disclaimer VII

Foreword 1

Part I: Who Makes the Rules 7

1. State Law vs. City Law 9
2. Why New York Tenant Law Is Unlike Anywhere Else 21
3. The HSTPA and Why Everything Changed in 2019 31

Part II: Rent Control, Rent Stabilization & Legal Rent 41

4. Rent Control vs. Rent Stabilization 43
5. Is Your Apartment Rent-Stabilized? 53
6. Legal Rent, Rent Increases and Renewal Leases 65
7. Overcharge Claims 75
8. Reading Your Lease Like a Tenant Lawyer 85
9. Lease Renewals, Non-Renewals and Holdover Status 99

Part IV: Evictions and Just Cause 109

10. What "Just Cause" Eviction Means in New York 111
11. Owner Use, Demolition and Other Common Eviction Claims 121
12. Eviction Notices 131
13. What Actually Happens in New York Housing Court 143

Part V: Security Deposits, Fees & Move-Out Money 153

14. Security Deposit Limits and Strict Deadlines 155
15. Illegal Deductions and Triple-Damage Penalties 165
16. Application Fees, Move-In Fees and Illegal Charges 177

Part VI: Your Rights While Living In The Unit 187

17. Repairs, Habitability and Rent Withholding 189
18. Landlord Entry, Privacy and Harassment 201
19. Retaliation 211
20. Nonpayment of Rent and Late Fees 221
Part VII: Special Rental Situations 231
21. Roommates, Sublets and Unauthorized Occupants 233
22. Succession Rights 245
23. Illegal Apartments and Certificate of Occupancy Problems 257
Part VIII: The Endgame: Buyouts, Negotiation & Strategy 269
24. Small Landlords, Owner-Occupied Buildings and Exemptions 271
25. Buyouts, Cash-for-Keys and Tenant Waivers 283
26. When You're Not Perfectly in the Right 295
27. When to Fight, When to Negotiate, When to Get Help 307
28. Using New York Tenant Rights Without Burning Out 319
Appendices 327
Appendix A 329
Appendix B 343
Appendix C 355
Appendix D 361
Appendix E 375
About the Author 385

Legal Disclaimer

Important Notice to Readers

THIS BOOK IS PROVIDED FOR INFORMATIONAL AND EDUCATIONAL PURPOSES ONLY AND IS NOT INTENDED TO CONSTITUTE LEGAL ADVICE.

No Attorney-Client Relationship

The information contained in this book does not create an attorney-client relationship between the author, publisher, and any reader or user of this material. Reading this book, accessing its content, or using any information contained herein does not establish any professional relationship or create any duties or obligations on the part of the author or publisher to any reader.

Not a Substitute for Professional Legal Counsel

The content of this book is general in nature and may not apply to your specific situation. Legal matters are highly fact-specific and jurisdiction-dependent. Laws, regulations, court decisions, and legal interpretations change frequently and vary significantly between jurisdictions. Nothing in this book should be used as a substitute for competent legal advice from a licensed attorney in your jurisdiction who is familiar with the specific facts of your case.

YOU SHOULD ALWAYS CONSULT WITH A QUALIFIED ATTORNEY BEFORE MAKING ANY LEGAL DECISIONS OR TAKING ANY ACTION BASED ON INFORMATION CONTAINED IN THIS BOOK.

Accuracy and Currency of Information

While every effort has been made to ensure the accuracy of the information contained in this book at the time of publication, the author and publisher make no representations or warranties regarding the completeness, accuracy, reliability, or currency of the information provided. Laws and legal precedents change constantly, and what may have been accurate at the time of writing may no longer be current or applicable.

The information in this book reflects the law as understood by the author as of the publication date. Legal developments occurring after the publication date are not reflected in this material.

Jurisdictional Limitations

Laws vary significantly among different countries, states, provinces, and localities. The information in this book may be based primarily on the laws of specific jurisdictions and may not be applicable in your location. Local laws should always be consulted, and local legal counsel should be retained for matters involving specific jurisdictions.

Limitation of Liability

TO THE FULLEST EXTENT PERMITTED BY LAW, THE AUTHOR, PUBLISHER, EDITORS, CONTRIBUTORS, AND DISTRIBUTORS OF THIS BOOK DISCLAIM ALL LIABILITY FOR ANY LOSS, DAMAGE, OR INJURY ARISING FROM THE USE OF OR RELIANCE ON THE INFORMATION CONTAINED HEREIN, WHETHER SUCH LIABILITY ARISES IN CONTRACT, TORT, STRICT LIABILITY, OR OTHERWISE.

This limitation applies to all damages or injuries, including but not limited to:

- Direct, indirect, incidental, and consequential damages
- Lost profits or business opportunities
- Legal fees and costs

- Punitive or exemplary damages
- Any other economic or non-economic losses

No Warranties

THIS BOOK IS PROVIDED "AS IS" WITHOUT WARRANTY OF ANY KIND, EXPRESS OR IMPLIED, INCLUDING BUT NOT LIMITED TO WARRANTIES OF MERCHANTABILITY, FITNESS FOR A PARTICULAR PURPOSE, OR NON-INFRINGEMENT.

Individual Circumstances

Every legal situation is unique. The examples, case studies, and scenarios presented in this book are for illustrative purposes only and may not reflect the full complexity of actual legal situations. The outcomes described may not be achievable in your circumstances, and past results do not guarantee future outcomes.

Updates and Revisions

The author and publisher are under no obligation to update or revise the content of this book to reflect changes in the law or legal practice. Readers are encouraged to verify all information with current legal sources and qualified legal professionals.

Third-Party Content and References

Any references to third-party materials, websites, organizations, or publications are provided for informational purposes only and do not constitute an endorsement of such materials or entities. The author and publisher are not responsible for the content, accuracy, or availability of third-party materials.

Compliance with Professional Rules

Readers who are legal professionals should ensure that their use of any information in this book complies with applicable professional conduct rules, ethical requirements, and licensing obligations in their jurisdiction.

Intellectual Property Notice

This book is protected by copyright and other intellectual property laws. The information provided is for personal, educational, and non-commercial use only. Any commercial use, reproduction, or distribution requires express written permission from the copyright holder.

Severability

If any portion of this disclaimer is held to be invalid or unenforceable, the remaining portions shall remain in full force and effect.

BY READING AND USING THIS BOOK, YOU ACKNOWLEDGE THAT YOU HAVE READ, UNDERSTOOD, AND AGREE TO BE BOUND BY THE TERMS OF THIS DISCLAIMER.

IF YOU DO NOT AGREE WITH THESE TERMS, DO NOT USE THIS BOOK.

Foreword

The Apartment on Flatbush

Maria signed the lease on a Thursday.

The apartment was a one-bedroom in a prewar building off Flatbush Avenue. Original hardwood, high ceilings, a kitchen window that actually opened. The rent was $2,150 a month. The landlord's representative said it was market-rate, handed her a stack of papers, and told her the standard move-in costs were first month, last month, and a security deposit equal to six weeks' rent.

Maria paid it all. She was relocating from North Carolina, had seventy-two hours before her new job started, and didn't want to lose the apartment. She didn't ask questions. She didn't know there were questions to ask.

For the first year, things were fine. The heat worked. The super was slow but responsive. She paid rent on time, every time.

Then the letter arrived.

Her landlord was not renewing the lease. She had sixty days to vacate. The letter cited a provision of New York State law and included language about the tenancy reverting to month-to-month status. It looked official. It sounded final.

Maria started packing.

She mentioned it to a coworker, casually, the way you mention something you've already accepted. The coworker, who had lived in Brooklyn for eleven years, said five words that changed everything:

Have you checked the rent history?

Maria didn't know what rent history was. She didn't know she could request one. She didn't know her building was rent-stabilized, or that the term meant anything specific, or that it applied to her unit regardless of what the landlord called it.

She requested the records. They arrived three weeks later.

Her apartment had been rent-stabilized continuously for over thirty years. The legal rent, the maximum her landlord was allowed to charge, was $1,740. She had been paying $410 more than that every month since move-in. The "last month's rent" she'd paid upfront was illegal. The security deposit exceeded the legal cap by hundreds of dollars. And the non-renewal notice? In a rent-stabilized apartment, her landlord couldn't simply refuse to renew. He needed a legally recognized reason, and he didn't have one.

Maria didn't move out.

She filed an overcharge complaint. She recovered thousands of dollars. Her rent dropped to the legal amount. Her lease was renewed. And the non-renewal notice, the letter that had felt like a verdict, turned out to be unenforceable before she ever opened it.

None of this happened because Maria found a loophole. There was no trick, no technicality, no aggressive legal maneuvering. The law had been on her side the entire time. She just hadn't known it existed.

Everything Maria lost (the overcharged rent, the illegal fees, the weeks of stress and apartment hunting) she lost because of one thing: she didn't know the rules. And her landlord was counting on that.

Maria's story is a composite, but nothing in it is invented. Every element, the illegal deposit, the inflated rent, the bogus non-renewal, the stabilization status hidden in plain sight, comes from real New York tenant disputes. They happen every day, across every borough, to renters who are smart, careful, and still blindsided.

They happen because New York tenant law is powerful but not intuitive. The protections are real. The penalties are serious. The leverage is substantial. But none of it activates automatically. Tenant rights in New York only become real when a tenant knows enough to invoke them.

That gap, between what the law provides and what renters actually know, is where landlords operate. Not always through fraud. Often through silence, selective explanation, and the reasonable assumption that most tenants won't look further.

This book exists to close that gap.

Tenant Power: New York was written for renters, not lawyers. It translates New York tenant law into language you can actually use: when a rent increase arrives, when a deposit disappears, when a notice shows up on your door, when something feels wrong but you can't name why. It explains what the law requires, where landlords cut corners, and how to tell the difference between a legitimate demand and an illegal one.

You shouldn't have to learn these lessons the hard way. Maria almost did. This book exists so you don't have to.

How to Use This Book

You can read *Tenant Power: New York* two ways, and both are intentional.

Cover to cover if you want the full picture. The book is structured to build understanding progressively, from the legal system itself, to rent regulation, to eviction, to money, to daily life in the apartment, to endgame strategy. Each chapter connects to the ones around it. Reading in order gives you the framework to handle situations you haven't encountered yet.

Surgically if you have a problem right now. Each chapter is self-contained enough to use on its own. If you just got a rent increase, you don't need to read about eviction notices first. If you're staring at a security deposit deduction, you don't need the history of rent stabilization to understand your rights.

The guide below will get you to the right chapter fast.

Find Your Situation

I just signed a lease and want to understand what I agreed to. Go to Chapter 8: Reading Your Lease Like a Tenant Lawyer.

I'm not sure which laws apply to my apartment. Go to Chapter 1: State Law vs. City Law.

I think my apartment might be rent-stabilized. Go to Chapter 5: Is Your Apartment Rent-Stabilized?

My rent just went up and I'm not sure it's legal. Go to Chapter 6: Legal Rent, Rent Increases & Renewal Leases.

I think I've been overcharged on rent. Go to Chapter 7: Overcharge Claims: How to Get Your Money Back.

My landlord says my lease won't be renewed. Go to Chapter 9: Lease Renewals, Non-Renewals & Holdover Status.

I received an eviction notice. Go to Chapter 12: Eviction Notices: Why Many Are Invalid.

My landlord says they need the apartment for personal use. Go to Chapter 11: Owner Use, Demolition & Other Eviction Claims.

I have to go to housing court. Go to Chapter 13: What Actually Happens in Housing Court.

My landlord is keeping my security deposit. Go to Chapter 14: Security Deposit Limits and Strict Deadlines.

I was charged suspicious deductions after move-out. Go to Chapter 15: Illegal Deductions & Triple-Damage Penalties.

I was charged fees before moving in that seem too high. Go to Chapter 16: Application Fees, Move-In Fees & Illegal Charges.

Something is broken and my landlord won't fix it. Go to Chapter 17: Repairs, Habitability & Rent Withholding.

My landlord keeps entering my apartment. Go to Chapter 18: Landlord Entry, Privacy & Harassment.

I complained and now my landlord is retaliating. Go to Chapter 19: Retaliation: What It Is and How to Prove It.

I'm behind on rent and worried about eviction. Go to Chapter 20: Nonpayment of Rent & Late Fees.

I want to add a roommate or sublet my apartment. Go to Chapter 21: Roommates, Sublets & Unauthorized Occupants.

A family member lived here and I want to stay. Go to Chapter 22: Succession Rights.

My apartment might not be a legal unit. Go to Chapter 23: Illegal Apartments & Certificate of Occupancy Problems.

My landlord says they're exempt from tenant protections. Go to Chapter 24: Small Landlords, Owner-Occupied Buildings & Exemptions.

My landlord offered me money to leave. Go to Chapter 25: Buyouts, Cash-for-Keys & Tenant Waivers.

I made a mistake and I'm not sure where I stand. Go to Chapter 26: When You're Not Perfectly in the Right.

I need to decide whether to fight, negotiate, or get help. Go to Chapter 27: When to Fight, When to Negotiate, When to Get Help.

I need sample letters, checklists, or agency contacts. Go to the Appendices.

A Note Before You Begin

This book is not legal advice. It is legal information, written to help you understand a system that affects your home, your money, and your stability. It will help you spot problems, ask better questions, and know when professional help is worth the investment.

New York tenant law is powerful. But it is not self-executing. The protections in this book exist on paper whether you read them or not. They only protect you when you use them.

That's what this book is for.

Part I: Who Makes the Rules

(And Why It's So Confusing)

1

State Law vs. City Law

Which Rules Control Your Apartment?

If renting in New York feels confusing, it's because the law is layered on purpose.

New York tenant rights don't come from a single rulebook. They come from multiple overlapping systems, and which one controls your apartment depends on where you live, what kind of building you're in, and which law gives you more protection. Understanding how those layers work is the foundation of everything else in this book. It is also the first place landlords start exploiting what tenants don't know.

The Basic Rule Most Renters Never Learn

The principle is simple, even if the application is not.

State law sets the floor. City law can raise the ceiling.

New York State law applies everywhere in the state. It establishes baseline protections that every landlord must follow, regardless of location. But cities, and New York City in particular, are allowed to pass local tenant-protection laws that go further than state law, as long as they don't directly contradict it. When city law gives tenants more rights than state law, city law controls.

This means three things in practice.

State law is the minimum protection any New York renter receives. City law can add stronger, more specific rules on top of that minimum. And when a conflict arises, landlords must follow whichever rule benefits the tenant more.

Most tenants never learn this. They assume one set of rules applies everywhere, or they assume the lease is the final word, or they take their landlord's explanation at face value. Each of those assumptions can cost real money and real housing.

How the Layers Actually Stack

To understand how the system works, it helps to see the full picture.

At the top level, New York State statutes create the framework. The Real Property Law, the Real Property Actions and Proceedings Law, and the General Obligations Law all contain provisions that affect tenants. These statutes apply statewide. A renter in Syracuse is covered by the same baseline rules as a renter in the Bronx.

Below that, New York City has its own body of housing law. The New York City Administrative Code, the Housing Maintenance Code, and the Rent Stabilization Code all create protections that apply only within the five boroughs. These laws don't replace state law. They build on top of it, filling gaps and raising standards.

Then there are agency regulations. The Division of Housing and Community Renewal (DHCR, now part of Homes and Community Renewal or HCR) issues rules governing rent-stabilized apartments. The New York City Department of Housing Preservation and Development (HPD) enforces the housing code. These agencies interpret the law through administrative decisions that shape how rules actually work in practice.

Finally, there is case law. Court decisions, from Housing Court to the Court of Appeals, interpret statutes and regulations in ways that create binding precedent. A statute might say one thing on paper, but a court ruling might narrow, expand, or clarify what it means in a real dispute.

The result is a system where your rights as a tenant can depend on the intersection of a state statute, a city ordinance, an agency regulation, and a court decision that interpreted all three. No single source tells the whole story.

This complexity is not accidental. It reflects decades of legislative responses to housing crises, each adding new protections without fully replacing the old ones. For tenants who understand the system, that complexity creates leverage. For tenants who don't, it creates vulnerability.

When City Law Overrides State Law

City law overrides state law when three conditions are met.

First, the city must have legal authority to regulate housing. New York City has this authority through its charter and through specific grants of power from the state legislature. This is well established and rarely contested.

Second, the local rule must provide greater tenant protection than the comparable state rule. The standard is not whether the rules are different, but whether the local rule gives tenants more.

Third, the local rule must not directly contradict a state mandate. If the state legislature has explicitly preempted a particular area of housing law (meaning it has declared that only state rules apply), local law cannot override it. But preemption is the exception, not the rule. In most areas of tenant protection, cities retain the power to go further.

In practice, city law overrides state law constantly in New York City. This happens in areas that affect nearly every renter.

Eviction standards are stricter in the city than the state requires. Where state law might allow a landlord to terminate a tenancy with proper notice and no stated reason, city law may require just cause, meaning the landlord must have a legally recognized reason for the eviction.

Notice requirements are more demanding. State law sets minimum notice periods for lease terminations. City law, and local regulations governing rent-stabilized apartments, often require longer notice periods, additional disclosures, or specific forms that state law does not mandate.

Rent regulation enforcement is more aggressive locally. Rent stabilization is administered primarily through city-level systems, with rules that go well beyond what state law requires for unregulated apartments.

Harassment protections are broader in New York City. The city defines landlord harassment more expansively than state law, covering conduct like repeated buyout pressure, frivolous court filings, and deliberate service reductions.

Procedural rules in Housing Court create additional safeguards that do not exist in courts elsewhere in the state. These include mandatory pre-trial conferences, specific service requirements, and filing procedures designed to slow down improper evictions.

Tenants outside New York City may have fewer of these protections, or none at all, depending on whether their municipality has enacted its own local tenant laws. This is why location matters so much, and why advice from someone in a different part of the state can be unreliable.

Why NYC Renters Have Different Rights Than the Rest of the State

New York City is not treated like any other municipality in the state, and that distinction runs deep.

The city's housing laws reflect legislative findings, repeated over decades, that New York City faces unique housing conditions requiring heightened protection. Those conditions include extreme population density, a chronic shortage of affordable housing, a long and sometimes volatile history of rent regulation, and a rental market where the power imbalance between landlords and tenants is especially acute.

Because of these findings, NYC renters often have protections that simply do not exist elsewhere in the state.

Eviction defenses are stronger. In many upstate jurisdictions, a landlord who follows proper notice procedures can end a tenancy without stating a reason. In New York City, tenants in covered units cannot be removed without a legally valid cause, even when the lease has expired.

Notice requirements are more layered. NYC landlords must comply with both state notice rules and city-specific requirements, and the city rules are often more demanding. A notice that would be valid in Albany may be defective in Brooklyn.

Landlord compliance standards are stricter. The city enforces building and housing codes more aggressively, with a dedicated inspection apparatus and a court system designed specifically for housing disputes.

Harassment definitions are broader. Conduct that might be considered unpleasant but legal in other parts of the state can constitute actionable harassment in New York City, with civil penalties attached.

Procedural safeguards in court are more robust. Housing Court in New York City operates under rules designed to protect tenants from being rushed through the eviction process. Conferences, adjournments, right-to-counsel programs, and mandatory filings create multiple checkpoints that don't exist in many other courts.

The practical consequence is significant. A renter in Westchester, Buffalo, or Rochester may be subject to the same state statute as a renter in Queens, but the NYC-specific overlays can change what that statute actually means in practice. Two tenants reading the same law can reach different conclusions about their rights, and both can be correct, because the answer depends on where they live.

This is why advice from friends, online forums, or even attorneys who practice outside the city can be dangerously wrong when applied to a New York City apartment. Location is not a detail. It is the starting point of the entire analysis.

The Most Common Landlord Tactic: Selective Law Quoting

One of the most effective landlord strategies is not lying. It is telling the truth selectively.

Landlords and their representatives routinely cite real laws, real statutes, and real legal principles when communicating with tenants. What they leave out is often more important than what they include.

The pattern is predictable. A landlord will cite a state statute that sounds authoritative and final. They will frame the issue as settled law, using language like "under New York law" or "as required by statute." They will omit any reference to stricter city rules that apply to the same situation. And they will present their interpretation as the only reasonable reading.

This works because tenants make a series of reasonable but incorrect assumptions. They assume the landlord knows the law. They assume laws are uniform statewide. They assume that if a landlord cites a specific statute, that statute must be the controlling one. And they assume that challenging a legal claim requires hiring a lawyer.

None of those assumptions are reliably true.

Landlords are not required to know the law comprehensively. Many rely on property managers, template letters, or outdated legal advice. Some know the law well and choose their citations strategically. Others genuinely believe the state statute is the final word because no one has ever told them otherwise.

The result is the same either way. Tenants receive communications that sound definitive, cite real legal authority, and lead to conclusions that are wrong.

A common example involves lease termination. A landlord sends a notice stating that the lease will not be renewed, citing a state statute that allows termination at the end of a lease term with proper notice. The notice is formatted professionally. The statute is real. The citation is accurate.

But if the apartment is in New York City and covered by local tenant protections, the state statute may not be the controlling law. City law may require the landlord to have just cause for non-renewal. The notice may be legally meaningless, no matter how official it looks.

The landlord cited a real law. It just wasn't the right one.

This pattern repeats across nearly every area of tenant law: rent increases, security deposits, entry rights, eviction procedures, and fee collection. In each case, the landlord's position may be based on a real rule that doesn't actually apply, either because city law provides greater protection or because the specific circumstances trigger a different standard.

The only reliable defense is verification. Tenants who treat landlord legal explanations as claims rather than conclusions, and who check those claims against the full body of applicable law, consistently fare better than those who accept them at face value.

Why "My Lease Says..." Is Often Irrelevant

After selective law quoting, the second most common source of tenant confusion is the lease itself.

Many tenants believe the lease is the supreme document in the landlord-tenant relationship. They assume that if they signed it, they agreed to it, and that agreement is binding no matter what. This belief is understandable. In most areas of life, a signed contract is the final word.

In New York tenant law, it is not.

Leases cannot waive tenant protections granted by law. If a lease clause conflicts with a state or city tenant protection, the clause is unenforceable. It does not matter that the tenant signed it. It does not matter that the tenant read it. It does not matter that the tenant understood it at the time. If the law prohibits the waiver, the waiver has no legal effect.

This principle applies broadly.

A lease that says the tenant waives the right to a habitable apartment is unenforceable. The warranty of habitability cannot be waived in New York, regardless of what any document says.

A lease that imposes a security deposit greater than one month's rent is unenforceable as to the excess. The statutory cap applies whether the lease acknowledges it or not.

A lease that purports to shorten notice periods below what the law requires is unenforceable. The tenant retains the longer, legally mandated period.

A lease that includes a clause allowing the landlord to enter without notice is unenforceable to the extent it conflicts with the tenant's right to reasonable notice and quiet enjoyment.

A lease that waives the tenant's right to a renewal in a rent-stabilized apartment is unenforceable. Renewal rights are statutory and cannot be bargained away.

This is especially important in New York City, where landlords routinely use lease templates that contain provisions banned by local law. Some landlords use out-of-state forms purchased online. Others use templates drafted years or decades ago, before current protections took effect. Still others include unenforceable clauses deliberately, knowing that most tenants will comply with whatever the lease says without checking whether the law supports it.

The practical takeaway is this: if city law gives you more protection than what's written in your lease, the lease loses. Every time.

This does not mean leases are meaningless. Valid lease provisions that do not conflict with statutory protections are enforceable. Lease terms governing things like pet policies, guest rules, and maintenance responsibilities may be binding if they fall within the range the law allows. But the lease is always subordinate to the law. It can add obligations. It cannot subtract rights.

When a tenant says "my lease says," the correct response is often: "What does the law say?"

Legal Ambiguity Is a Feature, Not a Bug

From the tenant's perspective, New York's housing system feels unnecessarily complex. There are too many laws, too many agencies, too many exceptions, and too many situations where the answer depends on facts that aren't obvious.

From a landlord's perspective, that complexity is often useful.

Ambiguity creates several advantages for landlords. It discourages tenants from asserting rights, because the system feels too complicated to navigate. It allows landlords to pressure tenants into "voluntary" compliance, because tenants assume the landlord's position is correct when the rules seem unclear. It makes disputes feel risky and uncertain, pushing tenants toward inaction. And it shields landlord conduct from scrutiny, because misconduct only surfaces when someone challenges it.

The reality is that many tenant rights only become real when a tenant invokes them. The law does not send inspectors to every apartment. Agencies do not audit every rent registration. Courts do not review every notice. The system is largely complaint-driven, which means it depends on tenants knowing enough to complain.

Silence favors the landlord. Every time a tenant accepts an illegal rent increase without questioning it, every time a tenant moves out based on a defective notice, every time a tenant pays an unlawful fee because it feels easier than fighting, the landlord's position is reinforced, not by the law, but by the absence of challenge.

Knowledge changes that balance. It does not change the law. The law was there all along. What changes is the tenant's ability to use it.

This is why the complexity of New York tenant law, frustrating as it is, is not an argument against learning the system. It is the strongest argument for learning it. The tenants who understand the layers, who know which law controls, who verify before they comply, are the tenants who keep their housing, recover their money, and force landlords to follow rules that were always on the books.

The complexity is real. But it is not random. Once you see the structure, the system becomes navigable. And once it's navigable, it becomes powerful.

The Location Test: A Framework for Every Dispute

Before analyzing any housing dispute in New York, there is a threshold question that must be answered first.

Where is the apartment?

The answer determines which body of law controls, which agency has jurisdiction, which court will hear the case, and which protections are available. It is the single most important fact in any tenant law question, and it is the fact most often overlooked.

If the apartment is in New York City, the tenant has access to the full stack of protections: state law, city law, rent regulation (if applicable), Housing Court procedures, HPD enforcement, and local harassment and anti-retaliation rules.

If the apartment is outside New York City but within a municipality that has enacted its own tenant protections, the tenant has state law plus whatever local protections exist. These vary significantly from place to place.

If the apartment is in a jurisdiction with no local tenant protections beyond state law, the tenant has state law only, which provides important but more limited rights.

The location test is not a technicality. It is the foundation of the entire analysis. Every chapter in this book builds on it.

When you face a housing question, start here. Before researching the issue, before reading the lease, before responding to the landlord, ask: which law controls this apartment?

The answer will tell you where to look, what to expect, and how much leverage you actually have.

Real-World Example: When State Law Was the Wrong Law

A first-time renter in New York City received a termination notice stating that their lease would not be renewed. The landlord cited New York State law allowing termination at the end of a lease term with proper notice. The notice was printed on letterhead. It included a statute number. It gave a move-out date. Everything about it looked official and final.

The tenant assumed it was valid. They began searching for a new apartment.

Before signing a new lease, the renter spoke with a housing counselor at a community organization. The counselor asked one question: where is the building located?

Because the apartment was in New York City, and because the building was covered by local tenant protections, the landlord could not simply refuse to renew the lease without a legally recognized reason. City law required just cause for termination, regardless of what the state statute allowed in other parts of the state.

The landlord had cited a real law. The statute was accurate. The notice period was correct under that statute.

But it wasn't the controlling law.

The tenant challenged the notice. The landlord withdrew it. The tenant stayed.

The difference was not a loophole or a technicality. It was not a clever argument or an aggressive legal strategy. It was one question, asked at the right time: which law actually applies?

That question saved a tenancy. It can save yours.

What to Take From This Chapter

New York tenant law is layered by design. State law provides the floor. City law raises the ceiling. Lease clauses cannot lower either one.

If you rent in New York, especially in New York City, the following principles should guide every interaction with your landlord.

Never assume state law is the final word. Always ask whether city law adds protections that go further.

Treat landlord legal explanations as claims, not conclusions. Verify before you comply.

Remember that leases are subordinate to statutory protections. Signing a document does not waive a right the law says you cannot waive.

Start every analysis with location. The answer to "which law controls?" determines everything that follows.

And understand that the complexity of the system, while genuinely frustrating, is not your enemy. It is the terrain. The landlords who exploit it are counting on you not learning it. The tenants who learn it gain leverage that simply does not exist anywhere else in the country.

The rest of this book builds on that foundation. Once you know which law governs your apartment, you can start using it strategically instead of defensively.

2

Why New York Tenant Law Is Unlike Anywhere Else

If you've rented in another state before, New York can feel upside-down.

Things landlords treat as "automatic" elsewhere, ending a lease, raising rent, refusing renewal, removing a tenant, often don't work the same way here. That's not accidental. New York's tenant laws are the product of more than a century of housing shortages, political fights, and deliberate choices to slow displacement even when the market pushes hard in the opposite direction.

Understanding why New York law is different makes it easier to spot when something feels wrong, and to recognize when a landlord is relying on out-of-state assumptions that don't apply here.

The History That Shaped Everything

New York's tenant protections didn't appear all at once. They grew in response to repeated housing crises, each one adding new rules without fully replacing the old ones.

The first wave came during World War I. Rapid population growth collided with limited housing supply, producing extreme rent hikes and mass evictions. Lawmakers responded by freezing rents and restricting removals. What began as an emergency measure became a long-term policy, because the conditions that created the emergency never fully went away.

The second wave came during and after World War II. Returning veterans flooded the housing market. Federal and state governments imposed rent controls to prevent a repeat of the World War I crisis. In New York City, those controls took root deeply and never fully lifted.

The third wave came in the 1960s and 1970s, when the city created the rent stabilization system. Rent stabilization was designed to cover a broader class of apartments than old-style rent control, applying to buildings based on age and size rather than individual tenant history. It introduced regulated increases, renewal rights, and registration requirements that still govern hundreds of thousands of apartments today.

The fourth wave came in 2019 with the Housing Stability and Tenant Protection Act (HSTPA), which dramatically strengthened tenant protections by closing deregulation loopholes, expanding overcharge lookback periods, and tightening the rules landlords must follow when claiming rent increases. The HSTPA is covered in detail in Chapter 3.

Each of these waves left a permanent mark on the law. The result is a system built in layers, where protections from different eras coexist, sometimes reinforcing each other and sometimes creating complexity that benefits whoever understands it better.

That history matters because it explains why New York law doesn't behave like tenant law in other states. This isn't a system designed from scratch with clean logic. It's a system that evolved under pressure, repeatedly, over more than a hundred years. The complexity is the history.

Why Rent Regulation Isn't Just About Rent

When most people hear "rent regulation," they think about price. How much the landlord can charge. How much the rent can go up each year.

That's part of it, but it's not the whole picture. In New York, rent regulation influences far more than the dollar amount on the lease.

Rent regulation affects eviction standards, because landlords of regulated units face stricter requirements for removing tenants. It affects lease renewal rights, because tenants in stabilized apartments are generally entitled to renewals that landlords cannot refuse without cause. It affects notice requirements, because regulated units trigger specific timing and disclosure rules. And it affects landlord behavior under scrutiny, because violations of rent regulation carry penalties that create real financial exposure.

Even apartments that are no longer regulated exist in a legal environment shaped by that history. Courts, agencies, and legislators all operate within a framework where rent regulation is the backdrop, not the exception. Understanding the regulatory environment helps tenants in unregulated apartments too, because the principles, the procedural expectations, and the enforcement culture all flow from the same source.

Why Eviction Timelines Are Longer in New York

In many states, eviction is designed to be fast. A landlord gives notice, files a case, and gets a court date within days or weeks. The assumption is that landlords should be able to recover their property quickly when tenants fail to pay or violate the lease.

New York takes a fundamentally different approach. Here, eviction is designed to be deliberate.

The law assumes that eviction is a serious event with consequences that extend beyond the landlord-tenant relationship. Losing housing affects employment, education, health, and family stability. Because of those broader consequences, New York law builds in multiple checkpoints before a tenant can be removed.

Landlords must give advance written notices before filing cases. Those notices must meet strict content and timing requirements. Tenants have the right to court review before any physical removal. Procedural errors by landlords can halt or restart entire cases. And courts are structured to give tenants time to respond, raise defenses, and seek legal help.

The result is that eviction timelines in New York are significantly longer than in most other states. This is not because the courts are inefficient. It is because the law prioritizes due process and housing stability over speed.

For tenants who understand the process, this creates breathing room. A defective notice can invalidate an entire case. A service error can force a restart. A missed deadline can shift leverage entirely. These are not technicalities in the pejorative sense. They are the rules, and they exist because the legislature decided that getting eviction right matters more than getting it done quickly.

For landlords accustomed to faster systems, New York feels hostile. For tenants who learn the process, it creates options that don't exist anywhere else.

Why "Standard Leases" Don't Mean Standard Rights

One of the most dangerous myths in New York renting is the idea of the "standard lease."

Tenants hear this phrase from landlords, brokers, and even well-meaning friends. It implies that leases are uniform, that signing one is routine, and that the terms inside are more or less the same everywhere. None of that is true.

There is no single lease that defines tenant rights in New York. Instead, the law operates independently of the lease in many critical areas. Statutes override contracts. City law overrides boilerplate. Regulated units follow separate rules entirely. And courts regularly ignore lease clauses that violate tenant protections.

Landlords frequently use lease forms that are outdated, inapplicable, or flatly illegal. Some use out-of-state templates purchased from office supply companies or downloaded from the internet. Some use forms written for unregulated apartments in buildings that are actually regulated. Some include clauses that were banned years or even decades ago but were never removed from the template.

The problem is compounded by the fact that tenants rarely read leases carefully, and even when they do, they assume the document is legally sound because it looks official. A professionally formatted lease with numbered paragraphs and legal language creates an impression of authority. That impression is often misleading.

Signing a lease does not mean you agreed to waive your rights. In New York, many rights cannot be signed away, even voluntarily, even with full knowledge of what you're doing. The law protects tenants from their own agreements when those agreements conflict with statutory protections.

This is why two tenants with identical leases may have entirely different legal outcomes. The controlling rights come from law, not paper. The lease is a starting point, not the final word.

How New York Compares to Other Major Cities

If you're moving to New York from another city with strong tenant protections, you might assume you already know how renter-friendly laws work. That assumption can be misleading, because New York's system differs from other major cities in important ways.

Compared to Los Angeles, New York's rent regulation system is broader in scope but operates through different mechanisms. Los Angeles has a significant rent stabilization ordinance (the RSO) that covers apartments built before October 1978 and limits annual rent increases. In that respect, it resembles New York's system. But Los Angeles allows landlords to pass through certain capital improvement costs to tenants more easily, and the city's just cause eviction protections, while real, historically developed more recently and with different enforcement infrastructure. Los Angeles also relies heavily on a single city agency (the Los Angeles Housing Department) for rent regulation, while New York splits authority between state and city agencies in ways that create both redundancy and complexity. A tenant coming from LA will recognize the concept of rent stabilization but will find that New York's rules around renewal leases, registration requirements, and overcharge claims operate under a different and often stricter framework.

Compared to San Francisco, New York shares a similarly layered and tenant-protective legal environment, but the two cities diverge on key structural points. San Francisco's rent ordinance covers units built before June 1979, and the city has strong just cause eviction protections. However, San Francisco's system relies more heavily on the San Francisco Rent Board as a centralized adjudicatory body, where tenants and landlords can petition for resolution of disputes. New York's system is more fragmented, with disputes handled across Housing Court, HCR, HPD, and other agencies depending on the issue. San Francisco also allows certain types of owner move-in evictions under conditions that differ from New York's rules, and the city's Ellis Act (a state law allowing landlords to withdraw units from the rental market entirely) has no direct equivalent in New York. A tenant arriving from San Francisco will find New York's protections familiar in spirit but different in structure, with more procedural complexity and a less centralized enforcement system.

Compared to Chicago, the differences are more dramatic. Illinois repealed its statewide rent control preemption decades ago, but Chicago has not enacted a comprehensive rent stabilization system. The city passed the Residential Landlord and Tenant Ordinance (RLTO), which provides important protections around security deposits, notice requirements, and lease disclosures, but it does not regulate rent amounts or guarantee lease renewals the way New York's stabilization system does. Chicago tenants have strong security deposit protections (including penalty provisions that can be quite powerful), but they generally lack the rent regulation infrastructure, renewal rights, and just cause eviction framework that New York tenants in covered units rely on. A tenant moving from Chicago to New York will find familiar concepts around deposits and notices but will need to learn an entirely new system of rent regulation and eviction defense that simply does not exist in Illinois.

The common thread is that every city's tenant protections reflect its own history, politics, and housing conditions. New York's system is not just "more protective" than other cities. It is structurally different, with layers of regulation, agency oversight, and procedural requirements that create both stronger protections and greater complexity. Assuming that experience in another city translates directly to New York is one of the most common and costly mistakes transplants make.

Why New York Protects Tenants More Aggressively

New York's tenant protections are strict because lawmakers repeatedly concluded that the housing market alone does not produce fair outcomes for renters.

The legislative findings behind New York's housing laws return to the same themes across decades. The housing market does not self-correct in ways that protect vulnerable tenants. Displacement harms communities, labor markets, and public health. Instability increases homelessness and imposes costs on public systems. And the power imbalance between property owners and individual renters consistently favors owners unless the law intervenes.

As a result, New York law does more than set rules. It regulates behavior. It punishes noncompliance with penalties. It gives tenants procedural tools that shift leverage. And it expects landlords to know and follow the rules without being reminded.

This doesn't mean tenants always win. It means landlords must play by very specific rules, and many don't. When landlords cut corners, skip steps, or rely on tenant ignorance, the law creates consequences. But those consequences only materialize when someone invokes them.

The aggressive posture of New York tenant law is not abstract. It shows up in specific ways that affect daily life. Rent increases must be justified and documented. Eviction notices must be precise. Security deposits must be returned on strict timelines. Fees must fall within statutory caps. Entry must be on notice. Harassment must stop or face penalties.

None of these protections are automatic. All of them require tenants to know they exist and to act on them. But the protections themselves are among the strongest in the country, and they exist because New York decided, over and over again, that housing stability is too important to leave entirely to the market.

The Out-of-State Trap

The biggest mistakes happen when renters import assumptions from other states.

In many places, leases end when they end. Month-to-month means the landlord can terminate with minimal notice. Eviction is mostly administrative. Security deposit rules are loose. And tenant protections are limited to whatever the lease provides.

In New York, every one of those assumptions can be wrong.

Leases may not end simply because the term expires, if the tenant is protected by just cause rules. Month-to-month tenancies may require longer notice periods than tenants expect, based on length of occupancy. Eviction is a court-supervised process with multiple procedural requirements. Security deposits are capped, must be returned on a strict timeline, and carry penalties for noncompliance. And the lease is subordinate to statutory protections that the tenant may not even know about.

The out-of-state trap catches two groups of tenants. The first group is tenants who moved to New York from states with weaker protections. They assume the landlord's position is correct because it would be correct where they came from. They don't challenge rent increases, accept non-renewal notices, or move out voluntarily, all because the rules they internalized elsewhere told them they had no choice.

The second group is tenants who grew up in New York but absorbed assumptions from national media, online forums, or friends in other states. They hear that "landlords can do whatever they want" or that "you can't fight an eviction" and assume those statements apply here. They don't, at least not in the way other states define those concepts.

Both groups lose rights not because the law failed them, but because they applied the wrong legal framework to their situation. The fix is simple in theory and difficult in practice: learn the New York rules, and stop assuming that what's normal elsewhere is normal here.

Real-World Example: The Month-to-Month Mistake

A renter relocated from Florida to New York City and signed a one-year lease. When the lease expired, the landlord sent an email stating the tenancy would continue month-to-month and could be ended with 30 days' notice.

The renter assumed this was normal. In Florida, it would have been.

Months later, the landlord issued a termination notice with 30 days to vacate. The renter began preparing to move, believing they had no defense.

Only after speaking with a tenant advocate did the renter learn that New York law required a longer notice period based on length of occupancy. The renter had lived in the apartment for more than one year, which triggered a notice requirement significantly longer than 30 days. Beyond the notice period issue, local tenant protections limited the landlord's ability to terminate without cause.

The 30-day notice was insufficient under New York law. The termination itself may have been impermissible.

Because the renter acted on out-of-state assumptions, they almost gave up a valid defense. They almost moved out of an apartment they had every legal right to remain in, based on rules that applied in Florida but not in New York.

The landlord wasn't relying on deception. They were relying on the tenant's familiarity with the wrong legal system. And that reliance almost worked.

What to Take From This Chapter

New York tenant law is different because it was built to be.

History matters. The layers of protection that exist today grew out of real crises, real displacement, and real legislative responses accumulated over more than a century. The system is complex because the problems it addresses are complex.

Process matters. Eviction timelines are longer because the law treats housing loss as serious. Procedural requirements exist because shortcuts produce unjust outcomes. Courts move deliberately because due process requires it.

Location matters. New York's protections differ from those in Los Angeles, San Francisco, Chicago, and virtually every other city in the country. Experience renting elsewhere does not translate directly, and assumptions imported from other states are among the most common sources of tenant mistakes.

Assumptions are risky. "Standard leases" are not standard. Month-to-month does not mean unprotected. Lease expiration does not mean the tenancy is over. And what a landlord says the law requires may not be what the law actually requires.

If you rent here, the safest question is never "What usually happens?" It's "What does New York law actually require?"

In the next chapter, we'll tackle the single most important piece of tenant legislation in recent New York history: the Housing Stability and Tenant Protection Act of 2019, what it changed, and why advice written before it passed may no longer be reliable.

3

The HSTPA and Why Everything Changed in 2019

If there is a single date that divides modern New York tenant law into "before" and "after," it is June 14, 2019.

That is when the Housing Stability and Tenant Protection Act (HSTPA) was signed into law. It was the most significant overhaul of New York's tenant protections in a generation, and it changed the rules so fundamentally that advice written before it passed, whether from a lawyer, a website, a landlord, or a well-meaning friend, may no longer be accurate.

This chapter explains what the HSTPA did, why it matters, and how it affects nearly every topic covered in this book. If you rent in New York and you're relying on information that predates 2019, this is the chapter that tells you why that's dangerous.

What the HSTPA Was Responding To

For decades, New York's rent regulation system had been slowly shrinking.

The mechanisms were technical, but the effect was simple: apartments were leaving the regulated system faster than new ones were entering it. Landlords had legal tools to deregulate apartments permanently, and they used them aggressively. Tenants who didn't understand the process often didn't realize their apartment had been deregulated until it was too late to challenge it.

The primary engines of deregulation were vacancy decontrol, high-rent vacancy increases, and landlord claims for capital and apartment improvement costs. Each of these tools allowed landlords to raise the legal rent on a stabilized apartment, sometimes dramatically, and once the rent crossed a statutory threshold, the apartment could be permanently removed from regulation.

The result was predictable. Thousands of apartments that had been rent-stabilized for decades were deregulated, often through a combination of legal maneuvers that tenants never saw. A landlord could wait for a tenant to move out, claim improvement costs, stack a vacancy increase on top, push the rent above the deregulation threshold, and the apartment was permanently lost to the stabilization system. The next tenant would pay market rent with no regulatory protections and no idea what the apartment's history looked like.

By 2019, advocates, researchers, and legislators had concluded that the existing system was designed to fail tenants slowly. The HSTPA was the response.

The End of Vacancy Decontrol

Before the HSTPA, landlords could permanently deregulate a rent-stabilized apartment once the legal rent exceeded a threshold (which at various times was set at $2,500 or $2,774 per month) and the apartment became vacant.

This was called high-rent vacancy decontrol, and it was one of the most powerful tools landlords had.

The incentive was obvious. If a landlord could push the legal rent above the threshold, all they needed was a vacancy. Once the tenant moved out, the apartment left the stabilization system forever. No more regulated increases. No more renewal rights. No more registration requirements.

Landlords used every available mechanism to inflate the legal rent toward the threshold. They claimed improvement costs, applied vacancy bonuses, and stacked increases in ways that were technically lawful but strategically aggressive. Some tenants were pressured to leave through buyouts or harassment. Others left voluntarily without realizing their departure would trigger permanent deregulation.

The HSTPA eliminated vacancy decontrol entirely.

Under current law, there is no rent threshold that triggers automatic deregulation. A rent-stabilized apartment remains stabilized regardless of how high the legal rent becomes. Vacancy alone no longer changes the apartment's regulatory status.

This single change preserved hundreds of thousands of apartments in the stabilization system and removed the financial incentive for landlords to inflate rents purely for the purpose of deregulation.

For tenants, it means that a stabilized apartment stays stabilized. The landlord cannot deregulate it by raising the rent. The next tenant inherits the same protections. And the building's regulated status is no longer a countdown clock that landlords can accelerate.

Limits on Major Capital Improvements

Before the HSTPA, landlords could pass the cost of building-wide improvements through to tenants as permanent rent increases.

These were called Major Capital Improvements, or MCIs. The concept was straightforward: if a landlord replaced the roof, upgraded the boiler, or installed a new elevator, they could apply to the state housing agency for permission to increase the rent on every apartment in the building to recoup the cost.

The problem was how the math worked in practice. MCI increases were permanent. Once added to the legal rent, they never went away. Over time, a series of MCI increases could raise the legal rent substantially, pushing apartments toward the deregulation threshold that existed before 2019.

Landlords also had financial incentives to over-invest in MCIs, or to characterize routine maintenance as capital improvements, because the permanent rent increase more than paid for the work over time. Tenants bore the cost indefinitely, even after the landlord had fully recouped the original expense.

The HSTPA changed MCI rules in several important ways.

MCI rent increases are no longer permanent. They now expire after 30 years, meaning the increase is eventually removed from the legal rent.

The total amount a landlord can collect through MCIs is capped more tightly. Annual MCI increases are limited to a smaller percentage of the tenant's rent than was previously allowed.

The approval process was tightened, with stricter documentation requirements and greater scrutiny of claimed costs.

And because vacancy decontrol was eliminated, MCI increases can no longer be used as a stepping stone to deregulation.

For tenants, this means that MCI increases still exist but are smaller, temporary, and less likely to be abused as a deregulation strategy. When a landlord claims an MCI increase, tenants should verify that the claimed work qualifies, that the costs are documented, and that the increase complies with post-HSTPA caps.

Limits on Individual Apartment Improvements

Individual Apartment Improvements, or IAIs, were the apartment-level equivalent of MCIs.

Before the HSTPA, when a tenant vacated a rent-stabilized apartment, the landlord could make improvements to the individual unit (new kitchen, new bathroom, new flooring) and add a percentage of the cost to the legal rent as a permanent increase. Like MCIs, IAI increases never expired. And like MCIs, they could be stacked to push the rent toward the deregulation threshold.

The system created a perverse incentive. Landlords benefited financially from tenant turnover, because each vacancy was an opportunity to make improvements, raise the legal rent, and move the apartment closer to deregulation. In some cases, the improvements were genuine. In others, landlords inflated costs, performed cosmetic work at premium prices, or used related-party contractors to maximize the rent increase on paper.

The HSTPA imposed strict new limits on IAIs.

There is now a hard cap on the total amount a landlord can spend on IAIs and add to the rent. The cap applies over a 15-year period, preventing landlords from front-loading improvements to maximize rent increases.

IAI increases are no longer permanent. Like MCIs, they now expire after 30 years.

Landlords must provide documented proof of the actual cost of improvements, not estimates or inflated invoices. The documentation requirements are significantly stricter than before.

And again, because vacancy decontrol is gone, IAI increases can no longer serve as a pathway to permanent deregulation.

For tenants, the practical impact is significant. If you move into a rent-stabilized apartment and the rent seems high relative to comparable regulated units, IAI claims may be part of the reason. You have the right to review the rent history, examine what improvements were claimed, and challenge increases that don't comply with post-HSTPA rules.

New Security Deposit Rules

The HSTPA didn't just change rent regulation. It also overhauled security deposit rules statewide.

Before 2019, New York's security deposit rules varied and enforcement was uneven. Landlords routinely collected deposits exceeding one month's rent, charged last month's rent in advance, required pet deposits, or imposed other move-in charges that functioned as additional deposits under different names.

The HSTPA imposed a hard cap: security deposits are limited to one month's rent, period. No exceptions for pets, credit history, income level, or any other factor. Advance payment of last month's rent is prohibited. And any deposit that exceeds one month's rent is illegal, regardless of what it's called.

The law also tightened the return timeline. Landlords must return the deposit (or provide an itemized statement of deductions) within 14 days after the tenant vacates. Missing that deadline carries consequences, including potential forfeiture of the right to claim any deductions at all.

These rules apply statewide, not just in New York City, and they apply to all residential rentals, not just rent-stabilized apartments.

Security deposits are covered in detail in Chapters 14 and 15, but it's important to understand here that the rules you may have encountered before 2019, or the rules a landlord may cite from memory or habit, may no longer be the law. The HSTPA changed the baseline, and landlords who haven't updated their practices are violating it.

Strengthened Overcharge Lookback Periods

One of the most consequential changes the HSTPA made was to the overcharge lookback period.

Before 2019, tenants who believed they were being overcharged on rent could file a complaint, but the investigation was generally limited to the previous four years of rent history. If the overcharge originated before that four-year window, it was often unreachable. Landlords knew this, and some structured their rent increases to exploit the limitation. By the time a tenant discovered the problem, the evidence of the original violation had aged out of the reviewable period.

The HSTPA changed the lookback rules significantly.

The overcharge examination period was expanded. While the specifics have been the subject of ongoing litigation and regulatory interpretation, the general direction of the HSTPA was to allow the housing agency to look back further than four years when examining rent history, particularly when there is evidence of fraud or irregularity.

The law also changed how damages are calculated, allowing treble (triple) damages for willful overcharges and making it harder for landlords to claim that overcharges were accidental.

For tenants, this means that overcharge claims filed today may be able to reach further back into the rent history than was possible before 2019. If you suspect your rent is higher than it should be, the expanded lookback period may allow recovery of overcharges that would previously have been time-barred.

Overcharge claims are covered in detail in Chapter 7, but the key point here is that the HSTPA removed one of the landlord's most reliable defenses: the passage of time.

The End of Vacancy Bonuses and Longevity Increases

Before the HSTPA, landlords were entitled to automatic rent increases when a rent-stabilized apartment became vacant. These vacancy bonuses (typically 20 percent for a two-year lease) allowed landlords to raise the legal rent significantly between tenants, even without making any improvements to the apartment.

The rationale was that landlords needed incentives to maintain apartments and absorb turnover costs. The effect was that every time a tenant left, the rent jumped, often substantially. Combined with IAIs and MCIs, vacancy bonuses could push rents up dramatically over a short period.

The HSTPA eliminated vacancy bonuses entirely.

When a rent-stabilized tenant moves out, the landlord may no longer apply an automatic percentage increase to the legal rent. The incoming tenant's rent is based on the prior legal rent plus any lawful RGB increase, not on a vacancy windfall.

The HSTPA also eliminated longevity increases, which had allowed landlords to add additional rent based on how long the previous tenant had occupied the apartment.

For tenants, this means that the rent you're offered in a newly vacated stabilized apartment should be closely tied to the prior legal rent. If it seems significantly higher than what the previous tenant paid, and the landlord has not documented lawful IAIs, something may be wrong.

Why Pre-2019 Advice Is Dangerous

The HSTPA changed so many fundamental rules that advice written before June 2019 is often not just outdated but affirmatively wrong.

Before the HSTPA, it was true that apartments could be deregulated once the rent crossed a threshold. That is no longer true.

Before the HSTPA, it was true that MCI and IAI increases were permanent. That is no longer true.

Before the HSTPA, it was true that vacancy bonuses allowed significant rent jumps between tenants. That is no longer true.

Before the HSTPA, it was true that overcharge claims were generally limited to a four-year lookback. That is no longer true in many circumstances.

Before the HSTPA, it was true that security deposits could exceed one month's rent in certain situations. That is no longer true.

The internet is full of pre-HSTPA advice. Blog posts, forum threads, legal guides, and even some attorney websites still describe the old rules as current law. Tenants who rely on that information may accept rent increases that are no longer lawful, fail to file overcharge claims they would win, or believe their apartment has been deregulated when it hasn't been.

Landlords, too, sometimes operate under pre-HSTPA assumptions, either because they haven't updated their practices or because the old rules were more favorable to them. A landlord who tells you that your apartment was "deregulated" based on high rent may be citing a rule that no longer exists.

The safest approach is to treat any tenant law advice that doesn't specifically reference the HSTPA with skepticism. If it was written before mid-2019 and doesn't mention the changes described in this chapter, it may be describing a legal landscape that no longer exists.

How the HSTPA Connects to the Rest of This Book

The HSTPA didn't create a new system. It reformed the existing one. That means its effects are woven throughout every topic this book covers.

Chapter 4 (Rent Control vs. Rent Stabilization) reflects the post-HSTPA reality that stabilized apartments can no longer be deregulated through high rent or vacancy.

Chapter 5 (Is Your Apartment Rent-Stabilized?) explains how to verify stabilization status in a world where deregulation claims based on pre-HSTPA rules may no longer be valid.

Chapter 6 (Legal Rent, Rent Increases & Renewal Leases) incorporates the elimination of vacancy bonuses and the new limits on MCI and IAI increases.

Chapter 7 (Overcharge Claims) covers the expanded lookback periods and enhanced damages that the HSTPA created.

Chapters 14 and 15 (Security Deposits) reflect the HSTPA's hard cap on deposits and strict return timelines.

Chapter 16 (Application Fees, Move-In Fees & Illegal Charges) addresses the HSTPA's limits on fees that landlords can charge before move-in.

If a topic in this book involves rent regulation, deposits, fees, or overcharges, the HSTPA is part of the analysis. The law didn't just change a few rules. It changed the framework.

Real-World Example: The Deregulation That Didn't Happen

A tenant moved into a one-bedroom apartment in 2021. The landlord advertised it as market-rate and charged $2,900 per month. The lease made no mention of rent stabilization. The landlord told the tenant, truthfully, that the previous tenant had paid less and that the rent had been adjusted to reflect market conditions.

The tenant assumed this was normal. The rent was high but not unusual for the neighborhood.

Two years later, the tenant requested the apartment's rent history from the state housing agency. The records showed that the apartment had been rent-stabilized for decades. The prior legal rent had been approximately $1,600. The landlord had claimed IAI costs after the previous tenant moved out, applied a vacancy bonus, and pushed the rent above the old deregulation threshold.

Before the HSTPA, that sequence might have been lawful. After the HSTPA, it was not.

Vacancy bonuses had been eliminated. The IAI costs exceeded the new caps. And vacancy decontrol no longer existed, meaning the apartment could not have been lawfully deregulated regardless of the rent amount.

The tenant filed an overcharge complaint. The apartment was confirmed as rent-stabilized. The legal rent was recalculated. The tenant recovered a substantial refund and had their rent reduced to the lawful amount going forward.

The landlord had followed the old playbook. The old playbook no longer applied.

What to Take From This Chapter

The HSTPA is the most important piece of tenant legislation in recent New York history. It eliminated vacancy decontrol, capped MCI and IAI increases, removed vacancy bonuses, strengthened overcharge lookback periods, and imposed strict new security deposit rules.

If you rent in New York, especially in a rent-stabilized apartment, understanding the HSTPA is not optional. It is the foundation of the current legal landscape.

Any advice that predates June 2019 should be treated with caution. The rules it describes may no longer exist. The strategies it recommends may no longer work. And the assumptions it reflects may lead you to surrender rights you actually have.

The HSTPA didn't just give tenants more protection. It took away tools that landlords had used for decades to erode those protections quietly. The system is still complex, but the balance shifted in 2019, and tenants who understand that shift have leverage that previous generations of renters did not.

In the next chapter, we'll move from the legislative framework to the practical question that affects more tenants than any other: rent control versus rent stabilization, what the difference actually means, and why getting it wrong costs real money.

Part II: Rent Control, Rent Stabilization & Legal Rent

4

Rent Control vs. Rent Stabilization

What's the Difference?

Few topics in New York housing law generate more confusion than rent control and rent stabilization. Tenants mix them up constantly. Landlords encourage that confusion. And the consequences of misunderstanding the difference are not abstract. They show up in the rent you pay, the rights you have, and the leverage you hold in every interaction with your landlord.

These are two separate systems with different histories, different rules, different coverage, and different implications for your tenancy. This chapter explains what each system actually is, how they work, where they overlap, and why the distinction matters more than most tenants realize.

Rent Control: The System That Is Disappearing

Rent control is the older of the two systems, and it is vanishing.

True rent-controlled apartments exist almost exclusively in New York City, and they survive only when all of the following conditions are met. The building was constructed before 1947. The tenant, or a qualifying family member who succeeded to the tenancy, has lived there continuously since before July 1, 1971. And the apartment has never been lawfully deregulated.

Those conditions are extraordinarily narrow. As original rent-controlled tenants pass away or move out, the apartments leave the rent control system. No new rent-controlled apartments are being created. The population of rent-controlled units shrinks every year, and it will eventually reach zero.

Under rent control, rents are set by a formula administered by the city, and increases are determined by the Maximum Base Rent (MBR) system. The MBR is recalculated periodically, and landlords may apply for increases based on that recalculation, but the process is distinct from how rent stabilization works. Rent-controlled tenants also have strong protections against eviction and are generally entitled to remain in their apartments for life, subject to narrow exceptions.

Because rent control is so limited in scope, most renters will never encounter it directly. The apartments that remain under rent control tend to be occupied by long-term, often elderly tenants who have lived in the same unit for decades. The rents are frequently far below market, which creates enormous financial pressure on landlords to find ways to end those tenancies and bring the apartments into a more profitable status.

For most readers of this book, rent control is not the system that governs your apartment. But understanding it matters for two reasons.

First, rent control creates a shadow that affects how tenants think about regulation generally. When people hear "rent control" in casual conversation, they often imagine a system that freezes rent at absurdly low levels and applies broadly. That image is inaccurate, but it shapes public perception in ways that make tenants skeptical that regulation could apply to them. Landlords benefit from that skepticism.

Second, rent control and rent stabilization interact in specific situations, particularly around succession rights and building-wide regulatory status. If a rent-controlled tenant dies and a family member seeks to remain, the rules governing that succession are different from the rules in stabilized apartments. Understanding which system applies is critical to knowing which rules control.

Rent Stabilization: The System That Actually Matters

Rent stabilization is the system that governs the vast majority of regulated apartments in New York. It is the system most likely to affect you, and it is the system that this book focuses on most heavily.

Rent-stabilized apartments are generally found in buildings that meet one of two criteria. Either the building was constructed before 1974 and contains six or more units, or the building received certain tax benefits (such as 421-a or J-51 tax abatements) that brought it into the stabilization system regardless of when it was built.

The first category is the larger one. Tens of thousands of prewar and mid-century buildings across New York City fall into it. The second category is significant because it means that even newer buildings can be stabilized, sometimes temporarily, depending on the terms of the tax benefit.

Rent stabilization operates through a set of interconnected rules that together create a regulated framework for the entire tenancy, not just the rent amount.

Rent increases are set annually by the Rent Guidelines Board (RGB), a city body that determines the maximum percentage increase landlords may apply to renewal leases. Landlords cannot charge more than the RGB-approved increase for one-year and two-year renewal terms. They cannot invent their own increases, apply future RGB rates early, or substitute "market" logic for the regulated rate.

Tenants have the right to renewal leases. This is one of the most important features of rent stabilization and one of the least understood. In a stabilized apartment, the landlord cannot simply decline to renew your lease when the term expires. You are entitled to a renewal, and the landlord must offer it in the proper form, within the proper time window, with the correct rent amount. Refusal to renew requires a legally recognized justification, not just a preference for a different tenant or a higher rent.

Landlords must register each stabilized apartment annually with the state housing agency (HCR). The registration must include the legal rent, the tenant's name, the lease dates, and any changes to the rent. Failure to register has consequences, including the potential freezing of rent increases.

Deregulation is heavily restricted. As discussed in Chapter 3, the HSTPA eliminated vacancy decontrol, meaning apartments can no longer leave the stabilization system simply because the rent reached a certain level. A stabilized apartment remains stabilized regardless of the rent amount, and regardless of whether the tenant changes.

Overcharges carry penalties. If a landlord charges more than the legal rent, the tenant can file an overcharge complaint, recover the excess, and potentially receive treble damages if the overcharge was willful. The expanded lookback periods created by the HSTPA make these claims more powerful than they were before 2019.

Together, these rules create a system where stabilization is not just a price cap. It is a comprehensive regulatory framework that governs the entire relationship between landlord and tenant, from the amount of rent to the right to stay to the landlord's obligations around transparency and compliance.

Why So Many Tenants Don't Know They're Stabilized

One of the most striking facts about rent stabilization is how many tenants live in stabilized apartments without knowing it.

This happens for several reasons, and none of them are accidental.

Landlords are not required to volunteer the information proactively in every context. While there are disclosure requirements (including the obligation to provide a rent stabilization lease rider and to register the apartment), compliance is uneven. Many landlords simply don't mention stabilization. They market apartments as "market-rate" or "free market" without further explanation. They use standard-looking leases that omit any reference to regulation. And they present the rent as a straightforward negotiation between landlord and tenant, as if no regulatory framework existed.

Tenants, for their part, often associate rent stabilization with a particular image: elderly tenants in old buildings paying very low rent. If the apartment doesn't match that image, if the rent is high, the unit is renovated, or the building looks modern, the tenant assumes stabilization doesn't apply. That assumption is frequently wrong. Stabilization follows the building and the unit, not the tenant's profile or the rent amount. A renovated apartment with a $3,000 rent can be stabilized. A unit occupied by a 25-year-old who moved in last year can be stabilized. The criteria are structural, not demographic.

The combination of landlord silence and tenant assumptions means that many New Yorkers are paying rents they could challenge, accepting increases they could reject, and lacking renewal protections they actually possess, all because no one told them the truth about their apartment's regulatory status.

Chapter 5 explains exactly how to determine whether your apartment is stabilized. But the threshold point is this: you cannot rely on what the landlord tells you, what the listing said, or what the lease implies.

Stabilization status is a matter of public record, and the only reliable way to know is to check.

Legal Rent vs. Paid Rent: The Number That Matters

Understanding rent stabilization requires understanding a concept that confuses many tenants: the difference between legal rent and the rent you actually pay.

Legal rent is the maximum amount a landlord is legally permitted to charge for a rent-stabilized apartment. It is created by a chain of documented, lawful steps: the base rent, plus RGB increases, plus any approved MCI or IAI adjustments, all properly registered with the state housing agency.

The rent you pay may or may not match the legal rent.

If you are paying the legal rent, your rent is at the regulated maximum. Any increase must come from an RGB order or another lawful source.

If you are paying less than the legal rent, you may be receiving what is called a preferential rent. A preferential rent is a voluntary discount the landlord offers below the legal maximum. Preferential rents are common, particularly in neighborhoods where the legal rent exceeds what the market will bear, or when landlords want to attract tenants quickly.

If you are paying more than the legal rent, you are being overcharged. This is illegal, and it can be challenged through a complaint to the state housing agency. Overcharges can result in rent reductions, refunds of excess payments, and treble damages for willful violations.

The critical point is that you may not know which category you fall into unless you check. Landlords are required to disclose the legal rent on the rent stabilization lease rider, and the legal rent should appear in the apartment's registration records. But many tenants never see the rider, never request the records, and simply assume the rent they were quoted is the rent the law allows.

It often isn't.

How Preferential Rent Creates Confusion

Preferential rent is one of the most commonly misunderstood features of rent stabilization, and it is frequently a source of disputes.

Here is how it works in principle. A landlord has a stabilized apartment with a legal rent of $2,200. The market in the neighborhood supports only $1,800. The landlord offers the apartment at $1,800, which becomes the preferential rent. The tenant pays $1,800. The legal rent remains $2,200.

Before the HSTPA, landlords could, upon renewal, jump the rent from the preferential level back up to the legal rent (or close to it), sometimes resulting in increases of hundreds of dollars that tenants were not expecting. This was technically lawful under the old rules but created enormous hardship and confusion.

The HSTPA changed the preferential rent rules significantly. Under current law, the preferential rent generally must be used as the base for calculating future increases. The landlord cannot simply abandon the preferential rent and leap to the legal rent at renewal. Increases on preferential rents must generally follow the same RGB percentages as increases on legal rents, applied to the preferential amount, not the higher legal amount.

This is an area where the details matter and where pre-HSTPA advice is particularly dangerous. If your landlord is attempting to raise your rent from a preferential level to the full legal rent, or is applying RGB increases to the legal rent rather than the preferential rent, they may be violating current law. Chapter 6 covers this in detail.

For now, the key takeaway is that preferential rent is not a gift with no strings attached. It has rules. Those rules changed in 2019. And landlords who haven't updated their practices, or who are hoping you haven't noticed, may be collecting more than the law allows.

Why the Confusion Between the Two Systems Costs Real Money

The confusion between rent control and rent stabilization is not just academic. It has direct financial consequences for tenants who get it wrong.

When tenants misunderstand these systems, they make predictable and costly mistakes.

They accept rent increases without verifying whether the increase complies with RGB guidelines, because they assume their apartment isn't regulated.

They fail to demand renewal leases, because they don't realize they have a statutory right to one.

They miss overcharge claims, because they assume the rent they're paying must be the legal rent.

They waive defenses in eviction cases, because they don't realize their landlord needs just cause to remove them.

They move out voluntarily when their lease expires, because they believe the landlord has an absolute right not to renew, when in fact the landlord has no such right in a stabilized apartment without a legally recognized cause.

Each of these mistakes transfers money or leverage from the tenant to the landlord. And in many cases, the transfer is irreversible. Once a tenant moves out based on a false belief, recovering the lost apartment is far more difficult than staying would have been.

The financial stakes are not hypothetical. A tenant paying $300 per month above the legal rent loses $3,600 per year. Over a five-year tenancy, that's $18,000 in overcharges, not counting treble damages. A tenant who moves out of a stabilized apartment unnecessarily loses not just the apartment but the below-market rent that comes with it, which in New York City can represent tens of thousands of dollars in annual savings compared to market-rate alternatives.

Knowledge isn't just leverage. It's money.

What Landlords Gain From the Confusion

The confusion between rent control and rent stabilization serves landlord interests in a specific way that goes beyond the general advantage of tenant ignorance discussed in Chapter 1.

Rent control has become, in the public imagination, a symbol of something rare, extreme, and nearly extinct. When tenants hear "rent control," they picture apartments frozen at $400 per month in buildings that haven't been updated since the Kennedy administration. They assume that kind of protection is irrelevant to them, because their apartment doesn't look like that and their rent doesn't feel like that.

That image is not entirely wrong as a description of rent control. But it bleeds into how tenants think about rent stabilization, which is a different system entirely. When a tenant conflates the two, or when a landlord encourages the conflation, the result is that the tenant dismisses the possibility of regulation without investigating it.

A landlord who says "that's rent control, not stabilization" is making a factual statement that sounds informative but functions as misdirection. The tenant hears "your apartment isn't protected." The accurate message would be "your apartment isn't rent-controlled, but it might be rent-stabilized, and rent stabilization carries a full set of protections including regulated rent, renewal rights, and overcharge remedies."

Landlords don't deliver that second message. They don't have to. The confusion does the work for them.

The remedy is straightforward. Stop asking whether your apartment is rent-controlled. Start asking whether it's rent-stabilized. And then verify the answer yourself, using the process described in Chapter 5.

Real-World Example: The Apartment That Wasn't Market-Rate

A tenant rented an apartment advertised as market-rate in a prewar building in Brooklyn. The rent was $2,400 per month. The lease was a standard-looking document with no mention of regulation. The landlord described the apartment as a "free market" unit and presented the rent as a straightforward ask-and-offer negotiation.

The tenant paid the rent for two years without questioning it. The apartment was in good condition. The neighborhood was desirable. The rent, while high, seemed consistent with the market.

Then a neighbor mentioned, in passing, that she had requested her apartment's rent history from the state housing agency. She explained that the process was free, that it didn't require the landlord's permission, and that the records showed whether the apartment was registered as stabilized.

Curious, the tenant did the same.

The records showed that the apartment had been rent-stabilized for decades. The legal rent, according to the most recent registration, was approximately $1,900. The tenant had been paying $500 per month more than the legal maximum for the entire tenancy.

The landlord had never registered the current rent. The lease rider disclosing the apartment's stabilized status had never been provided. The "market-rate" description was not a legal classification. It was a marketing choice.

The tenant filed an overcharge complaint with the state housing agency. The apartment was confirmed as stabilized. The rent was reduced to the legal amount. The tenant recovered thousands of dollars in overcharges for the period they had been overpaying.

The tenant hadn't found a secret. The information had been available the entire time. It was sitting in a government database, waiting for someone to request it.

The landlord had been counting on no one asking.

What to Take From This Chapter

Rent control and rent stabilization are two different systems. Rent control is rare, old, and shrinking. Rent stabilization is common, current, and the source of most regulated tenant protections in New York.

Legal rent is the maximum a landlord may charge in a stabilized apartment. It is not necessarily the rent in your lease, the rent in the listing, or the rent the landlord quoted you. It is a regulated number created by documented, lawful steps, and it can be verified.

Preferential rent is a discount below the legal maximum. Under current law, landlords generally cannot jump from preferential rent to full legal rent at renewal. The rules changed in 2019, and pre-HSTPA practices may no longer be lawful.

The confusion between the two systems benefits landlords and costs tenants real money. Misunderstanding whether your apartment is regulated, or which system applies, can lead to overpayment, lost renewal rights, and unnecessary displacement.

If you rent in New York, the right question is never "Is this apartment rent-controlled?" It's "Is this apartment rent-stabilized, and how do I verify it?"

The next chapter answers that question step by step, using records landlords hope you never request.

5

Is Your Apartment Rent-Stabilized?

How to Find Out

Many New York renters live in rent-stabilized apartments without knowing it.

This is not a marginal problem affecting a handful of tenants in obscure situations. It is a widespread condition that costs tenants real money every month. Landlords rarely advertise stabilization unless legally compelled to. Listings say "market-rate." Leases look ordinary. Rent increases are presented as non-negotiable. And tenants, trusting the presentation, never think to question whether the apartment they're paying market prices for is actually subject to a regulatory system that caps their rent, guarantees their renewal, and gives them leverage they've never used.

For tenants in this position, the only way to know the truth is to check the records yourself. This chapter explains what those records are, how to get them, and what to do with what you find.

The Core Rule: Stabilization Follows the Apartment, Not the Tenant

Whether an apartment is rent-stabilized depends on the building and its history, not on who currently lives there.

This is one of the most important and least understood principles in New York tenant law. Stabilization is a characteristic of the unit itself, determined by factors like when the building was constructed, how many units it contains, and whether it received certain tax benefits. It does not depend on the tenant's age, income, length of tenancy, or any other personal characteristic.

An apartment may still be stabilized even if the rent is high. Even if the previous tenant moved out. Even if the landlord says it isn't regulated. Even if the lease makes no mention of stabilization. Even if the apartment has been renovated from floor to ceiling.

The law follows the unit. If the apartment was never lawfully deregulated, it remains stabilized, no matter how it's marketed, no matter what the landlord claims, and no matter what the lease says.

This means that the question "Is my apartment rent-stabilized?" cannot be answered by looking at the rent amount, the lease language, or the landlord's representations. It can only be answered by looking at the records.

Which Buildings Are Typically Stabilized

Rent stabilization generally applies to two categories of buildings.

The first category is buildings constructed before 1974 that contain six or more residential units. This is the largest group. Tens of thousands of prewar and mid-century apartment buildings across New York City fall into this category. If your building was built before 1974 and has six or more apartments, there is a strong chance that some or all of the units are stabilized.

The second category is buildings that received certain tax benefits, regardless of when they were built. The two most common programs are the 421-a tax exemption and the J-51 tax abatement. Buildings that received these benefits are generally required to keep their apartments rent-stabilized for the duration of the benefit period. In some cases, that obligation extends for decades. In others, it may have expired, potentially affecting the stabilization status of units in the building.

There are additional situations that can bring an apartment into the stabilization system, including certain conversions, government-financed construction, and regulatory agreements. But the two categories above cover the vast majority of stabilized apartments in the city.

Knowing your building's age and size gives you a starting point. It does not give you a definitive answer. The definitive answer comes from the registration records.

What Landlords Are Required to Do: Registration

Landlords of rent-stabilized apartments are required to register each unit every year with the state housing agency.

The agency is the New York State Division of Housing and Community Renewal (DHCR), which operates within a larger entity called New York State Homes and Community Renewal (HCR). The administrative arm that handles rent regulation is the Office of Rent Administration (ORA). You will see these names and acronyms used interchangeably in official documents, court filings, and tenant advocacy materials. They all refer to the same regulatory system.

Annual registration must include the apartment's legal regulated rent, the tenant's name (or vacancy status), the lease start and end dates, and any lawful changes to the rent since the prior registration.

Registration is not optional. It is a legal obligation, and failure to comply has consequences.

When landlords don't register, rent increases may be frozen. Under the HSTPA, a landlord who fails to register a stabilized apartment cannot collect rent increases for the unregistered years. This means that gaps in registration don't just create paperwork problems. They create financial exposure for the landlord and potential refund claims for the tenant.

Registration records are also a critical piece of evidence in overcharge disputes, eviction cases, and deregulation challenges. When a landlord claims that an apartment is no longer stabilized, the registration history is often where the claim is tested.

Landlords sometimes skip registration hoping tenants won't notice. Many tenants don't. The system works only when tenants check.

The Rent History: The Single Most Powerful Tenant Document

If you remember one thing from this chapter, let it be this: you have the right to request your apartment's rent history, and doing so is the single most important step you can take to understand your legal position as a tenant.

A rent history is the official record maintained by DHCR of every rent that a landlord has registered for a specific apartment over the years. It is a printout of the annual registration filings, going back as far as records exist, and it shows the registered rent for each year, the type of lease (renewal or vacancy), and codes indicating the reason for any rent changes.

This document reveals whether the apartment has been registered as stabilized. It shows the legal rent over time. It shows increases claimed by the landlord and the basis for those increases. And it reveals gaps, irregularities, or suspicious patterns that may indicate overcharges or improper deregulation.

For many tenants, requesting the rent history is the moment when assumptions collapse. What the landlord said was market-rate turns out to be stabilized. What looked like a normal rent turns out to exceed the legal maximum. What seemed like a straightforward tenancy turns out to involve years of unregistered increases, unexplained rent jumps, or deregulation claims that don't hold up.

The rent history does not require a lawyer to obtain. It does not require the landlord's permission. It does not cost money. And the landlord is not notified when you request it.

How to Request Your Rent History: Step by Step

There are several ways to request your apartment's rent history from DHCR. Each method reaches the same records. The choice depends on your preference for speed, convenience, and documentation.

The online method is the most common starting point. DHCR operates an online inquiry portal where tenants can submit requests. You visit the HCR website and use the "Submit your Inquiry" function. When prompted for the reason for your inquiry, select "Apartment Rent History" or "Am I Rent Stabilized?" (both options will produce the same result). You will need to provide your full name, your email address (or indicate that you don't have one), and the building address including your apartment number and zip code. After submission, the rent history will be printed and mailed directly to your apartment address. Processing typically takes two to four weeks, though it can take longer during busy periods.

The email method is an alternative. You can email your request directly to RentInfo@hcr.ny.gov. Include your full name, the complete building address with apartment number, and a clear statement that you are requesting the rent history for your unit. This method produces the same result as the online portal, with a similar processing timeline.

The phone method is available for tenants who prefer to make the request verbally. You can call DHCR's Rent Info Line at 833-499-0343. Listen for the menu option to request your rent history and stay on the line. Hold times can be long, so plan accordingly.

The text message method is also available. You can text "RENT HISTORY" to (646) 783-0627 to initiate a request.

The in-person method is generally the fastest but requires a trip to a DHCR borough rent office. You must bring a state-issued photo identification and a copy of your lease. If you are not the named tenant on the lease (for example, if you are a family member, roommate, or subtenant), you may be denied a copy through this method. Borough rent offices are located in the Bronx (2400 Halsey Street, 1st Floor), Brooklyn (55 Hanson Place, 6th Floor), Lower Manhattan (25 Beaver Street, 2nd Floor), Upper Manhattan (163 West 125th Street, 5th Floor), and Queens (92-31 Union Hall Street, 6th Floor). In-person visits are by appointment only.

Whichever method you use, keep a record of when you submitted the request and through which channel. If you need the rent history for a court proceeding or a time-sensitive complaint, submit your request as early as possible and alert your attorney or advocate to the timeline.

What You Don't Need to Request Rent History

Tenants often hesitate to request rent history because they believe the process is complicated, adversarial, or requires resources they don't have. It is none of those things.

You do not need a lawyer. The request is administrative, not legal. You are asking a government agency for records it is obligated to provide.

You do not need the landlord's permission. The records belong to the regulatory system, and tenants have a right of access as a matter of law. The landlord is not a gatekeeper.

You do not need to pay a fee. Rent history requests from tenants are free.

You do not need to explain why you want it. You are not required to state a reason, allege wrongdoing, or justify your curiosity.

You do not need to worry about retaliation. Requesting records from a government agency is a protected activity. It is not a confrontation, a complaint, or a legal filing. It is an information request.

The barrier to requesting rent history is not procedural. It is psychological. Tenants don't request it because they don't know it exists, because they assume the process is difficult, or because they're afraid of what they might find. None of those are good reasons to stay in the dark about your own apartment.

The Building Search: A Quick First Check

Before requesting your full rent history, you can do a preliminary check using DHCR's Rent Regulated Building Search tool, available online at apps.hcr.ny.gov/BuildingSearch/.

This free, public tool allows you to search by address and see whether a building has filed rent regulation records with DHCR at any point from 1984 to the present. If your building appears in the database, it means that at least one apartment in the building has been registered as rent-regulated at some point.

The building search is useful as a starting point, but it has important limitations.

It tells you about the building, not your specific apartment. A building can contain both stabilized and non-stabilized units, particularly in buildings that have undergone co-op or condo conversions.

It reflects registration filings, not current status. A building that appears in the database may have units that were lawfully deregulated at some point. Conversely, a building that does not appear may have units that should have been registered but weren't.

It does not replace the full rent history. The building search tells you whether to investigate further. The rent history tells you the answer.

If your building appears in the search results, request your rent history. If it doesn't appear but your building was built before 1974 and has six or more units, request your rent history anyway. The absence of a registration filing may itself be a violation.

Third-Party Tools: JustFix and RentHistory.org

In addition to DHCR's own resources, several third-party tools can help tenants investigate their building's regulatory status.

JustFix.nyc offers a tool that aggregates building records from multiple city agencies, including HPD violations, Department of Buildings records, and ownership information. It can help you build a fuller picture of your building's history beyond what rent registration alone shows.

RentHistory.org provides a rent history analysis tool that can flag potential overcharges, identify suspicious deregulation patterns, and cross-reference DHCR data with HPD violations, building permits, and ownership records. Some of its services are available to tenants directly, while others are designed for attorneys and housing organizers.

These tools are supplements, not substitutes. The official rent history from DHCR is the authoritative record. But third-party tools can help you understand what the official record means and identify issues you might otherwise miss.

How to Read Your Rent History

When your rent history arrives, you will be looking at a table of annual registration entries. Each row typically includes the registration year, the type of filing (initial, annual, or amendment), the legal regulated rent, the type of lease (renewal or vacancy), and a code indicating the basis for any rent change.

Reading this document is not difficult, but it requires attention to a few key things.

Look at whether the apartment has been continuously registered as stabilized. If it has, the apartment is stabilized, regardless of what the landlord told you. If registration stops at some point, ask why. Was the apartment lawfully deregulated? Was the landlord simply not filing? The answer matters.

Look at the legal rent over time. Does it increase gradually, consistent with RGB guidelines? Or does it jump suddenly, particularly between tenants? Large jumps may indicate vacancy bonuses (which are no longer lawful under the HSTPA), IAI claims (which are now capped), or increases that were never properly documented.

Look for gaps in registration. Years where no registration was filed may mean the landlord was not complying with the registration requirement. Under the HSTPA, rent increases during unregistered years may be invalid.

Compare the last registered rent before your tenancy began to the rent you were charged when you moved in. Under current law, the legal regulated rent is based on the prior legal rent plus permissible increases. If the rent you were offered was substantially higher than the last registered amount, and the landlord has not documented lawful IAIs or other approved adjustments, you may have been overcharged from day one.

If you have difficulty interpreting the rent history, tenant advocacy organizations like Met Council on Housing, Legal Aid Society, and Legal Services NYC can help you understand the document and assess whether action is warranted.

Red Flags for Illegal Deregulation

Some apartments were deregulated lawfully under the rules that existed before the HSTPA. Many were not.

Illegal deregulation typically leaves traces in the rent history, and knowing what to look for can reveal whether the landlord's "market-rate" claim holds up.

Watch for sudden, large rent increases between tenants that exceed what RGB guidelines and lawful adjustments would allow. These may indicate stacked increases (vacancy bonuses plus inflated IAIs) designed to push the rent above the old deregulation threshold.

Watch for gaps in registration records. If the landlord stopped registering the apartment and then began marketing it as deregulated, the deregulation may never have been lawful.

Watch for deregulation claims based solely on high rent. Before the HSTPA, apartments could be deregulated when the rent exceeded a statutory threshold. But even under the old rules, the rent had to reach that threshold through lawful increases. If the increases themselves were improper (inflated IAIs, unauthorized fees, or improperly calculated vacancy bonuses), the rent never lawfully reached the threshold, and the deregulation was invalid.

Watch for claims tied to "luxury" renovations without documentation. Landlords sometimes assert that extensive renovations justified a rent increase large enough to trigger deregulation. But IAI claims require documented proof of actual costs, and the amounts are now capped. Vague references to renovations without invoices, permits, or receipts are a red flag.

Watch for silence. When landlords refuse to discuss rent history, deflect questions about stabilization status, or become vague when asked about the apartment's regulatory background, it often signals that the full story does not support their position.

Not every red flag means the apartment is illegally deregulated. But every red flag means the question deserves investigation.

Why Tenants Don't Check, and Why They Should

Tenants hesitate to request rent history and investigate stabilization status for reasons that are understandable but ultimately self-defeating.

Some fear retaliation. They worry that investigating their apartment's status will anger the landlord and lead to consequences. But requesting records from a government agency is not an act of aggression. It is an exercise of a legal right. And New York law prohibits landlords from retaliating against tenants who assert their rights.

Some fear souring the relationship. They have a decent rapport with their landlord and don't want to disrupt it. This is a reasonable concern, but it should be weighed against the possibility that you are paying hundreds of dollars per month more than the law allows. A good relationship built on an illegal rent is not as good as it seems.

Some fear being wrong. They worry about going through the process and discovering that their apartment isn't stabilized after all, that they'll feel foolish for checking. But confirming that your apartment is not stabilized is itself valuable information. It tells you exactly where you stand and eliminates uncertainty.

Some simply don't know. They've never heard of rent history, don't know they can request it, and have never had anyone explain the process. This is the most common reason, and it is the reason this chapter exists.

The risk of checking is almost always lower than tenants expect. The upside can be transformative. A rent reduction. A refund of overcharges. Renewal rights. Protection against eviction. The difference between knowing and not knowing is often thousands of dollars per year.

Real-World Example: The $500 Answer

A renter in Queens signed a lease at a rent they believed was market-rate. The landlord assured them the apartment had been deregulated years ago. The building was old, but the unit had been renovated with new fixtures, appliances, and flooring. Everything about the apartment said "market-rate."

After hearing about rent stabilization from a coworker, the tenant requested rent history from DHCR. The process took about three weeks. The records arrived by mail.

The rent history showed that the apartment had been rent-stabilized continuously. The legal rent, according to the most recent registration before the tenant moved in, was more than $500 per month lower than what the tenant was paying. The landlord had claimed IAI costs after the previous tenant vacated, but the claimed amounts exceeded the post-HSTPA caps. The apartment had never been lawfully deregulated. The "market-rate" label was a description of how the landlord chose to market the unit. It was not a legal status.

The tenant filed an overcharge complaint with DHCR. The apartment was confirmed as stabilized. The rent was reduced to the lawful amount. The tenant recovered thousands of dollars in overcharges covering the period of overpayment.

The entire process started with a single request the landlord hoped would never be made. It took three weeks to receive the document. It took one look at the numbers to see the problem. And it changed the tenant's financial position by more than $6,000 per year.

What to Take From This Chapter

Rent stabilization follows the apartment, not the tenant. High rent, renovated conditions, and landlord assurances do not determine whether an apartment is stabilized. Only the records do.

Landlords must register stabilized apartments annually. Failure to register has consequences, including the potential freezing of rent increases for unregistered years.

The rent history is the most powerful document a tenant can request. It is free, it does not require landlord permission, and it reveals whether the apartment is stabilized, what the legal rent is, and whether overcharges exist.

You can request your rent history online, by email, by phone, by text, or in person. The process is straightforward and typically takes two to four weeks.

Red flags in the rent history, including sudden rent jumps, registration gaps, and unsupported deregulation claims, warrant further investigation.

If you're unsure whether your apartment is rent-stabilized, checking is the smartest move you can make. The cost is zero. The potential value is enormous. And the only person who benefits from you not checking is your landlord.

In the next chapter, we'll break down how legal rent is calculated, what increases are actually allowed, and how landlords commonly get it wrong.

6

Legal Rent, Rent Increases and Renewal Leases

In a rent-stabilized apartment, rent is not whatever the landlord asks and the tenant agrees to. It is a regulated number with rules, limits, and paperwork behind it. When those rules aren't followed exactly, the increase may be illegal, even if the tenant paid it for months or years without objection.

This chapter explains how legal rent is established, how the increase process works, what makes a renewal lease valid, and why many rent hikes that look routine are actually unlawful. If you live in a stabilized apartment, this is the chapter that tells you whether the rent you're paying is the rent the law allows.

Legal Rent: The Number That Actually Matters

Legal rent is the maximum amount a landlord is permitted to charge for a rent-stabilized apartment. It is not a suggestion, not an approximation, and not a negotiating position. It is a regulated ceiling created by a chain of documented, lawful steps.

Legal rent is not the advertised rent. A landlord can advertise an apartment at any price, but advertising does not establish legal rent. If the advertised rent exceeds the legal maximum, the advertisement is irrelevant to what the landlord is actually allowed to collect.

Legal rent is not the rent in your lease if the lease is unlawful. A lease can state any number, but if that number exceeds the legal rent, the excess is an overcharge. The lease does not make an illegal rent legal.

Legal rent is not the rent the previous tenant paid if that rent was wrong. If the prior tenant was overcharged, the overcharge does not become the new baseline simply because it was collected without challenge. The legal rent is what the law allows, not what the landlord managed to collect.

Legal rent is created by a specific sequence. It begins with the prior legal rent, properly registered with HCR. To that base, the landlord may add only lawful increases: RGB renewal increases, approved MCI adjustments, documented IAI costs within post-HSTPA caps, and any other increase specifically authorized by law. Each step must be documented, registered, and compliant with the rules in effect at the time.

If any step in that chain is skipped, improperly documented, or unauthorized, the legal rent may be lower than what the landlord is charging. In some cases, it may be significantly lower. And in some cases, the rent may need to be rolled back to the last point where everything was done correctly.

How the Rent Guidelines Board Sets Increases

Most rent increases in stabilized apartments come from the Rent Guidelines Board (RGB).

The RGB is a nine-member panel appointed by the mayor of New York City. Each year, the board conducts research, holds public hearings, and votes on the maximum percentage increases landlords may apply to renewal leases for the coming year. The process typically runs through the spring, with the final vote in June and the new rates taking effect for leases commencing on or after October 1 of that year through September 30 of the following year.

The RGB sets separate percentages for one-year and two-year renewal leases. For the current guideline year (leases commencing between October 1, 2025 and September 30, 2026), the approved increases are 3 percent for a one-year renewal and 4.5 percent for a two-year renewal.

These percentages are ceilings, not floors. A landlord may charge less than the RGB-approved increase, but may not charge more. And the increase may only be applied when a proper renewal lease is offered and accepted. The RGB rate alone does not authorize a rent increase. The increase must be delivered through the renewal process described later in this chapter.

Several things that landlords sometimes do are not permitted under the RGB system.

Landlords cannot invent their own increases. The percentage must match the applicable RGB order for the lease term being offered.

Landlords cannot apply future RGB rates early. If a renewal lease commences in September 2026, the applicable rate is from the guideline year covering that start date. The landlord cannot apply next year's rate in advance.

Landlords cannot combine multiple years of RGB increases into a single jump. Each increase corresponds to a specific renewal. If the landlord failed to offer renewals for several years, they cannot retroactively stack all the missed increases into one.

Landlords cannot substitute "market" reasoning for the regulated rate. In a stabilized apartment, the market is irrelevant to the renewal increase. The increase is what the RGB says it is, period.

If the renewal lease itself is defective, the increase built on it often fails as well. The RGB rate means nothing without a valid renewal to carry it.

The Renewal Lease: Where Most Landlords Slip

In rent-stabilized apartments, tenants have the right to a renewal lease. This right is statutory. It cannot be waived, bargained away, or eliminated by landlord preference. And the process for offering a renewal is governed by specific rules that landlords must follow exactly.

A valid renewal lease must meet several requirements.

It must be offered within the required time window. In New York City, the landlord must send the renewal offer by mail or personal delivery no more than 150 days and no less than 90 days before the existing lease expires. This window is mandatory, not advisory. A renewal sent too early or too late is not timely, and an untimely renewal has consequences.

It must be on the correct form. Renewals in New York City must be offered on the DHCR Renewal Lease Form (RTP-8) or an approved facsimile. An informal letter, an email, or a conversation does not satisfy the requirement. The form must also be accompanied by the Rent Stabilization Lease Rider, which explains the tenant's rights, describes how the proposed rent was calculated, and discloses the legal regulated rent.

It must include the correct legal rent. The renewal must reflect the current legal rent plus the applicable RGB increase for the lease term the tenant selects. If the rent on the renewal is wrong, the renewal is defective.

It must offer both one-year and two-year terms. The tenant has the right to choose between a one-year and a two-year renewal. The landlord cannot offer only one option.

It must preserve the same terms and conditions as the expiring lease. A renewal lease cannot change the fundamental terms of the tenancy unless a specific law or regulation requires the change. Adding new restrictions, eliminating existing rights, or attaching riders that alter the deal is generally not permitted.

Once the tenant receives the renewal offer, they have 60 days to select a lease term, sign, and return it. After the tenant returns the signed renewal, the landlord must send back a fully executed copy within 30 days.

Failure to comply with any of these requirements is not a minor technicality. It is a regulatory violation with real consequences.

What Happens When the Landlord Misses the Window

When a landlord fails to offer a timely renewal, the consequences fall on the landlord, not the tenant.

If the renewal is offered late (fewer than 90 days before the lease expires), the landlord forfeits the right to collect the rent increase as early as they otherwise could. The tenant has the option of choosing the lease start date: either the date the lease would have commenced had the offer been timely, or 90 days after the date the landlord actually makes the offer. The new rent cannot take effect before 90 days after the late offer is made, regardless of which option the tenant selects.

If no renewal is offered at all, the tenant's rights continue. The tenant is not required to move out. The tenant cannot be charged more than the current rent. And the landlord's failure to offer a renewal can be the basis of a DHCR complaint, using Form RA-90, which may result in an order directing the landlord to offer a proper renewal.

This is one of the most important and least understood protections in rent stabilization. Many tenants assume that if the lease expires without a renewal, they must leave or their tenancy becomes precarious. The opposite is true. A tenant in a stabilized apartment who does not receive a renewal continues on the same terms at the same rent. The landlord's failure to act does not diminish the tenant's rights. It diminishes the landlord's.

Preferential Rent: The Discount That Creates Confusion

Some tenants in stabilized apartments pay a preferential rent, meaning a rent lower than the legal regulated maximum.

Preferential rents are common, particularly in neighborhoods where the legal rent exceeds what the market will bear. A landlord with a legal rent of $2,400 might offer the apartment at $1,900 to attract a tenant quickly. The $1,900 becomes the preferential rent. The $2,400 remains the legal rent.

Before the HSTPA, preferential rents were a source of enormous confusion and hardship. Many leases contained language allowing the landlord to eliminate the preferential rent at renewal and jump the collected rent to the full legal amount. Tenants who had been paying $1,900 would suddenly face a renewal at $2,400, an increase that had nothing to do with the RGB and everything to do with the landlord exercising a contractual option.

The HSTPA changed this dramatically.

Under current law, tenants who were paying a preferential rent as of June 14, 2019 retain the preferential rent for the duration of the tenancy. The landlord may apply RGB increases to the preferential rent, but may not jump from the preferential amount to the full legal rent during the tenancy. The higher legal rent can generally be collected only after the tenant vacates and a new tenant moves in.

This means that if you are currently paying a preferential rent, your renewal increase should be calculated based on the preferential amount, not the legal rent. A landlord who applies the RGB percentage to the legal rent rather than the preferential rent is overcharging you.

This is an area where the details are critical and where pre-HSTPA practices are particularly dangerous. If your landlord is attempting to raise your rent from a preferential level to the full legal rent, or is calculating your increase based on the legal rent rather than the preferential rent, they may be violating current law. The remedy is an overcharge complaint with DHCR, covered in Chapter 7.

Common Illegal Rent Increases

Illegal rent increases are not rare. They are common, and they often hide in plain sight.

The most frequent form is increasing rent without a proper renewal lease. Landlords sometimes raise the rent by simply stating a new amount, by sending an email or letter, or by charging a higher amount and hoping the tenant pays without objection. In a stabilized apartment, a rent increase is not valid unless it is delivered through a compliant renewal lease. An increase without a renewal is an overcharge.

Another common violation is charging RGB increases without offering the required renewal terms. The landlord applies the percentage but skips the formal renewal process, or offers only a one-year option instead of both terms, or uses an improper form. Each of these defects can invalidate the increase.

Applying increases after missing the renewal window is another frequent problem. As discussed above, landlords who fail to offer timely renewals lose the right to collect increases as soon as the law would otherwise allow. Landlords who charge the increase anyway are overcharging.

Stacking multiple increases at once occurs when a landlord has failed to offer renewals for several years and then attempts to apply all the missed RGB increases in a single renewal. This is generally not permitted. Each increase must correspond to a specific renewal period. Combining them inflates the rent beyond what any single renewal would allow.

Raising rent during a registration lapse is another violation. When a landlord fails to register a stabilized apartment with HCR, rent increases for the unregistered period may be invalid. The HSTPA strengthened this rule, making registration compliance a prerequisite for lawful increases.

Adding charges that are not part of the legal rent is a subtler form of overcharging. Landlords sometimes add fees for amenities, services, or building features that were previously included in the rent. If these charges effectively raise the amount the tenant pays above the legal rent, they function as illegal increases regardless of how they are labeled.

Each of these violations has the same remedy. The tenant can challenge the increase through an overcharge complaint with DHCR, and may recover the excess plus damages.

Why Paying an Illegal Increase Does Not Make It Legal

One of the most important protections in New York tenant law is a principle that surprises many tenants: paying an illegal rent does not legalize it.

Tenants do not waive their rights by paying rent. If the legal rent is $1,800 and the landlord charges $2,200, paying $2,200 every month does not transform $2,200 into the legal rent. The overcharge remains an overcharge, recoverable through complaint and subject to penalties.

Tenants do not waive their rights by signing a defective lease. If the renewal lease contains an illegal rent, signing it does not make the rent lawful. The law controls, not the paper.

Tenants do not waive their rights by renewing under pressure. A tenant who accepts a renewal because they fear losing their apartment has not voluntarily agreed to an illegal term. The term is unenforceable regardless of the circumstances under which it was signed.

Tenants do not waive their rights by failing to object immediately. New York law provides overcharge lookback periods that allow tenants to challenge rents that were wrong for years before the complaint was filed. The HSTPA expanded these lookback periods significantly. The passage of time weakens some claims, but paying without objection does not extinguish the right to challenge.

This principle exists because the alternative would be unworkable. If paying an illegal rent made it legal, landlords would have every incentive to overcharge and simply wait for the tenant to pay. The law eliminates that incentive by ensuring that illegality is measured by compliance, not by collection.

If you are paying more than the legal rent, you have the right to challenge it. The fact that you've been paying it for months or years does not eliminate that right. It may, in fact, increase the amount you can recover.

The Renewal Lease as Leverage

Most tenants think of the renewal lease as paperwork. Something that arrives, gets signed, and goes in a drawer.

In reality, the renewal lease is one of the strongest tenant protections in New York law, and it creates leverage that tenants rarely use because they don't realize it exists.

The renewal lease locks in the tenant's right to stay. Once a proper renewal is offered and accepted, the tenancy continues on regulated terms. The landlord cannot terminate without just cause. The rent is fixed for the lease term. And the terms of the tenancy are preserved.

The renewal lease constrains the landlord's ability to increase rent. The increase is limited to the RGB percentage applied to the correct base rent. The landlord cannot charge more, cannot impose additional increases mid-lease, and cannot alter the terms of the deal.

The renewal lease creates a compliance record. Each renewal that is offered, signed, and registered creates a documented link in the chain of legal rent. Breaks in that chain, whether from missed renewals, improper forms, or unregistered increases, create vulnerabilities for the landlord and opportunities for the tenant.

And the failure to offer a proper renewal creates direct consequences for the landlord. It delays increases, freezes rent, and provides grounds for DHCR complaints.

Tenants who understand the renewal process treat each renewal not as routine paperwork but as a checkpoint. They verify the rent amount, confirm the RGB rate, check the form, note the timing, and keep copies of everything. Each renewal is an opportunity to catch errors, document compliance (or noncompliance), and build a record that protects the tenancy.

Real-World Example: The Renewal That Never Came

A tenant in a rent-stabilized apartment in the Bronx was told their rent would increase at renewal. The landlord sent an email in March stating the new monthly amount and began charging it when the lease term ended in June. No formal renewal lease was offered. No RTP-8 form was sent. No lease rider was provided. The tenant received no paperwork at all, just a higher number on the next rent statement.

The tenant paid the increased amount for eight months, assuming it was valid. The email had included a percentage that sounded like it could be the RGB rate. The landlord had been professional in all other dealings. There was no reason to suspect anything was wrong.

Then the tenant mentioned the increase to a neighbor who had recently gone through a lease renewal dispute of her own. The neighbor asked a simple question: did you get a renewal lease form?

The tenant hadn't.

After consulting with a tenant advocacy organization, the tenant learned that rent-stabilized renewals must be offered on the proper form, within the required 150-to-90-day window, accompanied by the rent stabilization lease rider. Because the landlord had done none of this, the increase was unlawful. The email was not a valid renewal. The higher rent was an overcharge.

The tenant challenged the rent. The result: the rent was frozen at the prior legal amount for the period during which no valid renewal had been offered, and the landlord was required to offer a compliant renewal going forward. The tenant recovered the difference between what they had paid and what the law allowed.

The landlord hadn't broken the rules loudly. They had broken them quietly, in a way that looked like business as usual, and assumed the tenant would never notice the difference between a real renewal and an email with a number on it.

What to Take From This Chapter

Legal rent is created by compliance, not agreement. It is the product of a documented chain of lawful steps, and any break in that chain can freeze or reduce the rent.

RGB increases are the primary mechanism for lawful rent increases in stabilized apartments. They apply only when a proper renewal lease is offered and accepted, and they are limited to the percentages set for the applicable guideline year.

Renewal leases are mandatory, not optional. They must be offered in the correct form, within the correct time window, with the correct rent and both lease term options. Failure to comply delays or invalidates the increase.

Preferential rent is now protected under the HSTPA. Landlords generally cannot jump from the preferential amount to the full legal rent during the tenancy. Increases must be calculated on the preferential rent, not the legal rent.

Many rent increases fail because landlords miss procedural steps. Increases without renewals, increases on improper forms, increases outside the timing window, and increases during registration lapses are all potentially invalid.

Paying an illegal increase does not make it legal. Tenants retain the right to challenge overcharges regardless of how long they have been paying the wrong amount.

If you're paying more rent than last year, the key question is not "Is this increase normal?" It's "Was this increase done exactly the way the law requires?"

In the next chapter, we'll walk through the process of filing an overcharge complaint, calculating what you may be owed, and understanding why many tenants recover far more than they expect.

7

Overcharge Claims

How to Get Your Money Back

This is the chapter about money.

Everything covered so far, rent stabilization status, legal rent, RGB increases, renewal lease requirements, leads to a single practical question: what happens when the landlord has been charging more than the law allows?

The answer is that you can get the money back. Not just going forward, through a rent reduction. Going backward, through a refund of every dollar you were overcharged, potentially multiplied by three if the overcharge was willful.

Rent overcharge claims are one of the most powerful tools in New York tenant law. They are also one of the most underused, because tenants either don't know they exist, don't believe the amounts are worth pursuing, or assume the process is too complicated without a lawyer. This chapter explains the mechanics: how to identify an overcharge, how to calculate what you may be owed, how to file a complaint, what happens during the investigation, and what outcomes are possible.

The amounts are not small. For many tenants, an overcharge claim is worth more than a year's rent.

What Is a Rent Overcharge?

A rent overcharge occurs whenever a landlord collects more than the legal regulated rent for a rent-stabilized apartment.

The overcharge can be obvious or invisible. It can originate from a single event (an illegal rent increase at one point in the apartment's history) or from a compounding error that grows larger with every subsequent renewal. It can affect the current tenant, a previous tenant, or a chain of tenants stretching back years.

Common sources of overcharges include rent increases imposed without a valid renewal lease, RGB increases applied to the wrong base rent, IAI costs that exceed the post-HSTPA caps or that were never properly documented, vacancy bonuses applied after the HSTPA eliminated them, preferential rent increases calculated on the legal rent instead of the preferential amount, and rents set after fraudulent or improper deregulation claims.

What makes overcharges particularly damaging is that they compound. Once an illegal increase enters the rent, every subsequent increase builds on the inflated number. A $200 overcharge in year one becomes a $200-plus overcharge in year two after the RGB percentage is applied to the wrong base. By year five, the gap between what the tenant is paying and what the tenant should be paying may have widened substantially.

This compounding effect is why even a "small" overcharge at the beginning of a tenancy can produce a recovery worth tens of thousands of dollars by the time it is challenged.

The Lookback Period: How Far Back Can You Go?

The lookback period determines how far back DHCR or a court can examine the rent history when investigating an overcharge claim. This is one of the most contested and legally complex areas of New York tenant law, and it has changed multiple times in recent years.

Here is the current landscape, simplified as clearly as possible.

The HSTPA, enacted in June 2019, originally expanded the lookback period to six years and in some cases allowed DHCR and the courts to examine the full rent history of an apartment going back decades. This was a dramatic change from the prior rule, which generally limited the examination to four years before the complaint was filed.

In April 2020, the New York Court of Appeals issued a landmark decision in a case known as Regina Metropolitan. The court held that applying the HSTPA's expanded lookback provisions retroactively to overcharges that occurred before June 2019 would violate landlords' due process rights. The practical effect was to reinstate the four-year lookback for overcharges that accrued before the HSTPA took effect.

For overcharges that accrued after June 14, 2019, the HSTPA's six-year lookback generally applies. This means that a complaint filed today can reach back six years to examine rent history for the post-HSTPA period.

There is an important exception for fraud. If a tenant can show evidence of a fraudulent scheme by the landlord, whether to deregulate the apartment improperly or to overcharge systematically, the lookback period can extend further back than the standard four or six years. In 2024, the legislature passed additional legislation clarifying the definition of fraud in this context, establishing that a landlord can be deemed to have committed fraud based on the "totality of the circumstances" without requiring all elements of common-law fraud to be proven.

Additionally, claims challenging the regulatory status of an apartment (whether it was properly deregulated or should still be stabilized) are not subject to the same time limitations as overcharge claims. A tenant can challenge the stabilization status of their apartment at any time, regardless of when the alleged deregulation occurred.

The lookback rules are genuinely complicated, and the legal landscape continues to evolve through court decisions and legislative action. But the core message is straightforward: if you have been overcharged, the law provides a mechanism to reach back in time and recover what was taken, often going back many years.

For tenants who suspect an overcharge, the most important thing is to file sooner rather than later. The lookback period is measured from the date the complaint is filed. Every month you wait is a month that may fall outside the recoverable window.

How to Calculate What You May Be Owed

Calculating an overcharge precisely requires tracing the entire rent history and identifying where the legal rent diverged from the collected rent. That level of precision often requires professional assistance. But you can do a rough calculation yourself to understand the stakes before deciding whether to pursue a claim.

Here is a simplified example that illustrates how the math works.

Suppose you moved into a rent-stabilized apartment in 2020. The landlord charged you $2,200 per month. You have paid that amount, with RGB increases on top, for the past six years.

You request the rent history and discover that the legal rent at the time you moved in should have been $2,000. The landlord had claimed IAI costs that exceeded the post-HSTPA caps, inflating the rent by $200 per month from day one.

That $200 per month overcharge, compounded by RGB increases applied to the inflated base, grows over time. But even without accounting for the compounding effect, the simple math is striking.

$200 per month times 12 months equals $2,400 per year. Over six years, that is $14,400 in overcharges, not counting interest, not counting compounding, and not counting the RGB increases that were calculated on the wrong base.

When you add the compounding (because each year's RGB increase was applied to a base that was $200 too high), the actual total is higher. Over a six-year period, the additional overcharge from compounded RGB increases could add several thousand dollars more.

Now add treble damages. If DHCR or a court finds that the overcharge was willful, the refund amount is tripled. That $14,400 becomes $43,200. With compounding, it could exceed $50,000.

And the rent going forward is reduced to the correct legal amount, saving the tenant $200 or more every month for the remainder of the tenancy.

This is not a hypothetical exercise. These are the kinds of numbers that real tenants recover through real overcharge claims. The math is simple, but the amounts are not small.

How to File an Overcharge Complaint

Filing an overcharge complaint is an administrative process handled through DHCR's Office of Rent Administration. It does not require a lawyer, though legal assistance is strongly recommended for complex cases.

The process begins with obtaining your rent history, as described in Chapter 5. The rent history is the foundation of any overcharge claim. Without it, you are guessing. With it, you can trace every increase and identify where the numbers went wrong.

Once you have the rent history and believe an overcharge exists, you file a formal complaint using DHCR Form RA-89, titled "Tenant's Complaint of Rent and/or Other Specific Overcharges in Rent Stabilized Apartments." The form is available on the HCR website, at DHCR borough rent offices, or by calling 833-499-0343.

The form requires you to provide your contact information, the building address and apartment number, details of your lease, the rent you are currently paying, and a description of why you believe you have been overcharged. You are required to submit all supporting documentation with the complaint, including copies of your lease, rent receipts or bank statements showing what you have paid, the rent history, and any communications with the landlord about rent amounts.

You can submit the form by mail to DHCR's Office of Rent Administration at 92-31 Union Hall Street, Queens, NY 11433, or online through the HCR portal. Keep copies of everything you submit.

One important note about the form: DHCR's RA-89 asks you to specify the basis for your overcharge claim (MCI increase, IAI increase, registration lapse, and so on). Be careful with this question. DHCR has historically tended to limit its investigation to the specific basis you identify. If you are unsure where the overcharge originates, or if multiple issues may be involved, say so. Describe what you know and what the rent history shows, and avoid narrowing your claim unnecessarily. If you have access to a tenant advocate or attorney, this is a good moment to consult one.

What Happens After You File

After you submit the complaint, DHCR acknowledges receipt and assigns the case a docket number. The landlord is notified and given an opportunity to respond with documentation supporting the rent they charged.

The investigation process involves DHCR reviewing the rent history, the landlord's registration filings, the documentation both sides submit, and any other records relevant to calculating the legal rent. DHCR examines each increase in the chain, verifies whether it was lawful, and determines what the legal rent should be.

This process is not fast. Overcharge investigations at DHCR can take months, and in some cases years, depending on the complexity of the rent history, the volume of cases, and whether either party disputes the findings.

During the investigation, you should continue paying your current rent. Do not withhold rent based on a pending overcharge complaint. Withholding creates a separate legal issue (nonpayment) that can complicate your position and potentially lead to eviction proceedings while the overcharge claim is still being resolved. Pay what you are being charged, keep records, and let the process work.

If DHCR determines that an overcharge occurred, it issues a written order. That order establishes the correct legal rent, directs the landlord to refund the overcharged amount, and may include treble damages if the overcharge was willful.

Possible Outcomes: Rent Reduction, Refund, and Treble Damages

An overcharge order from DHCR can include several forms of relief.

The legal rent is recalculated and reduced to the correct amount. Going forward, the landlord may only charge the corrected legal rent plus lawful increases. This reduction is permanent for the duration of the tenancy and cannot be reversed by the landlord.

The landlord is directed to refund all overcharges collected within the applicable lookback period. This is a dollar-for-dollar refund of every cent the tenant paid above the legal rent during the recoverable period, plus interest.

If the overcharge is found to be willful, DHCR may impose treble damages, meaning the refund amount is multiplied by three. Willfulness does not require proof of evil intent. It generally means that the landlord knew or should have known that the rent exceeded the legal amount. Indicators of willfulness include failure to register the apartment, failure to provide the rent stabilization lease rider, large unexplained rent jumps between tenants, and a pattern of noncompliance.

The tenant can collect the overcharge award through one of two methods. The offset method allows the tenant to deduct the overcharge amount from future rent payments until the award is fully recovered. The judgment method allows the tenant to obtain a court judgment against the landlord for the overcharge amount, which can then be enforced through standard collection procedures.

DHCR vs. Housing Court: Where to File

Tenants have a choice about where to bring an overcharge claim. They can file with DHCR (the administrative route) or bring the claim in Housing Court or Supreme Court (the judicial route).

DHCR is the more common path for most tenants, particularly those without lawyers. The process is administrative, there is no filing fee, and DHCR conducts the investigation itself. The downside is speed: DHCR cases can take a long time, and the tenant has limited control over the timeline.

Housing Court or Supreme Court offers faster resolution in some cases and allows the tenant more control over the proceedings, but it requires more legal sophistication. Court proceedings involve formal pleadings, discovery, and potentially a trial. Most tenants who pursue overcharge claims in court do so with the assistance of an attorney.

You generally cannot pursue the same overcharge claim simultaneously in both forums. If you file with DHCR, that is the path until the case is resolved or you withdraw it. If you file in court, the court handles the claim.

For tenants without lawyers, DHCR is usually the better starting point. For tenants with complex cases, significant dollar amounts, or evidence of fraud, consulting an attorney about the judicial route is worth considering.

When to Get Help

Overcharge claims can be straightforward or extraordinarily complex. A case involving a single improper increase that is visible on the rent history can often be handled by a tenant alone through the DHCR process. A case involving decades of compounding errors, fraudulent deregulation, multiple ownership changes, and contested IAI claims is a different matter entirely.

Free and low-cost legal assistance is available through organizations that specialize in tenant representation. Legal Aid Society, Legal Services NYC,

Met Council on Housing, and borough-specific legal services organizations all handle overcharge cases. Many offer free consultations and can help you evaluate whether your case warrants filing, how strong the evidence is, and whether the judicial route would produce a better outcome.

If your rent history shows clear irregularities, if the potential recovery is substantial, or if the landlord has a history of noncompliance, getting professional help early is almost always worth it. An experienced attorney can calculate the overcharge more precisely, navigate the lookback rules, and maximize the recovery.

Real-World Example: Six Years of Invisible Overcharges

A tenant moved into a rent-stabilized one-bedroom in Washington Heights in 2019. The landlord charged $1,950 per month and presented the apartment as recently renovated. The lease made no mention of stabilization. No rent stabilization rider was provided. The landlord described the unit as market-rate.

The tenant paid the rent for six years without questioning it. The apartment was in good condition. The rent increased modestly at each renewal, and the increases felt reasonable.

In early 2025, after reading about rent stabilization online, the tenant requested the rent history from DHCR. The records arrived three weeks later.

The rent history showed the apartment had been continuously stabilized. The last legal rent before the tenant moved in had been $1,450. The landlord had claimed IAI costs of $40,000 for the renovation, producing a rent increase that pushed the legal rent to $1,950. But under the HSTPA's caps, the maximum allowable IAI increase for the apartment was based on $30,000 amortized over 15 years, which translated to roughly $179 per month, not the $500 per month the landlord had added.

The correct legal rent at move-in should have been approximately $1,629. The tenant had been overpaying by more than $300 per month from the first day.

Over six years, the base overcharge alone totaled more than $21,600. When compounded RGB increases applied to the inflated base were added, the total exceeded $25,000. DHCR found the overcharge was willful, noting the absence of the rent stabilization rider and the IAI costs that exceeded the statutory cap. Treble damages brought the total award to more than $75,000.

The tenant's rent was reduced to the correct legal amount. The landlord was ordered to refund the overcharges. And the tenant retained every protection of rent stabilization going forward.

The entire case started with a free request that took three weeks to process. The tenant had been paying the wrong rent for six years. The landlord had been counting on that continuing indefinitely.

What to Take From This Chapter

Overcharge claims allow tenants to recover every dollar paid above the legal regulated rent, potentially multiplied by three for willful violations.

The lookback period determines how far back the recovery can reach. For post-HSTPA overcharges, the lookback is generally six years. For pre-HSTPA overcharges, the standard is four years, with a fraud exception that can extend the window further. The rules are complex and continuing to evolve through litigation and legislation.

Filing a complaint requires your rent history, supporting documentation, and DHCR Form RA-89. The process is free and does not require a lawyer, though legal help is strongly recommended for complex cases.

DHCR investigates the complaint, determines the correct legal rent, and orders refunds and potentially treble damages. The process can be slow, but the outcomes are enforceable.

Even modest overcharges produce large recoveries over time. A $200 per month overcharge over six years, with treble damages, can exceed $50,000. These are not abstract numbers. They are real money that belongs to you if the law was not followed.

If you suspect your rent is higher than it should be, file sooner rather than later. Every month you wait is a month that may fall outside the recovery window. The clock is running. The complaint stops it.

In the next chapter, we'll move from the numbers to the document you hold in your hand every day: your lease. We'll walk through a typical New York City lease clause by clause and explain what's enforceable, what's not, and what matters more than it looks like it does.

8

Reading Your Lease Like a Tenant Lawyer

Most tenants sign their lease in a hurry.

The apartment is competitive. The broker is waiting. The landlord says the lease is "standard." There's pressure to sign quickly, and the document itself is dense, formal, and long enough that reading every clause feels impractical. So the tenant skims the rent amount, the move-in date, and the term length, signs at the bottom, and puts the lease in a drawer.

That lease may contain clauses that are illegal. It may omit disclosures that are legally required. It may include provisions the tenant could challenge, provisions the landlord will never enforce, and provisions that matter far more than they appear to. And it may be missing a document that, by its absence, tells the tenant something critically important about the apartment's regulatory status.

This chapter walks through a typical New York City residential lease the way a tenant lawyer would read it: clause by clause, sorting what matters from what doesn't, what's enforceable from what's not, and what you should pay attention to even when it looks like boilerplate.

Before You Read a Single Clause: What Kind of Lease Is This?

The first question is not about what the lease says. It's about what kind of lease you're holding.

If your apartment is rent-stabilized, the lease should be accompanied by a Rent Stabilization Lease Rider (we'll cover that in detail later in this chapter). The renewal lease should be on DHCR Form RTP-8 or an approved equivalent. The terms should reflect RGB-approved increases and the same conditions as the prior lease.

If your apartment is not stabilized, the lease is a private contract between you and the landlord. The terms are more negotiable, but the lease still cannot override statutory protections. Even in an unregulated apartment, the warranty of habitability applies, security deposit caps apply, notice period rules apply, and discriminatory provisions are unenforceable.

If you are unsure whether your apartment is stabilized, the lease itself may give you clues, but it is not definitive. A lease that makes no mention of stabilization does not prove the apartment is unregulated. As Chapter 5 explained, the only reliable way to know is to check the records. But a lease that does reference stabilization, or that arrives with the required rider, confirms that the landlord acknowledges the apartment's regulated status.

Knowing what kind of lease you're holding changes how you read every clause that follows.

The Rent Clause: More Than a Number

The rent clause states the monthly amount the tenant agrees to pay. In most leases, this looks straightforward. A dollar amount, a due date, an address for payment.

But in a rent-stabilized apartment, the number in this clause is not the whole picture. The rent clause should reflect the legal regulated rent, or, if a preferential rent is being offered, it should clearly state both the preferential rent (the amount you actually pay) and the legal rent (the maximum the landlord could charge). The distinction matters because it determines how future increases are calculated, as Chapter 6 explained.

If the lease states only one rent amount and the apartment is stabilized, ask whether that amount is the legal rent or a preferential rent. If the landlord is offering a preferential rent, both figures should appear on the lease or the rider. If only the higher number appears, you may be set up for confusion at renewal time.

Also look at how the rent is expressed. In stabilized apartments, the rent is often not a round number. A rent of $1,847.23 is a sign that the amount was calculated through RGB increases applied to a prior legal rent. A round number like $2,000 in a building you suspect is stabilized may indicate that the rent was set by the landlord rather than calculated through the regulatory process. That's not proof of a problem, but it's worth investigating.

The Lease Term: When It Starts, When It Ends, and What Happens After

The term clause specifies the duration of the lease, typically one or two years, along with the start and end dates.

In a stabilized apartment, you have the right to choose between a one-year and a two-year renewal. If the lease you're signing is an initial vacancy lease (your first lease in the apartment), the landlord may offer a specific term, but the renewal process is governed by statute, not by whatever this clause says about what happens when the lease expires.

In an unregulated apartment, the term clause has more significance. When the lease ends, the landlord has broader discretion about whether to offer a renewal and at what price. However, even in unregulated apartments, notice period requirements apply. Under state law, landlords must provide written notice before declining to renew or imposing a rent increase of 5 percent or more. The required notice period depends on how long you've lived there: 30 days for tenancy under one year, 60 days for one to two years, and 90 days for tenancy over two years.

Watch for "automatic renewal" language. Some leases include clauses stating that the lease automatically renews for another term unless the tenant provides notice by a certain date. These clauses can be enforceable in unregulated apartments and can trap tenants into terms they didn't intend to accept. If you see this language, note the notice deadline and calendar it.

In stabilized apartments, automatic renewal clauses are superseded by the statutory renewal process, so they have less practical effect. But their presence in a stabilized lease may be a sign that the landlord is using an outdated or inappropriate form.

The Security Deposit Clause: What the Law Caps

Security deposit clauses typically state the amount of the deposit and the conditions under which it may be withheld.

Under current New York law, the security deposit is capped at one month's rent. No exceptions. This cap applies to all residential rentals statewide, whether stabilized or not.

If the lease states a deposit amount that exceeds one month's rent, that clause is unenforceable as to the excess. If the landlord collected more than one month's rent as a deposit, the excess is illegal and recoverable.

The lease may also describe conditions for withholding the deposit at move-out. Common language references "damage beyond normal wear and tear," which is consistent with the law. But some leases include broader language, such as deductions for "cleaning," "repainting," or "restoring the apartment to its original condition." As Chapters 14 and 15 will explain, many of these deductions are illegal. Normal wear and tear is the landlord's responsibility. A lease clause that purports to make the tenant responsible for routine turnover costs does not override the law.

Also check whether the lease mentions the landlord's obligation to return the deposit. Under current law, the landlord must return the full deposit or provide an itemized statement of lawful deductions within 14 days of the tenant's departure. If the lease states a longer return period, the lease is wrong and the 14-day statutory deadline controls.

The Warranty of Habitability: It's There Whether the Lease Says So or Not

Some leases include a clause acknowledging the warranty of habitability. Many do not. It doesn't matter.

The warranty of habitability is implied in every residential lease in New York by operation of law. It requires the landlord to maintain conditions that are safe, sanitary, and fit for human habitation. It covers essentials like heat, hot water, functioning plumbing and electricity, freedom from infestation, structural safety, and working locks.

A lease clause that says the tenant accepts the apartment "as is" does not waive the warranty. A lease clause that says the tenant is responsible for all repairs does not waive the warranty. A lease clause that says the tenant agrees not to withhold rent for habitability issues does not waive the warranty. The warranty cannot be waived, period.

If your lease contains language suggesting otherwise, treat it as a red flag about the landlord's practices, not as a binding term. The clause is unenforceable, but a landlord who includes it may be the kind of landlord who will resist making repairs.

The Entry and Access Clause: What the Landlord Can and Cannot Do

Most leases include a clause granting the landlord the right to enter the apartment under specified circumstances.

Reasonable provisions include entry for necessary repairs, entry to show the apartment to prospective tenants or buyers near the end of the lease term, and entry in genuine emergencies (fire, flood, gas leak). These provisions are consistent with New York law, which allows landlord access for legitimate purposes with reasonable advance notice.

Watch for provisions that are broader than the law allows. A clause granting the landlord "unlimited access" is unenforceable. A clause allowing entry "at any time" without notice is unenforceable. A clause permitting entry for "inspections" without further definition is vague enough to be challenged if used as a basis for repeated intrusions.

The law requires reasonable notice and a legitimate purpose for non-emergency entry. The lease cannot grant more access than that. If your lease includes overly broad entry language, the practical effect is limited, but you should be aware of it in case the landlord later claims the lease authorizes conduct that the law does not.

Chapter 13 covers landlord entry, privacy, and harassment in detail.

The Subletting and Assignment Clause: Narrower Than It Sounds

Many leases contain an outright prohibition on subletting or assigning the lease. This language sounds absolute, but in practice, it is not.

New York law gives tenants in buildings with four or more units the right to request permission to sublet, subject to specific procedures. The landlord may impose reasonable conditions but cannot unreasonably withhold consent. If the landlord unreasonably refuses, the tenant may sublet anyway.

For rent-stabilized apartments, the subletting rights are even more defined. Tenants generally have the right to sublet under specific rules: the sublet must be for a limited duration, the tenant must maintain primary residence, the rent charged to the subtenant cannot exceed the stabilized rent (plus a limited surcharge for furnished apartments), and the tenant must follow formal procedures including written notice to the landlord.

A lease clause that says "no subletting under any circumstances" does not eliminate these rights. The clause may reflect the landlord's preference, but the law provides the tenant a process to sublet regardless of what the lease says.

Assignment (permanently transferring the lease to another person) is different from subletting and is more restricted. Landlords generally have broader discretion to refuse assignment. But even assignment clauses should be read against the backdrop of statutory rights, not taken at face value.

Chapter 21 covers roommates, sublets, and occupancy rules in full detail.

The Pet Clause: The Three-Month Rule

Pet clauses vary widely. Some leases prohibit all pets. Some allow certain animals with prior approval. Some are silent on the issue.

In New York City, the "pet law" (NYC Administrative Code Section 27-2009.1) provides that if a tenant openly and notoriously keeps a pet for three months or more, and the landlord or its agent knows or should have known about the pet, the no-pet clause is deemed waived. The landlord cannot later enforce the prohibition against that pet.

This means that a no-pet clause in the lease is not necessarily the final word. If you have been keeping a pet openly for more than three months and the landlord has been aware, the clause may no longer be enforceable against you.

However, the three-month rule has limits. It protects the specific pet you have been keeping, not future pets. It requires that the pet-keeping was open and obvious, not hidden. And it does not apply to situations where the pet creates a genuine nuisance or safety hazard.

Also note that in rent-stabilized apartments, a landlord cannot charge a pet fee or pet deposit. Any charge imposed as a condition of keeping a pet would constitute an illegal rent increase.

The Late Fee Clause: Capped by Law

Many leases include a late fee provision, typically charging a flat amount or a percentage of the rent if payment is not received by a certain date.

New York law provides a statutory grace period before rent is considered late. For monthly rent, the grace period is generally five days after the due date. Late fees cannot be imposed during the grace period.

Late fees must also be reasonable. New York courts have generally treated late fees exceeding $50 or 5 percent of the monthly rent (whichever is less) as potentially unenforceable. A lease that imposes a $200 late fee on a $2,000 apartment may not hold up if challenged.

Additionally, in nonpayment eviction cases, inflated late fees included in the rent demand can render the demand defective, potentially causing the entire case to be dismissed. Chapter 20 covers this in detail.

If your lease includes a late fee provision, check whether it respects the grace period and whether the amount is within reasonable bounds. If it doesn't, the clause may be unenforceable, but the landlord may still try to collect.

The Renewal Clause: What It Means in Regulated vs. Unregulated Apartments

In rent-stabilized apartments, the renewal process is governed entirely by statute. You have the right to a renewal lease, offered in the proper form within the proper time window, at the RGB-approved rate. The lease's own renewal language is secondary to the statutory process.

In unregulated apartments, the lease's renewal clause matters more. If the lease says nothing about renewal, the tenancy typically converts to month-to-month status after the lease expires, subject to applicable notice requirements. If the lease includes specific renewal terms, those terms may govern, as long as they don't conflict with statutory protections.

Watch for clauses that attempt to shorten notice periods or impose conditions on renewal that exceed what the law allows. These provisions may be unenforceable, but they create confusion that benefits the landlord.

The Escalation Clause: Old Language, Current Consequences

Some older leases, particularly in buildings that have been stabilized since the 1960s or 1970s, contain escalation clauses. These clauses allow the landlord to pass through increased operating costs (fuel, taxes, labor) directly to the tenant as a rent surcharge, separate from and in addition to RGB increases.

Escalation clauses are unusual in newer leases, but when they exist, they can add meaningful amounts to the rent. The RGB addresses escalation clauses in its annual orders, specifying how they interact with guideline increases.

If your lease contains an escalation clause, determine whether the landlord is actively collecting surcharges under it and whether those surcharges are calculated correctly. The rules are technical, and errors are common. If you are paying surcharges beyond your monthly rent, verify that they are authorized.

The Jury Trial Waiver: Common, Controversial, and Context-Dependent

Many residential leases include a clause in which the tenant waives the right to a jury trial in any dispute with the landlord.

These clauses are technically enforceable in certain contexts under New York law, but they are disfavored by courts and subject to scrutiny. The enforceability depends on whether the waiver was knowing, voluntary, and intentional, which is a high bar in a residential lease that most tenants never read carefully.

In practice, most landlord-tenant disputes in New York City are heard in Housing Court, which does not use juries. The waiver has limited practical significance in that context. However, if a dispute escalates to Supreme Court (for example, in a large overcharge claim), the waiver could theoretically be invoked.

If your lease includes a jury trial waiver, you should be aware of it, but it is unlikely to affect your day-to-day rights as a tenant. Courts are reluctant to enforce these waivers in adhesion contracts (take-it-or-leave-it agreements), and a tenant who can show they did not meaningfully consent to the waiver may be able to set it aside.

The Attorney's Fees Clause: A Two-Way Street

Some leases include a clause requiring the tenant to pay the landlord's attorney's fees if the landlord prevails in a legal dispute.

Under New York Real Property Law Section 234, any lease clause that entitles the landlord to recover attorney's fees automatically gives the tenant the reciprocal right to recover attorney's fees if the tenant prevails. This is true even if the lease mentions only the landlord's right to fees.

This means that an attorney's fees clause in your lease is actually a two-way street. If the landlord sues you and loses, you can recover your legal costs. If you challenge an illegal rent increase or eviction and win, you may be entitled to fees.

Many tenants don't realize this. Many landlords don't mention it. But the reciprocal right exists by operation of law, and it can be a significant source of leverage in disputes.

The Rent Stabilization Lease Rider: The Document That Changes Everything

If your apartment is rent-stabilized, the landlord is required to provide you with a Rent Stabilization Lease Rider at the time you sign the lease. This rider is not optional. It is mandated by law.

The rider explains how the proposed rent was calculated, discloses the legal regulated rent, states whether a preferential rent is being charged, describes the tenant's rights under rent stabilization (including the right to a renewal lease, the right to file complaints with DHCR, and the right to challenge the rent), and identifies the prior tenant's rent.

For vacancy leases (when you are the first tenant in the apartment or are replacing a prior tenant), the rider must disclose the rent charged to the immediately preceding tenant. This disclosure is critical because it allows the incoming tenant to verify that the rent was calculated properly and that any increase between tenants was lawful.

The rider is the single most important document for a rent-stabilized tenant, and its absence is one of the strongest red flags in New York tenant law.

If the landlord did not provide you with a rent stabilization rider, one of several things may be happening. The landlord may not know the apartment is stabilized (unlikely but possible). The landlord may know and is hoping you don't find out. Or the landlord may be deliberately concealing the apartment's regulatory status to charge a higher rent.

In any case, the absence of the rider does not eliminate your rights. If the apartment is stabilized, it is stabilized whether or not the rider was provided. But the missing rider is itself a violation, and it may be evidence of willfulness in an overcharge claim. Courts and DHCR take the failure to provide the rider seriously, because it deprives the tenant of the information needed to exercise their rights.

If you did not receive a rent stabilization rider, request your rent history immediately using the process described in Chapter 5. The rider's absence is not a reason to assume your apartment is unregulated. It is a reason to investigate.

Clauses That Sound Scary but Have No Teeth

Several categories of lease clauses create anxiety in tenants but are legally meaningless.

Clauses stating that the tenant waives all claims against the landlord for personal injury or property damage caused by the landlord's negligence are unenforceable under New York General Obligations Law Section 5-321. A landlord cannot contractually eliminate liability for their own negligence.

Clauses stating that the tenant agrees to vacate immediately upon any lease violation, without notice or court process, are unenforceable. New York law requires judicial process for eviction. Self-help eviction (lockouts, removal of belongings, shutting off utilities) is illegal regardless of what the lease says.

Clauses requiring the tenant to pay the landlord a penalty for breaking the lease early are often unenforceable to the extent they exceed the landlord's actual damages. New York law requires landlords to mitigate damages by making reasonable efforts to re-rent the apartment. A penalty that bears no relationship to actual loss may be struck down as an unenforceable liquidated damages provision.

Clauses prohibiting the tenant from having any guests or visitors are unenforceable. Tenants have the right to have guests, and the landlord cannot restrict that right through the lease.

These clauses persist in leases because they discourage tenants from asserting rights. They function as psychological deterrents, not legal instruments. Knowing the difference changes how you respond when the landlord invokes them.

Clauses That Matter More Than They Look

On the other side, some lease provisions that appear routine deserve careful attention.

The notice address clause specifies where the tenant must send notices to the landlord. If you ever need to send formal notice (requesting repairs, responding to a lease violation, asserting legal rights), using the wrong address can create complications. Verify the address, and send all important communications to the address listed in the lease, by certified mail, with proof of delivery.

The maintenance responsibility clause defines which repairs are the tenant's responsibility and which are the landlord's. In most residential leases, the landlord is responsible for structural repairs, building systems, and common areas, while the tenant is responsible for keeping the apartment clean and in reasonable condition. But the warranty of habitability overrides any clause that tries to shift essential repair obligations to the tenant.

The insurance clause may require the tenant to maintain renter's insurance. This is generally enforceable and is often a good idea regardless of whether the lease requires it. Renter's insurance is inexpensive and covers personal property loss, liability, and temporary displacement, none of which the landlord's insurance covers.

The alterations clause specifies what the tenant may and may not change in the apartment. Most leases prohibit alterations without landlord consent. This is generally enforceable for significant changes (removing walls, installing fixtures, painting in unusual colors). However, minor modifications that do not cause damage (hanging pictures, installing curtain rods) are typically permitted as ordinary use, regardless of what the clause says.

Real-World Example: The Lease That Told the Story

A tenant signed a lease for an apartment in a prewar building in Brooklyn. The lease was 12 pages long, printed in small type, and presented as "our standard form." The tenant signed it in the broker's office without reading every clause.

Two years later, facing a rent increase that felt too high, the tenant pulled out the lease for the first time since signing it.

Several things stood out. The lease made no mention of rent stabilization. No rider was attached. The security deposit clause stated an amount equal to six weeks' rent (illegal under current law). The subletting clause prohibited subletting entirely (overridden by statute for buildings with four or more units). And the late fee clause imposed a $150 penalty with no reference to the statutory grace period.

The tenant requested the apartment's rent history from DHCR. The records confirmed the apartment was rent-stabilized. The absence of the rider was a violation. The rent exceeded the legal amount by more than $200 per month.

The tenant filed an overcharge complaint, recovered thousands of dollars, and had the rent reduced to the correct legal amount.

The lease had told the story the entire time. The missing rider, the illegal deposit, the inflated rent, the overly restrictive clauses. Each one was a signal. The tenant just hadn't known how to read them.

What to Take From This Chapter

Your lease is important, but it is not supreme. Every clause must be read against the backdrop of New York tenant law, which overrides any provision that conflicts with statutory protections.

Unenforceable clauses persist because they discourage tenants from asserting rights. Recognizing them neutralizes their power.

Enforceable clauses deserve attention, particularly those governing notice addresses, maintenance responsibilities, insurance requirements, and renewal terms.

The Rent Stabilization Lease Rider is mandatory for stabilized apartments. Its absence is a serious red flag that warrants immediate investigation through DHCR.

The best time to read your lease carefully is before you sign it. The second-best time is right now.

In the next chapter, we'll cover what happens when your lease term ends: renewals, non-renewals, holdover status, and how notice periods work based on the length of your tenancy.

9

Lease Renewals, Non-Renewals and Holdover Status

The end of a lease is the moment when most tenants feel the most vulnerable. The term is expiring. The landlord may or may not offer a renewal. The rent may change. And the tenant often has no idea what happens next, legally, if the lease simply runs out without a new agreement in place.

In many states, the answer is simple: the lease ends, the tenancy ends, and the tenant either signs a new lease or leaves. New York is not one of those states. Here, the expiration of a lease does not automatically end a tenancy. What happens next depends on what kind of apartment you live in, how long you've lived there, what protections apply, and whether the landlord follows the correct procedures.

This chapter consolidates everything you need to know about the end of a lease term into one place: renewal rights, non-renewal rules, notice requirements, holdover status, and the protections that may apply even when you think they don't.

The Fundamental Principle: A Lease Ending Does Not Mean a Tenancy Ending

In New York, the expiration of a lease term does not give a landlord the automatic right to remove a tenant. This is the single most important concept in this chapter, and it is the one tenants most frequently get wrong.

The reason it confuses people is that in most contractual relationships, the end of the contract is the end of the relationship. You don't owe each other anything after the term expires. Both parties walk away.

Tenancy in New York doesn't work that way. The law treats housing as different from other contracts because the consequences of losing housing are more severe than the consequences of losing most other contractual relationships. Accordingly, the law imposes obligations on landlords that continue beyond the lease term, and it gives tenants rights that survive the expiration of the document they signed.

What those rights are, and how strong they are, depends on the category your apartment falls into.

Rent-Stabilized Apartments: Renewal Is a Right, Not a Request

If your apartment is rent-stabilized, you have a statutory right to a renewal lease. The landlord must offer it. The landlord cannot decline to offer it simply because the lease term expired or because they want a different tenant or a higher rent.

As Chapter 6 explained in detail, the renewal must be offered on the correct form (DHCR Form RTP-8 in New York City), within the correct time window (no more than 150 days and no less than 90 days before the current lease expires), with the correct rent (the current legal rent plus the applicable RGB increase), and with both one-year and two-year term options.

If the landlord fails to offer a timely renewal, the consequences fall on the landlord. The tenant's rent remains frozen at the current amount. The tenant cannot be charged a higher rent until a proper renewal is offered. And the tenant can file a complaint with DHCR using Form RA-90 for the landlord's failure to renew.

If the renewal is offered and the tenant does not respond within 60 days, the landlord may treat the failure to respond as a refusal to renew and may eventually seek to evict the tenant through a holdover proceeding. But even then, the eviction is not automatic. It must go through court, and the tenant has the right to raise defenses.

A landlord can refuse to renew a rent-stabilized lease only for specific, legally recognized reasons. These are narrow and strictly enforced. They include situations where the tenant is not maintaining the apartment as a primary residence, where the landlord or an immediate family member intends to occupy the unit (subject to significant restrictions, especially for senior and disabled tenants), or where the landlord seeks to withdraw the unit from the rental market entirely. Each of these requires specific procedures, specific proof, and in many cases, specific approvals.

The bottom line for stabilized tenants is unambiguous: when your lease expires, you do not have to leave. You are entitled to a renewal. The landlord must offer one. And if they don't, you stay on the same terms at the same rent until they do.

Good Cause Eviction: The New Protection for Many Unregulated Tenants

Before April 2024, tenants in unregulated apartments had significantly fewer protections when their leases expired. A landlord could decline to renew for any reason or no reason, as long as proper notice was given.

That changed with the passage of the Good Cause Eviction Law, which went into effect on April 20, 2024. This law extends eviction protections to many market-rate tenants in New York City and in municipalities across the state that have opted into the program.

If your apartment is covered by Good Cause, your landlord cannot evict you or refuse to renew your lease without proving one of several legally recognized reasons. These include nonpayment of rent (as long as the nonpayment is not based on an unreasonable rent increase), violation of a substantial lease obligation that was not corrected after notice, conduct that interferes with the comfort and safety of others, the landlord's intent to occupy the unit personally or for an immediate family member, and the landlord's intent to withdraw the unit from the rental market.

The law also limits rent increases. Annual increases above a set threshold (the lower of 10 percent or 5 percent plus the Consumer Price Index, which as of early 2026 works out to approximately 8 to 9 percent in the New York City area) are presumptively unreasonable. A landlord can still impose a higher increase, but only if they can justify it in court based on factors like significant repairs or increased operating costs.

Good Cause coverage depends on several factors. Your apartment is generally covered if it is unregulated, was built before 2009, is not in an owner-occupied building with fewer than 11 units, is not owned by a "small landlord" (defined as someone who owns no more than 10 units statewide), and the rent is below 245 percent of the Fair Market Rent for the unit size. As of the most recent figures, that threshold is approximately $6,000 per month for a one-bedroom apartment in New York City, meaning the vast majority of unregulated apartments are eligible.

Since August 2024, landlords have been required to include a notice in every lease, renewal, and predicate notice stating whether the apartment is covered by Good Cause, and if not, explaining why. If your landlord has not provided this notice, that is itself a violation that may be raised in court.

Good Cause does not replicate rent stabilization. It does not set specific rent increases by a regulatory board, does not require registration with a state agency, and does not provide the same renewal lease procedures. But it does something that did not exist before for unregulated tenants: it requires the landlord to have a reason before ending a tenancy. The burden of justification now falls on the landlord, not the tenant.

Unregulated Apartments Without Good Cause Coverage: What Still Applies

Some apartments are neither rent-stabilized nor covered by Good Cause. These include units in newer buildings (built after 2009), units rented at very high rents, units in small owner-occupied buildings, and units in municipalities that have not opted into Good Cause.

For tenants in these apartments, the landlord has broader discretion to decline renewal. But even here, the tenancy does not end silently when the lease expires. New York law imposes notice requirements that apply to all residential tenants regardless of regulatory status.

Under Real Property Law Section 226-c, enacted as part of the HSTPA in 2019, a landlord must provide written notice before refusing to renew a lease or imposing a rent increase of 5 percent or more. The required notice period depends on how long the tenant has occupied the unit.

For tenants who have lived in the apartment for less than one year, or who have a lease of less than one year, the landlord must provide at least 30 days' notice.

For tenants who have lived in the apartment for more than one year but less than two years, or who have a lease of at least one year but less than two years, the landlord must provide at least 60 days' notice.

For tenants who have lived in the apartment for two years or more, or who have a lease of at least two years, the landlord must provide at least 90 days' notice.

If the landlord fails to provide the required notice, the tenant has the right to remain in the apartment at the current rent until the landlord provides proper notice. The defective notice does not start the clock. The tenant stays until the landlord gets it right.

These notice requirements are minimum protections. They do not prevent the landlord from declining to renew. They ensure that tenants have adequate time to find alternative housing or negotiate. And they give tenants who receive deficient notice a clear legal defense.

Month-to-Month Status: What It Actually Means

When a lease expires and neither party takes action to renew or terminate, the tenancy typically converts to month-to-month status. This transition happens automatically under New York law.

Month-to-month status means that the tenancy continues on the same terms as the expired lease, but either party can end it with proper notice. The tenant can leave with notice. The landlord can seek to end the tenancy with notice, subject to whatever protections apply (rent stabilization, Good Cause, or the 30/60/90-day notice requirements described above).

Month-to-month does not mean unprotected. This is one of the most common misunderstandings in New York tenant law.

In a rent-stabilized apartment, a month-to-month tenancy after lease expiration does not reduce the tenant's rights. The tenant is still entitled to a renewal lease. The rent remains the same. The landlord still needs just cause to evict. The only thing that changes is that the formal lease document has lapsed, which is the landlord's problem, not the tenant's.

In a Good Cause-covered apartment, month-to-month status triggers the same protections as a lease. The landlord still needs good cause to terminate. The rent increase limits still apply. The tenant does not lose protection simply because there is no current written lease.

In an unregulated apartment not covered by Good Cause, month-to-month status provides less protection. The landlord can terminate the tenancy with the appropriate notice (30, 60, or 90 days depending on length of occupancy). But even here, the termination must follow proper procedures. A landlord cannot simply tell a month-to-month tenant to leave tomorrow.

The critical point is that month-to-month status is a legal status, not a vulnerability. It carries rights and protections that vary by category but always exist.

Holdover Status: When the Landlord Says Leave and the Tenant Stays

A holdover tenant is a tenant who remains in the apartment after the lease has expired or after the landlord has served a valid notice to terminate.

In New York, a holdover does not become a trespasser the moment the lease expires. The landlord cannot change the locks, remove belongings, shut off utilities, or otherwise engage in self-help eviction. These actions are illegal regardless of the tenant's holdover status.

To remove a holdover tenant, the landlord must file a holdover proceeding in Housing Court. This is a formal legal process that requires proper service of papers, a court hearing, and a judgment before any physical removal can occur. The marshal or sheriff executes the eviction only after the court issues a warrant.

Holdover proceedings are subject to the same procedural requirements as other eviction cases. The landlord must prove that the tenancy was lawfully terminated, that proper notice was given, that service was correct, and that the tenant has no valid defense. Defects in any of these elements can result in dismissal.

For rent-stabilized tenants, a holdover proceeding requires the landlord to prove a recognized ground for non-renewal, as described earlier. The burden is on the landlord, and the scrutiny is high.

For Good Cause-covered tenants, the landlord must prove good cause as defined by the statute.

For unregulated tenants not covered by Good Cause, the landlord must prove that proper notice was given and that the holdover is the result of a lawful termination. Even here, procedural defenses are available and frequently successful.

Holdover status is stressful for tenants, but it is not legally catastrophic. The tenant remains in the apartment. The court process takes time. And the landlord must satisfy every procedural requirement before removal is possible.

The Notice Trap: Why Timing Defeats So Many Landlord Cases

Notice requirements in New York are strict, and landlords get them wrong with remarkable frequency.

The most common errors involve timing. A landlord who provides 30 days' notice to a tenant who has lived in the apartment for more than two years has not satisfied the 90-day requirement. The notice is defective. The case fails.

Other common errors involve content. Under Good Cause, the notice must include a statement about whether the apartment is covered and, if the landlord is raising the rent or declining to renew, the justification. A notice that omits this information may be challenged.

Service errors are also frequent. Notices must be delivered in the manner prescribed by law, which may require personal delivery, delivery to a person of suitable age, or conspicuous placement plus mailing. A landlord who simply emails a termination notice or slides it under the door may not have satisfied service requirements.

Each of these errors creates a defense for the tenant. A tenant who receives a defective notice does not need to prove anything else. The landlord's failure is the defense.

This is why tenants who receive any notice related to non-renewal, termination, or rent increase should examine the notice carefully before assuming it is valid. The question is not "Did the landlord send something?" It's "Did the landlord send the right thing, at the right time, in the right way?"

Navigating the Transition: A Decision Framework

When your lease is approaching its end, the steps you take depend on what category your apartment falls into.

If your apartment is rent-stabilized, expect a renewal offer between 150 and 90 days before the lease expires. If you don't receive one, contact the landlord in writing and, if necessary, file Form RA-90 with DHCR. Continue paying your current rent. You cannot be charged more until a valid renewal is offered and accepted.

If your apartment is covered by Good Cause, your landlord cannot refuse to renew without a legally recognized reason and cannot raise your rent above the local standard without justification. If your landlord attempts to terminate or impose an unreasonable increase, you can challenge it in Housing Court. Since August 2024, the landlord should have provided you with a Good Cause notice stating your coverage status.

If your apartment is unregulated and not covered by Good Cause, the landlord has broader discretion but must still provide proper notice (30, 60, or 90 days depending on your length of tenancy). If the notice is defective, you are not required to leave until proper notice is given. If you receive proper notice, you may need to begin planning to relocate, but you should still verify that the notice meets all legal requirements before conceding anything.

In all cases, continue paying rent during the transition period. Do not withhold rent because a renewal is disputed or pending. Nonpayment creates separate legal exposure that can complicate your position.

Real-World Example: The Lease That Expired but the Tenancy That Didn't

A tenant in a rent-stabilized apartment in the Bronx received no renewal offer before her lease expired. The landlord said nothing. The lease term ended. The tenant continued paying rent at the same amount, and the landlord continued accepting it.

Six months later, the landlord sent a letter stating that because no lease was in effect, the tenancy was "at will" and could be terminated with 30 days' notice. The landlord offered a "new lease" at a rent $400 higher than the tenant had been paying, with a take-it-or-leave-it deadline.

The tenant nearly signed.

Before doing so, she contacted a tenant advocacy hotline. The advocate explained that in a rent-stabilized apartment, the landlord's failure to offer a renewal lease did not weaken the tenant's position. It weakened the landlord's. The tenant was entitled to remain at her current rent until a proper renewal was offered on the correct form, with the correct RGB increase, within the correct time window.

The "new lease" the landlord offered was not a valid renewal. It was not on the DHCR form. It did not reflect the RGB rate. And the rent increase bore no relationship to the regulated amount.

The tenant refused the offer and filed a complaint with DHCR for the landlord's failure to offer a proper renewal. DHCR directed the landlord to offer a compliant renewal lease at the correct rent. The $400 increase disappeared. The tenant stayed.

The landlord had been counting on the tenant's belief that an expired lease meant an expired tenancy. In New York, for a rent-stabilized apartment, that belief is wrong. The tenant's rights survived the lease. The landlord's obligations survived the lease. And the outcome depended entirely on who knew the rules.

What to Take From This Chapter

A lease ending does not mean a tenancy ending. In rent-stabilized apartments, renewal is a statutory right. In Good Cause-covered apartments, the landlord must prove a recognized reason to terminate. Even in unregulated apartments, notice requirements protect tenants from abrupt displacement.

Month-to-month status is a legal status with real protections, not a gap in coverage. Tenants in all categories retain rights during month-to-month tenancy.

Holdover tenants cannot be removed without court process. Self-help eviction is illegal in every circumstance.

Notice requirements are strict. Errors in timing, content, or service can invalidate a landlord's case entirely.

Good Cause Eviction, effective since April 2024, extends meaningful protections to hundreds of thousands of previously unregulated tenants. If your apartment is covered, your landlord cannot end your tenancy without proving a legally recognized reason.

If your lease is approaching its expiration, the most important question is not "What does my lease say?" It's "What protections apply to my apartment, and is my landlord following the rules?"

In the next chapter, we'll move from lease transitions to eviction itself, starting with the concept that governs everything: just cause, and what it means for landlords who want to remove a tenant from their home.

Part IV: Evictions and Just Cause

10

What "Just Cause" Eviction Means in New York

In many states, a landlord can end a tenancy for almost any reason, or no reason at all, as long as proper notice is given. The lease expires, the landlord declines to renew, and the tenant moves out. The landlord doesn't need to explain why. The tenant doesn't have the right to ask.

New York does not work that way.

Here, the concept of "just cause" eviction limits when a landlord can legally force a tenant out. For tenants in covered apartments, the surprise is often not that just cause exists, but how fundamentally it changes who has to justify what. Instead of tenants proving they deserve to stay, landlords must prove they have the right to remove. That shift, quiet as it sounds on paper, is the single most important structural protection in New York tenant law.

This chapter explains what just cause means in practice, which apartments it covers, what qualifies as a valid reason for eviction, and why the phrase "your lease expired" is almost never the end of the conversation.

What "Just Cause" Actually Means

Just cause means that a landlord must have a legally recognized reason to end a tenancy, refuse to renew a lease, or file an eviction case.

The reason must come from a defined list. It must be genuine. And it must be provable. A landlord who cannot identify and substantiate a valid cause cannot evict, regardless of whether the lease has expired, regardless of how long the case takes, and regardless of how much the landlord wants the apartment back.

This is a departure from what many tenants expect, especially those who have rented in other states. In most American jurisdictions, the default rule is that landlords can terminate tenancies without cause. New York inverts that default for covered apartments. The burden is on the landlord to justify removal, not on the tenant to justify staying.

Just cause requirements exist in New York through two distinct legal frameworks, each covering different categories of apartments.

For rent-stabilized apartments, just cause has been the rule for decades. Landlords of stabilized units have never been permitted to refuse renewal or evict without a recognized ground. The Rent Stabilization Code defines the permissible bases, and courts enforce them strictly.

For many previously unregulated apartments, just cause protections arrived with the Good Cause Eviction Law, which took effect in April 2024. As Chapter 9 explained, this law extended eviction protections to a broad class of market-rate tenants who previously had no right to remain after their leases expired.

The two frameworks operate independently, with different eligibility rules and somewhat different lists of permissible grounds. But the underlying principle is the same: the landlord needs a reason, and the reason must be real.

The Valid Grounds: What Landlords Can Actually Prove

The legally recognized reasons for eviction in New York fall into several categories. Not all grounds apply in all situations, and the procedural requirements vary. But the following covers the major categories that landlords rely on.

Nonpayment of rent is the most common ground for eviction in New York, and it is the one most tenants think of first. If a tenant fails to pay rent that is lawfully owed, the landlord can serve a rent demand and, if the rent remains unpaid, file a nonpayment proceeding in Housing Court. However, nonpayment cases are subject to strict procedural requirements (covered in Chapter 20), and the rent demanded must be the correct legal amount. A demand that includes illegal fees, inflated rent, or charges that were never lawfully imposed is defective.

Under Good Cause, there is an additional wrinkle: a tenant cannot be evicted for nonpayment if the nonpayment is based on a rent increase that exceeds the local rent standard and is found to be unreasonable. This means that a landlord who raises the rent above the Good Cause cap and then tries to evict for nonpayment of the higher amount may lose the case.

Lease violations that are not cured provide another common ground. If a tenant violates a substantial term of the lease, the landlord must first give the tenant notice of the violation and an opportunity to correct it. The notice period is typically 10 days for Good Cause-covered apartments and may vary for stabilized units depending on the nature of the violation. If the tenant corrects the problem within the notice period, the ground disappears. If the tenant does not correct it, the landlord may proceed.

The key word is "substantial." Minor violations, technical breaches, or provisions that the landlord never previously enforced are unlikely to support an eviction. Courts look at whether the violation is serious enough to warrant the loss of housing, not whether the lease technically permits termination.

Nuisance or objectionable conduct is a ground that applies across categories but is narrowly defined. The tenant must be engaging in behavior that substantially interferes with the comfort, safety, or enjoyment of other occupants or neighbors. This is not about personality conflicts, occasional noise, or lifestyle differences. Courts require evidence of persistent, serious conduct that rises above ordinary friction.

Owner or family occupancy is available as a ground under both rent stabilization and Good Cause, but it is subject to strict requirements. The landlord must demonstrate a genuine, good-faith intent to use the apartment as a primary residence for themselves or a qualifying family member. In rent-stabilized buildings, owner-use evictions are limited to one unit per building, and tenants who are 62 years of age or older or who have qualifying disabilities may be protected entirely. The landlord must also offer comparable housing in some circumstances. Chapter 11 covers owner-use claims in detail.

Withdrawal from the rental market is a ground that allows a landlord to remove a unit from residential use entirely. This is not the same as wanting to renovate, wanting to raise the rent, or wanting to convert the unit to another use temporarily. Withdrawal means permanently removing the apartment from the housing market. Courts scrutinize these claims carefully, and false withdrawal claims carry consequences.

Demolition or major structural alteration is available as a ground when a landlord intends to demolish the building or perform work so extensive that the apartment cannot remain occupied. Like withdrawal, this ground requires concrete evidence, not just plans or intentions. Approved permits, realistic timelines, and proof that the work cannot be done with tenants in place are all factors courts consider.

Court-ordered vacancy applies when a government agency or court has determined that the apartment must be vacated to correct a code violation or safety hazard. Importantly, this ground does not apply when the landlord created the condition that necessitates the vacancy. A landlord who allows a building to deteriorate and then seeks to evict tenants because of the resulting violations will find this ground unavailable.

What Is Not a Valid Ground

Understanding what does not constitute just cause is as important as understanding what does.

Wanting a higher-paying tenant is not a valid ground. This may seem obvious, but it is the underlying motivation behind many eviction attempts. A landlord who has a stabilized tenant paying $1,500 and could get $3,000 on the open market cannot evict simply to capture the difference. The rent stabilization system and Good Cause protections exist precisely to prevent this.

Lease expiration alone is not a valid ground. As Chapter 9 explained, in covered apartments, the end of the lease term does not give the landlord the right to remove the tenant. The lease may expire, but the tenancy continues unless the landlord can prove a recognized cause.

Retaliation is not a valid ground. A landlord who files an eviction case because the tenant complained about conditions, requested repairs, reported code violations, organized with other tenants, or asserted any legal right is retaliating. Retaliatory eviction is illegal in New York, and it is an affirmative defense that can result in dismissal of the case. Chapter 19 covers retaliation in detail.

The tenant asserting their rights is not a valid ground. A tenant who files an overcharge complaint, requests rent history, exercises their right to a renewal lease, or takes any other action protected by law cannot be evicted for doing so. Any eviction case that appears to follow one of these actions will face heightened judicial scrutiny.

Discrimination is not a valid ground. Eviction based on race, color, national origin, sex, gender identity, sexual orientation, age, disability, marital status, familial status, lawful source of income, immigration status, or any other protected characteristic is illegal under federal, state, and city human rights laws. Discriminatory eviction can be challenged not only as a defense to the eviction case but as an affirmative claim for damages.

Personal preference is not a valid ground. A landlord who simply doesn't like a tenant, disagrees with their lifestyle, or finds them unpleasant cannot evict. The law requires objective, provable grounds, not subjective dissatisfaction.

Covered vs. Exempt: Which Apartments Have Just Cause Protection

Not every apartment in New York is covered by just cause requirements. Understanding whether your apartment is covered is essential, and landlords frequently exploit uncertainty about coverage to pressure tenants into leaving.

Rent-stabilized apartments are fully covered by just cause requirements. This has been the law for decades and is not affected by the Good Cause Eviction Law, which explicitly excludes apartments already covered by rent stabilization.

Apartments covered by the Good Cause Eviction Law are covered by just cause requirements if they meet the eligibility criteria described in Chapter 9: generally, unregulated apartments in buildings constructed before 2009, rented below 245 percent of Fair Market Rent, and not exempt due to owner occupancy of a small building or small landlord status.

Apartments that are exempt from both rent stabilization and Good Cause have fewer protections. These include units in buildings constructed after 2009 (for a 30-year period following the certificate of occupancy), units rented above the Fair Market Rent threshold, units in owner-occupied buildings with fewer than 11 units (or fewer than 5 in some opt-in municipalities), units owned by small landlords (10 or fewer units statewide), and units in co-ops, condos, or public housing. Even in exempt apartments, the landlord must still comply with the 30/60/90-day notice requirements under Real Property Law Section 226-c, and self-help eviction remains illegal.

Coverage is a factual determination, not a landlord's assertion. Landlords frequently claim exemptions that don't apply. Chapter 24 addresses how tenants investigate and challenge exemption claims.

How Just Cause Shifts the Balance of Power

The practical effect of just cause requirements is not that tenants can never be evicted. Tenants who don't pay rent, who violate their leases, or who create genuine nuisance conditions can still be removed. The system does not protect tenants from the consequences of their own conduct.

What just cause does is change who has to justify the outcome. Without just cause, the landlord acts and the tenant reacts. The landlord decides not to renew, and the tenant must either negotiate or leave. The tenant has no legal right to demand a reason.

With just cause, the dynamic reverses. The landlord must state a reason. The reason must be valid under the law. The tenant can challenge it. And the court decides whether the landlord has met the burden.

This shift has several practical consequences.

It slows down improper evictions. A landlord who cannot articulate a valid cause cannot proceed. Cases filed on weak or pretextual grounds are dismissed, often before trial.

It exposes weak landlord claims. When a landlord must state a reason on the record, that reason becomes subject to scrutiny. Vague claims, shifting explanations, and after-the-fact justifications are treated skeptically by courts.

It creates leverage for negotiation. A tenant who knows the landlord lacks a valid ground is in a fundamentally different negotiating position than a tenant who believes they have no choice. Many disputes resolve before court because the landlord recognizes that the case cannot be won.

It discourages speculative filings. Landlords who know they must prove cause are less likely to file cases designed to pressure tenants into leaving. The cost of losing, in time, legal fees, and credibility, deters cases that exist only as leverage.

And it protects tenants who assert their rights. When eviction requires cause, tenants can request repairs, file complaints, and organize without fear that the landlord will respond by simply declining to renew. The just cause requirement is the foundation of anti-retaliation protection.

The Landlord's Burden: What "Prove It" Looks Like in Court

When a landlord files an eviction case based on a specific ground, the court evaluates whether the evidence supports the claim. The level of proof varies by the type of case, but the fundamental structure is the same: the landlord must present credible evidence, the tenant can challenge it, and the judge decides.

In nonpayment cases, the landlord must prove that the rent is lawfully owed and that the tenant received a proper demand. If the demand is defective or the rent is miscalculated, the case fails.

In holdover cases based on owner use, the landlord must prove genuine intent to occupy. Courts look at whether the landlord actually needs the unit, whether comparable units are available, and whether the claim is consistent with the landlord's conduct. If the landlord has made similar claims before or if the unit is re-rented after the tenant leaves, the claim collapses.

In cases based on lease violations, the landlord must prove that the violation is substantial, that the tenant received proper notice and an opportunity to cure, and that the violation was not corrected. Minor or technical violations rarely support eviction.

In cases based on nuisance, the landlord must prove persistent, serious conduct with credible evidence, typically from multiple witnesses or documented incidents. A single complaint from one neighbor is generally insufficient.

The common thread is that the landlord carries the burden. The tenant does not need to prove they are a perfect tenant. They do not need to prove they deserve to stay. They need only challenge the landlord's case, and if the case has weaknesses, the challenge will succeed.

Real-World Example: The Lease That Wasn't the End

A tenant in a Good Cause-covered apartment in Brooklyn received a notice stating that her lease would not be renewed and that she had 60 days to vacate. The notice did not state a reason for the non-renewal. It did not include the Good Cause Eviction notice required since August 2024. It simply stated that the lease was expiring and the landlord had elected not to renew.

The tenant had lived in the apartment for three years, paid rent on time, and had no lease violations. She assumed the notice was valid because she had never heard of Good Cause Eviction and believed that landlords could decline to renew for any reason.

She began looking for a new apartment.

Before signing a new lease, she mentioned the situation to a colleague who happened to know about the Good Cause law. The colleague suggested she call a tenant hotline.

The advocate who answered asked three questions: When was the building constructed? How many units does the landlord own? And what is the current rent? The answers confirmed that the apartment was covered by Good Cause. The landlord's notice failed on multiple levels. It did not state a cause. It did not include the required Good Cause disclosure. And the landlord had no recognized ground for non-renewal.

The tenant wrote to the landlord, citing the Good Cause Eviction Law and requesting a renewal lease. The landlord, after consulting with an attorney, withdrew the non-renewal notice and offered a renewal at the existing rent.

The tenant stayed. The lease that had "expired" was replaced by a new one. And the non-renewal that had felt like a foregone conclusion turned out to be legally groundless.

The landlord had relied on the tenant not knowing that the rules had changed. For thousands of tenants in similar situations, that reliance still works. For this tenant, one phone call was the difference.

What to Take From This Chapter

Just cause eviction means that landlords must have a legally recognized reason to remove a tenant. The concept applies to rent-stabilized apartments (where it has existed for decades) and to apartments covered by the Good Cause Eviction Law (which took effect in April 2024).

Valid grounds for eviction are limited and defined by law. They include nonpayment, substantial lease violations, nuisance, owner occupancy, withdrawal from the rental market, and demolition or major alteration. Each ground has specific procedural requirements.

Invalid grounds include wanting a higher rent, lease expiration alone, retaliation for asserting rights, discrimination, and personal preference.

Coverage depends on the apartment's characteristics. Rent-stabilized units are always covered. Good Cause covers many unregulated apartments built before 2009 and rented below the Fair Market Rent threshold. Exempt apartments still benefit from notice requirements and protection against self-help eviction.

Just cause shifts the burden of proof from tenant to landlord. The landlord must state a reason, prove it, and satisfy procedural requirements. The tenant's role is to challenge the claim, not to justify staying.

If your landlord says you must leave, the most important question is not "Did they give notice?" It's "Do they have a legally valid reason, and can they prove it?"

In the next chapter, we'll examine the most common reasons landlords claim in detail, starting with owner use, demolition, and family occupancy, and how tenants can tell when those claims don't add up.

11

Owner Use, Demolition and Other Common Eviction Claims

When landlords can't evict tenants freely, they often reach for the same handful of explanations. Claims that sound legitimate on their face, that are difficult for tenants to evaluate quickly, and that rely on tenants moving out before asking questions.

Owner occupancy. Family use. Demolition. Major renovation. Withdrawal from the market.

Each of these is a real legal ground for eviction in New York. Each one has specific conditions that must be met, procedures that must be followed, and evidence that must be produced. And each one is frequently abused, exaggerated, or asserted in bad faith by landlords who expect tenants to accept the claim and leave without investigating further.

This chapter explains what each ground actually requires, how the HSTPA tightened the standards, what additional protections exist for senior and disabled tenants, why the Golub Notice is one of the most important documents in a rent-stabilized eviction, and how tenants prove that a landlord's story doesn't match reality.

Owner-Occupancy Evictions: Narrower Than They Sound

Owner-use evictions are one of the most misunderstood and most frequently abused areas of New York tenant law.

The basic concept sounds reasonable: if the owner of a building wants to live in one of the apartments, they should be able to recover it. In principle, the law allows this. In practice, the requirements are so specific and the scrutiny so intense that many owner-use claims fail, either because the landlord cannot meet the legal standard or because the claim was never genuine in the first place.

Before the HSTPA, owner-use evictions were the most common method landlords used to remove rent-stabilized tenants. The standard was relatively loose. Landlords had to demonstrate "good faith" intent to occupy the unit, and courts gave landlords considerable benefit of the doubt. Tenant advocates estimated that at least half of owner-use claims were pretextual, meaning the landlord never actually intended to live in the apartment but used the claim as a tool to clear out a regulated tenant and reset the rent.

The HSTPA changed the standard dramatically.

Under current law, an owner seeking to evict a rent-stabilized tenant for personal occupancy must demonstrate an "immediate and compelling necessity" for the specific unit. This is a substantially higher bar than the old good-faith standard. The landlord must show not just that they want to live there, but that they need to live there, and that the need is both immediate (not speculative or future) and compelling (not merely convenient or preferable).

The owner is limited to recovering one unit per building for personal or immediate family use, even if the building has multiple owners or is held by an entity with multiple individual stakeholders. This prevents landlords from using owner-use claims to clear out multiple apartments in the same building through different family members or ownership interests.

The occupancy must be for the owner's primary residence. A landlord who wants the apartment as a pied-a-terre, a vacation home, a secondary residence, or a future investment does not have a valid owner-use claim. Primary residence means the place where the owner lives most of the time, where their personal and legal life is centered.

And the owner must actually move in and maintain the unit as a primary residence. If the owner recovers the apartment and then does not occupy it, or re-rents it, or uses it for a purpose other than what was claimed, the eviction was fraudulent and carries serious consequences.

The Golub Notice: The Document That Starts the Process

In rent-stabilized owner-use cases, the landlord's first formal step is serving what is commonly known as a "Golub Notice," named after the court case (*Golub v. Frank*, 65 N.Y.2d 900 (1985), 493 N.Y.S.2d 451) that established the requirement.

The Golub Notice is a written notice of non-renewal that the landlord must serve on the tenant between 150 and 90 days before the current lease expires. The notice must state that the landlord is declining to renew the lease, and it must specify the ground for the non-renewal, in this case, the owner's intent to occupy the apartment for personal use or the use of an immediate family member.

The Golub Notice is not a formality. It is a jurisdictional prerequisite. If the landlord fails to serve the notice, serves it outside the time window, or fails to include the required information, the holdover case that follows is defective. Courts dismiss cases where the Golub Notice was improperly served, regardless of the merits of the underlying claim.

The notice serves several important functions beyond satisfying a procedural requirement. It gives the tenant advance warning that the landlord intends to pursue an owner-use eviction, allowing the tenant to prepare a defense, consult a lawyer, and gather evidence. It puts the landlord's claim on the record early, creating a baseline against which future conduct can be measured. And it triggers the tenant's right to investigate the claim before any court proceeding begins.

When you receive a Golub Notice, do not panic and do not begin packing. The notice is the beginning of a process, not the end of a tenancy. Read it carefully. Note the stated ground. Note the date it was served. Note the family member identified, if any. And consult a tenant attorney or advocacy organization immediately, because the clock for building a defense starts when the notice arrives.

The Golub Notice requirement applies specifically to rent-stabilized apartments in New York City. For rent-stabilized apartments outside NYC and for rent-controlled apartments, the owner must apply to DHCR for a certificate of eviction by filing Form RA-54, which triggers a separate administrative process with its own requirements and timelines.

Under Good Cause Eviction, the procedures for owner-use claims are different. The landlord must prove the claim in court and must present "clear and compelling evidence" of their intent, but the formal Golub Notice procedure does not apply in the same way. However, the Good Cause law does require landlords to include the basis for non-renewal in the Good Cause notice attached to any predicate notice or petition, so the tenant still receives advance notice of the claim.

Who Qualifies as "Immediate Family"

Owner-use evictions can be pursued not only for the owner personally but for the owner's "immediate family." This term sounds broad, but it is legally defined and more limited than many landlords claim.

Under the Rent Stabilization Code, immediate family generally includes the owner's spouse, children, parents, siblings, grandparents, grandchildren, and in-laws. It does not include friends, distant relatives, employees, romantic partners who are not spouses, or business associates.

The family member must intend to use the apartment as their primary residence. A landlord who claims the apartment is needed for a child who currently lives in another state and has no immediate plans to relocate is making a speculative claim, not a compelling one. A landlord who claims the apartment is for a parent who already has suitable housing nearby faces the same problem.

Courts scrutinize family-use claims closely because they are easy to assert and difficult to verify without evidence. The landlord must show that the identified family member has a genuine and current need for the specific apartment, not just any apartment, but the one the tenant currently occupies.

Vague statements about future plans, general references to family convenience, and assertions that lack supporting documentation are insufficient. Intent matters, and proof of intent matters more.

Protections for Senior Citizens, Disabled Tenants, and Long-Term Occupants

The HSTPA significantly expanded the protections available to tenants who are most vulnerable to owner-use evictions.

For rent-stabilized apartments in New York City, the landlord cannot evict a tenant for owner use if the tenant or the tenant's spouse is a senior citizen (62 years of age or older) or is a person with a disability, unless the owner provides an equivalent or superior apartment at the same or lower regulated rent in a nearby area.

This is a substantial hurdle. Finding an equivalent apartment at a comparable rent in the same neighborhood is often impossible in New York City's housing market. Many owner-use claims against senior or disabled tenants fail not because the landlord's intent is questioned, but because the landlord cannot satisfy the relocation obligation.

The HSTPA extended similar protections to long-term tenants. Under current law, tenants who have been in occupancy for 15 years or more receive the same protections as senior and disabled tenants. This means that a landlord pursuing an owner-use eviction against a tenant who has lived in the apartment for 15 or more years must also provide equivalent or superior alternative housing.

For rent-stabilized apartments outside New York City, the protections for senior and disabled tenants are absolute: the owner cannot evict a disabled tenant for owner use at all.

For rent-controlled apartments statewide, DHCR must approve any owner-use eviction through the certificate of eviction process, and tenants who are 62 or older, disabled, or have been in occupancy for 20 years or more receive heightened protections, including the right to relocation assistance and equivalent housing.

These protections exist because the legislature recognized that the impact of displacement is most severe for tenants who are elderly, disabled, or deeply rooted in their community. An owner-use eviction that forces a 75-year-old tenant out of the apartment they've lived in for 30 years does not just change their address. It can disrupt medical care, sever social connections, and create hardship that goes far beyond the landlord-tenant relationship.

If you are a senior citizen, a person with a disability, or a tenant who has lived in your apartment for 15 years or more, and you receive an owner-use eviction notice, your protections are significant. An attorney experienced in rent stabilization law should be consulted immediately.

Demolition and Major Alteration Claims

Demolition is a recognized ground for eviction, but it is among the most demanding for landlords to prove.

A landlord claiming demolition must demonstrate that the building will be demolished, that the demolition is genuine and imminent, and that the work requires the apartment to be vacated. For rent-stabilized apartments, the landlord must file Form RA-54 with DHCR and obtain approval before proceeding. DHCR evaluates the application based on whether the plans are concrete, whether permits have been obtained, and whether the demolition is financially and practically feasible.

Courts and DHCR look for approved plans from the Department of Buildings, realistic construction timelines, evidence of financing, and consistency between the landlord's representations and their actual conduct. A landlord who files a demolition application but has not obtained permits, has not hired a contractor, and has not begun the approval process faces serious credibility problems.

Major alteration claims are similar but distinct. The landlord asserts that the work required on the building is so extensive that the apartment cannot remain occupied during construction. Unlike demolition, major alteration does not require the permanent removal of the unit. The expectation is that the tenant would be displaced temporarily and might have the right to return after the work is complete, depending on the circumstances.

Courts scrutinize alteration claims carefully because they can easily be used as pretexts. Cosmetic upgrades, routine maintenance, unit turnover improvements, and work that can be performed with tenants in place do not qualify. The alteration must be genuinely structural and genuinely incompatible with continued occupancy.

"Renovation" is not a synonym for "demolition" or "major alteration." A landlord who wants to renovate an apartment to charge a higher rent to a new tenant does not have a valid eviction claim. The desire to upgrade and re-rent is a financial motive, not a legal ground.

Withdrawal from the Rental Market

A landlord may claim the right to evict tenants by withdrawing the apartment from the rental market entirely. This means permanently removing the unit from residential use, not temporarily taking it off the market to renovate and re-rent.

Withdrawal claims require the landlord to demonstrate a genuine intent to stop renting the apartment permanently. Courts look at the totality of the circumstances: whether the landlord has other apartments in the building that remain rented, whether the withdrawal is economically rational, and whether the landlord's conduct before and after the claim is consistent with permanent withdrawal.

If a landlord withdraws a unit and then re-rents it within a relatively short period, the withdrawal was almost certainly pretextual. Courts can order reinstatement, impose penalties, and award damages.

In rent-stabilized buildings, withdrawal claims are particularly scrutinized because removing a unit from the stabilization system permanently reduces the stock of regulated housing. The regulatory framework treats each stabilized apartment as a public resource, not just a private asset, and the loss of regulated units is treated seriously.

When Landlords Lie: Strategic Exaggerations and False Claims

Not every questionable eviction claim is an outright fabrication. Many are strategic exaggerations, claims that contain a kernel of truth but are stretched beyond what the facts support.

A landlord who genuinely wants to move into a building they own but doesn't need the specific apartment the tenant occupies may assert owner use anyway, hoping the tenant won't challenge the "immediate and compelling necessity" standard.

A landlord who plans cosmetic renovations may frame them as "major alterations" requiring vacancy, knowing that the work could easily be done with the tenant in place.

A landlord who wants to re-rent at a higher price may claim withdrawal from the rental market, intending to re-list the apartment after a suitable interval.

These strategies work because they exploit the information gap between landlord and tenant. The landlord knows their own intentions. The tenant often does not. And because challenging the claim requires effort, money, and time, many tenants concede before the claim is tested.

The goal of a strategic exaggeration is often not to win in court. It is to avoid court entirely, by convincing the tenant to leave voluntarily before the claim has to be proved.

How Tenants Prove a Claim Was False

False eviction claims leave trails.

If the landlord claimed owner occupancy and then did not move in, the evidence is often visible. The apartment may appear on rental listings. Utility records may show no usage consistent with occupancy. Neighbors may confirm that no one moved in. Building records may show no change in mailbox labels or intercom listings.

If the landlord claimed demolition and then did not demolish, the building itself is the evidence. Department of Buildings records may show no permit applications. The building may remain standing and occupied. No construction activity may have occurred.

If the landlord claimed withdrawal and then re-rented, rental listings, lease records, and tenant testimony establish the fraud.

Tenants who suspect a false claim should begin documenting immediately.

Photograph the building and the apartment at regular intervals. Save any rental listings for the unit that appear online. Check Department of Buildings records for permit applications. Note whether construction activity begins. Keep records of communication with the landlord. Talk to neighbors and keep notes of what they observe.

Timing matters. Evidence that the claim was false is most powerful when gathered soon after the tenant's departure. Waiting months or years weakens the evidentiary trail.

If a landlord recovers an apartment through a false claim, the consequences can be severe.

In rent-stabilized cases, the tenant may be entitled to reinstatement in the apartment, monetary damages, and recovery of moving costs and rent differential. The landlord may face penalties from DHCR and credibility damage in all future proceedings.

Under Good Cause, a landlord who evicts based on a false owner-use claim and then re-rents the unit faces potential liability for wrongful eviction, and the tenant may raise the fraud as a defense in any subsequent proceeding.

False claims are not just bad behavior. They are legally actionable. But they are only actionable if someone checks.

Real-World Example: The Apartment That Came Back Online

A tenant in a rent-stabilized apartment in Manhattan received a Golub Notice stating the landlord intended to move into the apartment for personal use. The notice was served within the correct time window. It identified the owner by name. It stated that the owner had an immediate and compelling need for the unit as a primary residence.

The tenant was overwhelmed. The notice looked official. The landlord's attorney followed up with a letter offering a modest relocation payment if the tenant left voluntarily. The letter mentioned the cost and uncertainty of litigation, the possibility of an unfavorable outcome, and the stress of a court proceeding. It was polite, professional, and designed to make leaving feel like the rational choice.

The tenant moved out.

Three months later, the tenant saw the same apartment listed on a rental website at a significantly higher rent. The listing described the unit as "fully renovated" and "available immediately."

The tenant documented the listing, saved screenshots, and contacted a tenant attorney. The attorney filed a complaint with DHCR and initiated a proceeding challenging the eviction as fraudulent.

The landlord could not prove that any individual owner had ever moved into the apartment. There was no evidence of personal occupancy at any point after the tenant's departure. The apartment had been re-rented to a new tenant at a market-rate rent.

The tenant was entitled to remedies because the eviction was based on a false claim. The "immediate and compelling necessity" had never existed. The Golub Notice had been a tool to clear the apartment for profit, not a genuine assertion of need.

The landlord had counted on one thing: that no one would check after the tenant left.

Someone checked.

What to Take From This Chapter

Owner-use evictions require the landlord to prove immediate and compelling necessity for the specific unit, not merely a desire or preference. The standard was significantly tightened by the HSTPA.

The Golub Notice is a mandatory prerequisite for owner-use cases in rent-stabilized apartments. It must be served within the 150-to-90-day window before the lease expires. A defective or missing Golub Notice can result in dismissal of the entire case.

Only one unit per building can be recovered for owner or family use, regardless of how many owners or family members are involved.

Senior citizens (62 and older), disabled tenants, and tenants with 15 or more years of occupancy have heightened protections, including the right to equivalent or superior alternative housing at the same or lower rent.

Demolition and major alteration claims require concrete evidence, not just plans or intentions. Cosmetic renovations do not qualify. The work must be incompatible with continued occupancy.

False eviction claims leave evidence and carry consequences. Tenants who are evicted under pretextual claims may be entitled to reinstatement, damages, and penalties.

If your landlord says they need your apartment for personal reasons, the right response is not panic. It is verification. Check the notice for procedural defects. Investigate whether the claim is genuine. Consult an attorney. And remember that the burden is on the landlord to prove their case, not on you to prove you deserve to stay.

In the next chapter, we'll examine the eviction notices themselves, and why many are legally invalid before a case even starts.

12

Eviction Notices

Why Many Are Invalid

In New York, eviction doesn't start in court. It starts on paper.

Before a landlord can file an eviction case, they must serve the correct notice, in the correct form, at the correct time, and in the correct way. Miss any one of those requirements, and the entire case can fail. Not on the merits. Not because the tenant proved hardship. But because the eviction was never legally started.

This chapter is about those requirements. It explains the most common types of eviction notices, the specific rules each must follow, and the errors landlords make so frequently that many eviction cases are vulnerable before a tenant ever walks into a courtroom. If you receive an eviction notice, this chapter tells you what to look for before you assume the worst.

Why Notices Matter More Than Most Tenants Realize

Eviction notices are not warnings. They are not threats. They are not suggestions. They are legal prerequisites.

A notice is a mandatory step that the landlord must complete correctly before the court has authority to hear the case. If the notice is defective, the court lacks jurisdiction. If the court lacks jurisdiction, the case cannot proceed. The landlord must start over from scratch, with a new notice, properly prepared and properly served, and the clock resets.

New York courts enforce notice requirements strictly. This is not because judges enjoy technicalities. It is because eviction results in the loss of housing, and the law requires that a process with such serious consequences be initiated properly. Close enough is not good enough. Substantial compliance is not a recognized standard. The notice must meet every requirement, or it fails.

This strict approach creates a structural advantage for tenants who know what to look for. A defective notice is an absolute defense. It does not matter whether the tenant owes rent, whether the tenant violated the lease, or whether the landlord has a legitimate grievance. If the notice is wrong, the case is wrong.

Rent Demand Notices: The Gateway to Nonpayment Cases

The most common eviction case in New York is the nonpayment proceeding, and every nonpayment case begins with a rent demand notice.

Before a landlord can file a nonpayment petition in Housing Court, they must serve the tenant with a written demand for rent. This demand is a precondition to the case. Without it, the court lacks authority to proceed. With a defective demand, the result is the same.

A valid rent demand must meet several specific requirements.

The demand must state the correct amount of rent owed. This sounds obvious, but it is where many demands fail. The amount must reflect the legal regulated rent (in stabilized apartments), must exclude any charges that are not lawfully collectible as rent, and must accurately state the arrears for each period claimed. A demand that overstates the amount owed, even by a small margin, is defective.

The demand must clearly identify the rental periods covered. A demand that says "you owe $5,000" without specifying which months or periods are included does not give the tenant enough information to evaluate the claim. The tenant has the right to know exactly what is being demanded and for what time period.

The demand must give the tenant the required amount of time to pay or respond. Under current law, the tenant must receive a written rent demand at least 14 days before the landlord files a nonpayment petition. This 14-day period is mandatory and begins when the demand is properly served, not when the landlord mails it or thinks about it. Filing a petition before the 14-day period has elapsed is premature, and the case is subject to dismissal.

The demand must comply with formatting and delivery rules. It must be in writing. It must be served in a legally approved manner (discussed later in this chapter). And it must include the Good Cause Eviction notice, if applicable, informing the tenant whether their apartment is covered by the Good Cause law and the basis for that determination.

Common rent demand defects include inflated or incorrect rent amounts, inclusion of illegal late fees or penalties, demands for rent that is not legally due (such as amounts above the legal regulated rent in a stabilized apartment), demands that include non-rent charges (such as attorney's fees, repair costs, or administrative fees) that are not properly collectible as rent, and demands that use the wrong notice period.

Each of these defects can be fatal to the nonpayment case. A tenant who receives a rent demand should examine it line by line, comparing the demanded amount to the legal rent, checking for illegal charges, and verifying the time periods and dates. The math matters. The details matter. And the landlord's confidence in the demand does not make it correct.

Termination Notices: Ending a Tenancy the Right Way

For eviction cases other than nonpayment, landlords must serve a termination notice before filing a holdover proceeding.

Termination notices are used when the landlord seeks to end the tenancy itself, not just collect unpaid rent. The circumstances vary, but the notice requirements are consistently strict.

A valid termination notice must state a legally valid reason for termination when one is required. In rent-stabilized apartments, the notice of non-renewal (the Golub Notice discussed in Chapter 11) must specify the ground for the landlord's refusal to renew. In Good Cause-covered apartments, the notice must include the Good Cause disclosure and state the basis for the termination. Even in unregulated apartments, the notice must comply with applicable requirements, including the 30/60/90-day notice provisions of Real Property Law Section 226-c.

The notice must provide the correct notice period. The required period depends on the type of tenancy, the length of occupancy, and which legal framework applies. In rent-stabilized apartments, the Golub Notice must be served 150 to 90 days before the lease expires. For unregulated tenants, the notice period depends on length of occupancy: 30 days for tenancy under one year, 60 days for one to two years, and 90 days for tenancy over two years. Getting the notice period wrong by even one day can invalidate the notice.

The notice must correctly identify the parties. The landlord named in the notice must be the correct legal owner of the building. The tenant named must be the correct tenant of record. Errors in party identification, which happen more often than you might expect (particularly in buildings with complex ownership structures, LLCs, or recent ownership transfers), create jurisdictional problems that can derail the case.

The notice must comply with applicable disclosure requirements. Since August 2024, landlords must include the Good Cause Eviction notice with any predicate notice, lease, or renewal, stating whether the apartment is covered and, if not, why. Failure to include this disclosure is itself a defect that may be raised in court.

Common termination notice errors include citing the wrong legal ground, using state-law notice periods where city law or the Good Cause law requires a different standard, serving notices too early or too late relative to the required window, failing to include required disclosures, omitting the reason for non-renewal in situations where a reason is required, and naming the wrong owner or tenant.

Many termination notices look professional and authoritative. They are printed on letterhead, cite statutes, and include legal language designed to convey finality. None of that matters if the content, timing, or service is wrong. The appearance of a notice tells you nothing about its validity. Only the requirements tell you that.

The Predicate Notice: What It Is and Why It Matters

The term "predicate notice" refers to any notice that must be served before a case can be filed. It is the legal precondition, the predicate, to the court proceeding that follows.

In nonpayment cases, the predicate notice is the rent demand. In holdover cases, the predicate notice is the termination notice, cure notice, or notice of non-renewal, depending on the type of holdover.

The concept matters because courts evaluate predicate notices independently from the merits of the case. A judge reviewing a predicate notice is not asking whether the tenant owes rent or whether the tenant violated the lease. The judge is asking whether the landlord satisfied the prerequisite for being in court at all.

If the predicate notice fails, the case fails. The tenant does not need to address the substance. The landlord must go back, fix the notice, re-serve it, wait the required period, and only then file a new case. This process can add weeks or months to the landlord's timeline, during which the tenant remains in the apartment with all rights intact.

This is why experienced tenant attorneys always examine the predicate notice first. It is the foundation of the case. If the foundation is cracked, everything built on it collapses.

Notice to Cure: The Chance to Fix Before the Fight

Before a landlord can evict a tenant for a lease violation (other than nonpayment), they must generally serve a "notice to cure." This is a written notice that identifies the specific lease violation, describes the conduct the landlord considers objectionable, and gives the tenant a specified period to correct the problem.

The HSTPA extended the cure period for rent-stabilized tenants. Under current law, even after a tenant loses a lease violation case in court, the tenant has 30 days to cure the violation, up from 10 days under the prior law. And the tenant does not necessarily need to fully cure within that period. If the tenant can demonstrate that they are making substantial progress toward curing the violation, courts may extend the opportunity.

A notice to cure must be specific. It must tell the tenant exactly what the alleged violation is and what the tenant must do to fix it. A vague notice that says "you are in violation of your lease" without identifying the provision or the conduct is defective. The tenant has the right to know precisely what they are accused of and what compliance looks like.

Common notice to cure issues include vague or overbroad descriptions of the alleged violation, failure to identify the specific lease provision being violated, demands that are impossible to cure (such as demanding the tenant undo something that cannot be undone), and notices that are served for violations the landlord previously tolerated or condoned.

If you receive a notice to cure, read it carefully. Determine whether the alleged violation is real and substantial. If it is, cure it within the specified period and document that you did so. If it is not, or if the notice is defective, consult an attorney. The cure period is your opportunity to resolve the issue and remove the ground for eviction before the landlord can proceed to court.

If the tenant cures the violation within the allowed time, the ground for eviction disappears. The landlord cannot proceed. This is why the notice to cure exists: to give tenants a fair chance to correct problems before facing the loss of their housing.

Service Errors: How Notices Are Actually Delivered

Even a perfectly written notice is invalid if it isn't served correctly.

Service of process in New York is governed by specific rules that dictate how legal documents must be delivered to a tenant. These rules exist to ensure that tenants actually receive the notices they are entitled to, and courts enforce them seriously.

The rules vary depending on the type of notice and the stage of the proceeding, but the general framework involves a hierarchy of service methods.

Personal delivery is the preferred method. The notice is handed directly to the tenant. This is the most reliable form of service and the most difficult to dispute.

Substituted service is the next option, used when personal delivery cannot be accomplished after reasonable attempts. The notice is delivered to a person of suitable age and discretion at the tenant's residence or place of business, and a copy is mailed to the tenant. Both steps, delivery and mailing, are required. Substituted service without the follow-up mailing is incomplete.

Conspicuous place service (sometimes called "nail and mail") is used only after personal and substituted service have been attempted and failed. The notice is affixed to the door of the apartment in a conspicuous manner, and a copy is mailed. This method requires the process server to document the prior attempts and explain why they failed.

Each method has specific requirements about who can serve the notice, how many attempts must be made before escalating to the next method, and what documentation must accompany the service. The person who serves the notice must generally be someone other than the landlord. In many cases, a licensed process server is used, and the process server must file an affidavit of service describing exactly what was done, when, and to whom.

Common service mistakes are surprisingly frequent and include landlords serving notices themselves when the law requires service by a third party, improper "nail and mail" service without sufficient prior attempts at personal delivery, failure to complete the required follow-up mailing after substituted or conspicuous service, service at the wrong address or the wrong apartment, failure to file a proper affidavit of service, and serving the notice on someone who does not meet the "suitable age and discretion" standard.

Service errors deprive the court of jurisdiction over the tenant. If the court does not have jurisdiction, it cannot issue a judgment or a warrant of eviction. The case must be dismissed, and the landlord must start the entire process over.

Tenants often assume that service details don't matter. Courts consistently disagree. If you are served with eviction papers or a predicate notice, pay attention to how you received it. Was it handed to you personally? Was it left with someone else? Was it taped to your door? Was anything mailed? These details can determine whether the case against you is legally valid.

Timing Errors: When a Single Day Changes Everything

Notice timing in New York is unforgiving, and errors in timing are among the most common reasons eviction cases fail.

The rules vary by the type of notice, but the pattern is consistent: the law specifies a minimum number of days between when the notice is served and when the landlord can take the next step (filing a case, commencing a termination, or demanding the tenant vacate). That minimum is a hard line. Filing one day early can invalidate the proceeding.

In nonpayment cases, the landlord must wait at least 14 days after serving the rent demand before filing the petition. If the petition is filed on day 13, it is premature and subject to dismissal.

In holdover cases involving termination notices, the notice period depends on the type of tenancy and the applicable legal framework. The Golub Notice window (150 to 90 days before lease expiration) must be calculated precisely. The 30/60/90-day notice periods under RPL 226-c must be calculated from the date of service, not the date of mailing or the date the landlord decided to terminate.

Counting errors are common. Landlords or their attorneys miscalculate the number of days, forget to exclude (or include) the day of service, ignore holidays or weekends that affect filing deadlines, or confuse calendar days with business days.

A one-day mistake can invalidate a notice and force the landlord to restart the process. Courts do not grant extensions or forgive timing errors because the landlord was "close enough." The deadline is the deadline.

Why These Errors Are So Common

Notice defects are not rare events that happen only to careless landlords. They are common, recurring problems that affect a significant percentage of eviction cases in New York.

They happen because the notice rules are genuinely complex. Different types of cases require different notices, different notice periods, different service methods, and different content requirements. Keeping track of all the variables, especially when the rules have changed multiple times in recent years (HSTPA in 2019, Good Cause in 2024, NYC local amendments), is difficult even for experienced practitioners.

They happen because laws change and forms do not. Landlords and property managers often use notice templates that were drafted before the HSTPA or before the Good Cause law took effect. The templates may reflect notice periods, content requirements, or procedural standards that are no longer current. Using an outdated form is not a defense. The current law controls, regardless of what the template says.

They happen because landlords assume tenants won't challenge them. Many eviction cases proceed unchallenged. Tenants don't appear in court, don't raise defenses, and don't examine the notice. Landlords who have gotten away with defective notices in the past may not realize their practices are noncompliant until a tenant finally pushes back.

And they happen because speed works against precision. Landlords who are eager to recover possession often rush the process, filing too quickly, cutting corners on service, or skipping steps that feel like bureaucratic formalities. In New York, those formalities are legal requirements, and rushing past them creates the very defects that tenants can use to stop the case.

How to Evaluate a Notice You've Received

If you receive any notice related to eviction, whether a rent demand, a termination notice, a notice to cure, or court papers, do not assume it is valid. Examine it systematically.

Check the content. Does the notice state the correct rent amount? Does it identify the correct parties? Does it include the required disclosures (such as the Good Cause notice)? Does it state a valid reason for termination, if one is required? Does it match the type of proceeding the landlord is pursuing?

Check the timing. When was the notice served? When does the notice period expire? Has the landlord filed the case before the notice period elapsed? Is the Golub Notice window calculated correctly? Do the dates on the notice align with the dates on the affidavit of service?

Check the service. How did you receive the notice? Was it handed to you personally? Was it left with someone else? Was it taped to your door? Was a copy mailed? Does the affidavit of service match what actually happened? Was the server someone other than the landlord?

Check for the Good Cause disclosure. Since August 2024, every predicate notice, lease, and renewal must include a statement about whether the apartment is covered by the Good Cause Eviction Law. If the disclosure is missing, that may be a basis to challenge the proceeding.

If you find any defect, do not ignore it. Raise it in court, or provide the information to your attorney so they can raise it on your behalf. Notice defects are powerful defenses, but they must be asserted. A defect that is never raised cannot help you.

The Right to Counsel: Help You May Already Have

New York City's Right to Counsel program (also known as Universal Access to Counsel) provides free legal representation to tenants facing eviction in Housing Court. The program covers tenants in designated zip codes who meet income eligibility requirements, and it has expanded significantly since its inception in 2017.

If you are facing an eviction case, check whether you are eligible for free representation. The Housing Court Help Centers, located in each borough's courthouse, can provide information about the program and connect you with a legal services organization.

Having an attorney review your notice and your case is invaluable. Many of the defects described in this chapter are technical and require legal training to identify. An attorney who spots a notice defect on the first court date can get the case dismissed before it ever reaches the merits.

Even if you are not eligible for the Right to Counsel program, legal services organizations such as Legal Aid Society, Legal Services NYC, and Met Council on Housing may be able to help. Contact them as early as possible, ideally before your first court date.

Real-World Example: The Notice That Never Counted

A tenant in Brooklyn received an eviction notice taped to her door on a Monday evening. She was not home at the time. No one else in the apartment received the notice. No copy was mailed. The notice demanded rent and stated that the landlord would file an eviction case if the rent was not paid within five days.

The tenant assumed the notice was valid. The paper on the door felt official and urgent. She began gathering money to pay the arrears, worried about losing her apartment.

In court, the tenant's attorney (provided through the Right to Counsel program) examined the notice and the affidavit of service.

The affidavit claimed that the process server had attempted personal delivery twice before resorting to conspicuous place service. But the dates and times listed in the affidavit were inconsistent with the building's security camera footage, which the attorney obtained. The footage showed only one visit, not the required multiple attempts. No follow-up mailing had been sent, as required for conspicuous place service. And the notice period was five days, not the 14 days required under current law.

The judge dismissed the case.

The tenant didn't win because the rent issue disappeared. The rent was still owed, and the tenant eventually worked out a payment plan. She won because the eviction was never legally started. The notice was defective on multiple grounds. The service was improper. The timeline was wrong. And the landlord had to go back to the beginning, which gave the tenant time to stabilize her finances and negotiate from a position of strength rather than panic.

What to Take From This Chapter

Eviction notices are mandatory legal prerequisites, not optional warnings. A defective notice deprives the court of jurisdiction and can result in dismissal of the entire case.

Rent demand notices must state the correct amount, identify the correct periods, exclude illegal charges, and provide the required 14-day notice period. Inflated or inaccurate demands are fatal to nonpayment cases.

Termination notices must state the correct reason (when required), provide the correct notice period, identify the correct parties, and include all required disclosures, including the Good Cause notice.

Notices to cure must specifically identify the lease violation and give the tenant a meaningful opportunity to correct it.

Service must follow the prescribed hierarchy: personal delivery first, then substituted service, then conspicuous place service. Each method has specific requirements, and shortcuts invalidate the service.

Timing is unforgiving. Filing a case before the notice period expires, miscalculating the required days, or serving a notice outside the required window can each independently destroy the case.

If you receive an eviction notice, the first question is not "Is this serious?" It's "Was this done exactly the way the law requires?"

In the next chapter, we'll walk through what happens after the notice, when the case reaches Housing Court, and why most eviction cases never make it to trial.

13

What Actually Happens in New York Housing Court

Housing Court is one of the most feared and least understood parts of renting in New York.

Many tenants imagine eviction as a fast, one-way process: notice, court, lockout. A conveyor belt that moves in one direction, at one speed, toward one outcome. The landlord files. The judge rules. The tenant leaves.

That is not how it works. New York Housing Court is a process-driven system with multiple stages, multiple checkpoints, and multiple opportunities for cases to stall, collapse, or resolve long before anyone testifies. Most eviction cases never reach trial. Many are dismissed on procedural grounds. Others settle on terms the tenant finds acceptable. And some reveal defects so fundamental that the landlord has to start the entire process over from scratch.

If the previous three chapters explained what just cause means, what landlords claim, and why notices fail, this chapter explains what happens when a case survives all of that and actually reaches the courthouse. The process is more structured, more tenant-protective, and more navigable than most tenants expect.

How a Case Gets to Court

An eviction case begins when the landlord files a petition with the Housing Court clerk. The petition is the formal legal document that initiates the proceeding.

There are two main types of petitions.

A nonpayment petition alleges that the tenant has failed to pay rent that is lawfully owed. It must be supported by a valid rent demand that was properly served at least 14 days before the filing. The petition must state the correct amount of rent claimed, identify the rental periods covered, and name the correct parties.

A holdover petition alleges that the tenant's right to possession has ended and that the tenant remains in the apartment without the landlord's consent. It must be supported by a valid predicate notice, whether that is a Golub Notice, a termination notice, a notice to cure followed by a notice of termination, or another applicable notice, properly served within the required timeframe.

The petition itself must meet specific requirements. It must correctly identify the landlord (including the correct legal entity if the building is owned by an LLC, corporation, or trust). It must correctly identify the tenant of record. It must state the address and apartment number. It must describe the legal basis for the proceeding. And it must be verified, meaning someone with personal knowledge of the facts must sign it under oath or affirmation.

Errors in the petition, like errors in the predicate notice, can be grounds for dismissal. Naming the wrong landlord, naming the wrong tenant, misstating the legal basis, or failing to verify the petition are all defects that tenant attorneys look for immediately.

Service of Court Papers

After the petition is filed, the landlord must serve the tenant with the court papers, including the petition and a notice of the court date.

Service of the petition follows its own set of rules, which are separate from the service requirements for the predicate notice. In Housing Court, the petition and notice of petition must generally be served at least five days before the court date if served by personal delivery, or at least 10 days before the court date if served by substituted or conspicuous place service (with an additional five days added for mailing).

The same hierarchy of service methods applies: personal delivery first, then substituted service, then conspicuous place service, each with its own documentation requirements. The process server must file an affidavit of service with the court describing exactly what was done.

Improper service of the petition deprives the court of personal jurisdiction over the tenant. Without personal jurisdiction, the court cannot issue a judgment or a warrant of eviction, no matter how strong the landlord's underlying case might be.

This is one of the most important and least intuitive protections in the system. A landlord can have a valid claim, a valid notice, and a valid petition, and still lose the case because the petition was not delivered to the tenant in the manner the law requires. Service is not a formality. It is a constitutional requirement rooted in due process: the tenant has the right to know they are being sued and to have a meaningful opportunity to respond.

Tenants who were not properly served can raise a jurisdictional defense at any point in the proceeding. If the defense is sustained, the case is dismissed regardless of the stage it has reached.

The First Court Date: What Actually Happens

The first appearance in Housing Court is typically called a "return date" or an "initial conference." For many tenants, this is the most anxiety-producing moment in the process. The reality is usually less dramatic than they expect.

On the first court date, the judge or court attorney typically reviews the case for facial validity. This means checking whether the petition and predicate notice appear to comply with legal requirements on their face. If there are obvious defects (wrong parties, expired notice periods, missing predicate notices), the case may be addressed immediately.

Both sides are usually given an opportunity to speak or, more commonly, to meet with their attorneys. In New York City, the Right to Counsel program means that many income-eligible tenants are connected with a free attorney on their first court date. If you do not have an attorney when you arrive, ask the court clerk about the Right to Counsel program and the Housing Court Help Center before the case is called.

Several things may happen on the first court date.

The case may be adjourned. Adjournments (postponements) are extremely common on the first appearance. The court may adjourn the case to allow the tenant to obtain counsel, to allow both sides to review documents, or to schedule a conference or settlement discussion. An adjournment does not mean anything has been decided. It means the case will continue on a later date.

The case may be referred to a resolution part. Many Housing Courts have dedicated settlement or resolution parts where cases are sent before trial. These parts are designed to encourage negotiated outcomes. A mediator, court attorney, or judge may facilitate discussions about payment plans, repairs, lease terms, or other issues.

The case may be dismissed. If the judge identifies a defect in the petition, the notice, or the service, the case may be dismissed at the first appearance. This is more common when the tenant has an attorney who raises the issue, but judges can also identify defects on their own.

The case may proceed to a motion schedule. If the tenant has defenses that require formal briefing, the court may set a schedule for motions. This is discussed in the next section.

What almost never happens on the first court date is a trial. Trials require preparation, witness scheduling, and often multiple prior court appearances. The first date is the beginning of a process, not the end of one. Tenants who arrive expecting to lose their apartment that day are almost always wrong about the timeline.

Motions and Defenses: Challenging the Case Before Trial

If a case survives the initial review, either side may file motions, which are formal written requests asking the court to take a specific action.

The most powerful motion for tenants is a motion to dismiss. A motion to dismiss argues that the case should be thrown out for a legal deficiency, without the need for a trial on the facts. Common grounds for dismissal include defective predicate notice (wrong content, wrong timing, wrong service), improper service of the petition, lack of standing (the petitioner is not the legal owner or is not authorized to bring the case), failure to include required disclosures (such as the Good Cause Eviction notice), failure to state a cause of action (the petition does not allege facts that, even if true, would entitle the landlord to eviction), improper party identification (wrong landlord or wrong tenant named), and failure to comply with pre-suit requirements (such as the 14-day rent demand period).

Motions to dismiss are decided on the papers, meaning the judge reviews the written submissions without hearing testimony. If the motion is granted, the case is over without a trial ever taking place. If the motion is denied, the case proceeds to the next stage.

Tenants may also raise affirmative defenses in their answer to the petition. An answer is the tenant's formal written response, and it typically includes both denials of the landlord's allegations and affirmative defenses, which are legal arguments that, even if the landlord's facts are true, prevent the landlord from winning.

Common affirmative defenses in eviction cases include breach of the warranty of habitability (the landlord failed to maintain livable conditions, which may reduce or eliminate the rent owed), retaliatory eviction (the case was filed in response to the tenant exercising a legal right), waiver (the landlord accepted rent or condoned the conduct that forms the basis of the case after knowing about it), laches (the landlord unreasonably delayed in bringing the case), payment (the rent was paid and the landlord's records are wrong), and the apartment is subject to rent stabilization or Good Cause protections that the landlord has not acknowledged.

Each defense must be pleaded in the answer to be preserved. A defense that is not raised may be waived. This is one of the many reasons why having an attorney, even for the answer alone, is critically important.

Stipulations of Settlement: How Most Cases Actually End

The majority of eviction cases in New York Housing Court end not with a trial verdict but with a stipulation of settlement, which is a written agreement between the landlord and tenant that resolves the case on negotiated terms.

Stipulations are essentially contracts, but they are "so-ordered" by the judge, meaning they have the force of a court order. Both sides are bound by the terms, and violation of a stipulation can have immediate consequences.

In nonpayment cases, a typical stipulation might include an agreement by the tenant to pay the arrears on a specific schedule, a provision that if the tenant complies with the payment schedule the case is discontinued, and a provision that if the tenant defaults on the schedule the landlord may apply for a warrant of eviction without further court proceedings.

In holdover cases, stipulations might include an agreed move-out date in exchange for a waiver of claims, a withdrawal of the case in exchange for the tenant curing a violation, or a payment by the landlord to the tenant (a buyout) in exchange for a voluntary vacatur.

Stipulations can be powerful tools for tenants, but they can also be traps. A stipulation that seems reasonable on paper may include provisions that are difficult to comply with, timelines that are unrealistic, or consequences for default that are disproportionately severe.

Before signing any stipulation, read every word. If you have an attorney, discuss every term. If you don't have an attorney, ask the court for time to consult one. Once a stipulation is so-ordered by the judge, it is extremely difficult to modify or vacate. The time to negotiate is before you sign, not after.

Pay particular attention to "judgment clauses," which state that a judgment of possession is entered against the tenant immediately upon signing, with execution (the actual eviction) stayed as long as the tenant complies with the terms. If the tenant defaults, the landlord can execute the judgment without returning to court for a hearing. This means you could lose your right to be heard if you miss a payment or deadline. If a judgment clause is included, make sure you understand exactly what triggers execution and whether you have any opportunity to seek relief if circumstances change.

Discovery: When the Facts Need Investigation

In some eviction cases, particularly holdover cases involving disputed facts, the court may allow discovery, which is the formal process of exchanging information and evidence between the parties.

Discovery can include document requests (demanding the other side produce leases, rent records, registration filings, or other relevant documents), interrogatories (written questions that the other side must answer under oath), and depositions (oral questioning of witnesses under oath, conducted outside the courtroom).

Discovery is less common in Housing Court than in other types of litigation, but it can be critical in cases involving contested owner-use claims, disputed primary residence issues, fraud allegations, or complex rent histories. It allows tenants to obtain evidence that the landlord controls and that may reveal whether the landlord's claims are genuine.

In owner-use cases, for example, discovery might reveal that the landlord has no current address change on file, has not notified utility companies, or has made no preparations to actually move into the apartment. In nuisance cases, discovery might reveal that the landlord's claims are based on a single complaint rather than the persistent pattern required by law.

Discovery takes time, which generally benefits the tenant. The longer the case takes, the longer the tenant remains in the apartment, and the more pressure builds on the landlord to settle on reasonable terms.

Trial: The Rare Final Stage

Only a small fraction of Housing Court cases reach trial, but understanding what happens at trial is important for tenants who may face one.

At trial, the landlord bears the burden of proof. This means the landlord must present evidence sufficient to persuade the judge that every element of the case has been established. In a nonpayment case, the landlord must prove that the rent is owed, that the amount is correct, and that the predicate notice was proper. In a holdover case, the landlord must prove the ground for eviction, whether that is owner use, lease violation, nuisance, or another recognized cause.

The tenant has the right to cross-examine the landlord's witnesses, present their own evidence, call their own witnesses, and make legal arguments. The tenant does not need to prove anything. The tenant's job is to test the landlord's case and, if possible, show that it fails.

Trials in Housing Court are bench trials, meaning they are decided by a judge, not a jury. The judge evaluates the evidence, makes findings of fact, and issues a decision. If the landlord wins, the court enters a judgment of possession and issues a warrant of eviction. If the tenant wins, the case is dismissed.

Even after a judgment is entered, the tenant may have additional time before actual eviction. The court may stay (delay) execution of the warrant under certain circumstances, and the tenant may have the right to appeal.

After the Judgment: Warrants, Stays, and the Marshal

If the court enters a judgment of possession in favor of the landlord, the next step is the issuance of a warrant of eviction. The warrant authorizes the city marshal or sheriff to carry out the physical eviction.

The warrant does not mean the tenant is removed immediately. The marshal must serve the tenant with a notice of eviction, providing at least 14 days' notice before executing the warrant. During that period, the tenant may seek a stay of the warrant from the court, apply for emergency rental assistance, or negotiate a resolution with the landlord.

A stay is a court order that temporarily prevents the warrant from being executed. Courts may grant stays for various reasons, including pending appeals, applications for rental assistance, or changed circumstances that warrant additional time.

Only a city marshal or county sheriff can carry out a legal eviction. A landlord who attempts to remove a tenant without a warrant, whether by changing the locks, removing belongings, shutting off utilities, or using physical force, is committing an illegal eviction. Illegal evictions are crimes in New York City and can result in criminal charges, civil penalties, and orders restoring the tenant to possession.

Common Landlord Mistakes in Court

Landlords lose cases for reasons that have nothing to do with rent or behavior. The procedural requirements of Housing Court are demanding, and mistakes are common.

The most frequent errors include relying on outdated petition forms that do not reflect current law, miscalculating notice periods by one or more days, failing to register rent-stabilized apartments (which can undermine the landlord's standing or the validity of the rent demanded), naming the wrong legal entity as the petitioner (common in buildings owned by LLCs that have changed names or undergone ownership transfers), filing petitions before the predicate notice period has elapsed, failing to include the Good Cause

Eviction disclosure in the predicate notice or petition, and presenting rent demands that include illegal charges or overstate the amount owed.

Each of these errors creates an opportunity for the tenant. But the opportunity exists only if the tenant, or the tenant's attorney, identifies and raises the issue. Defects that are never raised cannot help. This is why legal representation, or at the very least careful review of every document in the case, is essential.

Real-World Example: Winning Before the Story Was Told

A tenant in a rent-stabilized apartment in Queens was served with a holdover petition alleging non-primary residence. The landlord claimed the tenant was not using the apartment as her primary home and sought to recover the apartment on that basis.

The tenant was terrified. She had been spending time at her partner's apartment in New Jersey and was worried that her absences would be used against her. She assumed the case would come down to her word against the landlord's, and she wasn't confident she would win.

Her attorney, assigned through the Right to Counsel program, took a different approach. Before looking at the factual dispute, the attorney examined the Golub Notice, the petition, and the affidavit of service.

The Golub Notice had been served 85 days before the lease expired. The required window was 150 to 90 days. Five days short.

The attorney filed a motion to dismiss based on the untimely Golub Notice. The judge granted the motion. The case was dismissed without the tenant ever having to testify about where she slept, how often she visited New Jersey, or whether the apartment was her primary home.

The factual questions were never reached. They didn't need to be. The case had a procedural defect that was fatal, and the attorney found it before the landlord could tell the story.

The tenant didn't win by proving her case. She won because the landlord's case was never properly started.

What to Take From This Chapter

Housing Court is procedural, not automatic. Every stage of the process, from filing to service to the first court date to trial, has specific requirements that the landlord must satisfy.

Most cases never reach trial. They are resolved through adjournments, settlements, motions to dismiss, or voluntary discontinuance. The outcome is often determined long before testimony begins.

Motions to dismiss are powerful tools. Procedural defects in the notice, service, or petition can end a case without the tenant having to address the merits.

Stipulations of settlement end most cases, but they must be read carefully. Judgment clauses and default provisions can have serious consequences if the tenant does not comply with every term.

Free legal representation may be available through the Right to Counsel program. Check eligibility as early as possible, ideally before your first court date.

If you're facing Housing Court, the key question is not "How bad is my situation?" It's "Did the landlord follow every required step?"

In the next chapter, we shift from eviction to money, starting with one of the most strictly enforced areas of New York tenant law: security deposits and move-out deadlines.

Part V: Security Deposits, Fees & Move-Out Money

14

Security Deposit Limits and Strict Deadlines

New York has some of the toughest security deposit rules in the country, and some of the least forgiving penalties for landlords who ignore them.

For tenants, this is one of the rare areas where the law is simple, strict, and heavily enforced. There is a clear cap on how much can be collected. There is a clear standard for what deductions are allowed. There is a mandatory process for documenting those deductions. And there is a hard deadline for returning what is owed. Miss the deadline, and the landlord's defenses start to disappear.

Many tenants lose money on security deposits not because the landlord's deductions were justified, but because the tenant didn't know the rules. This chapter explains every rule that matters, so that when you move out, you know exactly what the landlord is required to do, exactly when they are required to do it, and exactly what happens when they don't.

The One-Month Cap: No Exceptions, No Creativity

Under current New York law, a landlord may collect no more than one month's rent as a security deposit. This rule was established by the HSTPA in 2019 and applies statewide to all residential rentals, whether rent-stabilized or not.

The cap is absolute. It does not vary based on the tenant's credit score, income level, rental history, pet ownership, or any other factor. There is no "high-risk" exception. There is no "luxury apartment" exception. There is no exception for furnished units, short-term leases, or tenants without guarantors.

Before the HSTPA, landlords routinely collected deposits exceeding one month's rent, sometimes significantly. Deposits of two or three months' rent were common in certain market segments. The 2019 law eliminated that practice entirely.

The cap also extends to charges that function as security deposits regardless of what they are called. Landlords cannot lawfully collect last month's rent in advance. They cannot collect a separate "damage deposit." They cannot collect a "pet deposit." They cannot collect a refundable "move-in fee" that is held against future damage. If a charge is refundable, is collected at the start of the tenancy, and is held as security for the tenant's performance under the lease, it is a security deposit, and it counts toward the one-month cap.

Renaming the charge does not change the rule. A landlord who collects $2,000 as a "security deposit" and $1,000 as a "refundable cleaning fee" has collected $3,000 in security, which exceeds the one-month cap if the rent is $2,000 or less. The "cleaning fee" label is irrelevant. The substance determines the legality.

If you paid more than one month's rent as a deposit (under any name), the excess was illegally collected. You are entitled to a refund of the excess, and the illegal collection may be relevant to other claims, including overcharge complaints in rent-stabilized apartments.

What a Security Deposit Is Actually For

Security deposits exist for a single, narrow purpose: to cover tenant-caused damage beyond normal wear and tear.

This definition is important because it excludes far more than it includes. The deposit is not a general fund for the landlord to draw on whenever they want to charge the tenant for something. It is not a cleanup account. It is not a renovation budget. It is not a reserve for routine maintenance.

Specifically, the security deposit is not meant to cover routine painting between tenants. Repainting is a normal turnover expense that landlords bear as a cost of doing business, regardless of how long the tenant lived in the apartment.

It is not meant to cover ordinary cleaning. Unless the apartment was left in a condition that goes significantly beyond what any reasonable person would consider normal at the end of a tenancy, cleaning costs are the landlord's responsibility.

It is not meant to cover aging fixtures, worn appliances, or faded surfaces. These are the result of normal use over time, not tenant-caused damage. Carpet that is worn from years of walking is normal wear and tear. A countertop that shows signs of daily use is normal wear and tear. Light switches that are scuffed from regular contact are normal wear and tear.

The deposit covers damage that results from the tenant's negligence, misuse, or abuse, things that go beyond what would happen through ordinary, reasonable living. A hole punched in a wall is damage. A broken window caused by the tenant is damage. Burn marks on a hardwood floor from a dropped cigarette are damage. Extensive staining from a pet that was not properly cared for may be damage.

The distinction between normal wear and tear and actual damage is the central question in most deposit disputes. Landlords routinely blur this line because most tenants don't challenge it. Courts, however, recognize the difference and hold landlords to it.

Where the Deposit Must Be Held

New York law imposes requirements on how landlords hold security deposits, and these requirements are frequently ignored.

In buildings with six or more units, the landlord must hold the security deposit in a separate interest-bearing account at a New York banking institution. The deposit cannot be commingled with the landlord's personal or operating funds. The landlord must notify the tenant of the name and address of the bank where the deposit is held.

Interest earned on the deposit belongs to the tenant, minus a small administrative fee the landlord is entitled to retain. In practice, interest rates have been low enough in recent years that this provision has limited financial significance, but the legal requirement remains in effect.

For buildings with fewer than six units, the landlord must still hold the deposit in trust for the tenant. The deposit does not belong to the landlord. It belongs to the tenant and is held by the landlord as a fiduciary.

Landlords who commingle deposits with their operating accounts, who fail to place deposits in interest-bearing accounts, or who cannot account for the deposit funds when the tenant moves out are in violation of the law. These violations don't just create theoretical problems. They undermine the landlord's credibility in any dispute and may affect their ability to claim deductions.

The Itemization Requirement: Receipts or It Didn't Happen

If a landlord intends to keep any portion of the security deposit, they must provide the tenant with an itemized statement of deductions.

This is not optional. It is a legal requirement that applies regardless of the amount withheld, the reason for withholding, or the landlord's subjective belief that the deductions are justified.

The itemized statement must list each deduction separately. It must describe the specific damage or condition that justifies the charge. It must state the cost associated with each item. And it must be sent to the tenant within the 14-day deadline discussed in the next section.

Vague explanations do not satisfy the requirement. A statement that says "repairs: $500" is not an itemized statement. A statement that says "cleaning and maintenance: $800" is not an itemized statement. A statement that says "deductions for damages" with a single lump sum is not an itemized statement.

Each charge must be identified specifically enough that the tenant can evaluate whether it is legitimate. "Repair of two holes in bedroom wall: $150" is specific. "Replacement of kitchen faucet damaged by tenant misuse: $200" is specific. "General repairs: $350" is not.

The requirement exists because tenants have the right to challenge deductions they believe are improper. They cannot exercise that right if they don't know what they're being charged for. An itemized statement that is too vague to evaluate is functionally the same as no statement at all.

Landlords who fail to provide a proper itemized statement within the deadline weaken their position dramatically. Courts treat the absence of itemization as evidence that the landlord has no legitimate basis for the deductions, and the entire deposit may be ordered returned.

The 14-Day Rule: The Deadline That Changes Everything

New York law gives landlords 14 days after the tenant vacates to either return the full security deposit or return the balance along with an itemized statement of deductions.

This is the most consequential deadline in the entire security deposit process, and it is the one landlords violate most frequently.

The 14-day period begins when the tenant vacates, not when the lease expires, not when the tenant returns the keys, and not when the landlord inspects the apartment. If the tenant moves out on March 1, the landlord has until March 15 to return the deposit or provide the itemized statement. If the landlord does neither, the deadline has been missed.

The deadline is strict. Courts do not grant extensions because the landlord was waiting for contractor estimates. They do not excuse delays because the landlord was on vacation. They do not accept the explanation that the landlord "didn't have a forwarding address" (the landlord is responsible for making reasonable efforts to determine the address, including sending the statement to the apartment itself if no forwarding address is provided).

If the landlord misses the 14-day deadline, the consequences are significant.

The landlord may lose the right to claim any deductions at all. Courts have held that a landlord who fails to provide a timely itemized statement forfeits the right to withhold any portion of the deposit. The reasoning is that the itemization requirement exists to protect tenants, and allowing landlords to itemize late would undermine the purpose of the deadline.

The landlord may be required to return the full deposit regardless of whether actual damage existed. This is where the deadline becomes punitive rather than compensatory. Even if the tenant did cause damage, the landlord's failure to comply with the 14-day rule can result in the return of the entire deposit.

The landlord may be liable for additional damages. As discussed in detail in Chapter 15, bad-faith withholding can trigger statutory penalties, including treble (triple) damages.

The 14-day rule is one of the clearest and most measurable standards in New York tenant law. There is no gray area. Either the landlord met the deadline or they didn't. Either the statement was itemized or it wasn't. Either the deposit was returned or it wasn't. This clarity is what makes deposit claims among the most straightforward for tenants to pursue and among the most difficult for landlords to defend when they have not complied.

What Tenants Should Do at Move-Out

The strength of a security deposit claim depends heavily on what the tenant does when leaving the apartment. Documentation created at move-out is often the difference between recovering the deposit and losing it.

Before you move out, take photographs and video of every room in the apartment. Document the condition of walls, floors, ceilings, windows, fixtures, appliances, and any area the landlord might claim was damaged. Use a timestamp feature on your camera or phone, or include a newspaper or other date-verifiable item in the frame.

If possible, do the walkthrough with a witness. A friend, family member, or neighbor who can later testify about the apartment's condition at move-out adds significant credibility to your account.

Clean the apartment thoroughly before leaving. This does not mean you need to hire a professional cleaning service. It means the apartment should be left in a reasonably clean condition, free of personal belongings, garbage, and obvious mess. The standard is not perfection. It is reasonableness.

Provide the landlord with a forwarding address in writing. Send it by email, text, and certified mail so you have documentation. The forwarding address is where the landlord must send the deposit or the itemized statement. If you provide a forwarding address and the landlord claims they didn't know where to send the money, your documentation defeats that claim.

Keep copies of your lease, your move-in photos (if you took them), your rent payment records, and any correspondence with the landlord about the apartment's condition. If a dispute arises, these documents form the foundation of your case.

Return all keys and access devices, and document that you did so. A text message or email confirming that keys were returned on a specific date is sufficient. If you can get the landlord to acknowledge receipt in writing, even better.

The goal is to create a record that is clear, timestamped, and difficult to dispute. If the landlord later claims damage, your documentation will either confirm or refute the claim. If the landlord misses the 14-day deadline, your documentation of the move-out date establishes when the clock started.

What Happens When the Deadline Passes

When the 14-day deadline passes without a full return or a proper itemized statement, the tenant's position becomes significantly stronger.

At this point, the tenant should send a written demand to the landlord requesting the return of the full security deposit. The demand should reference the move-out date, the amount of the deposit, the 14-day deadline, and the fact that no deposit or itemized statement was received within the required period. Send the demand by certified mail with return receipt, and keep a copy.

If the landlord does not respond to the demand, or responds with an insufficient explanation, the tenant has several options.

Small claims court is the most accessible option for most tenants. In New York City, small claims court handles cases involving amounts up to $10,000 (or $5,000 in city courts outside NYC). The filing fee is modest, the process does not require an attorney, and the cases are typically heard within a few weeks. Security deposit cases are among the most common small claims court filings, and judges are familiar with the rules.

Housing Court may also have jurisdiction over deposit disputes in certain circumstances, particularly if the dispute is connected to an ongoing landlord-tenant relationship or an eviction case.

The tenant may also file a complaint with the New York State Attorney General's office, which handles consumer protection matters including security deposit violations. While the Attorney General's office may not resolve individual cases directly, complaints contribute to enforcement patterns and may prompt the landlord to comply.

In court, the tenant's burden is relatively straightforward. Prove the amount of the deposit, prove the date of move-out, prove that the 14-day deadline was not met, and prove that the deposit was not returned (or that the return was incomplete or the itemization was deficient). The landlord bears the burden of justifying any deductions, and if the itemization was late or deficient, the landlord may be unable to introduce evidence of deductions at all.

Deposits and Rent-Stabilized Apartments: Additional Considerations

In rent-stabilized apartments, security deposit rules interact with the broader regulatory framework in ways that create additional protections.

The security deposit in a stabilized apartment is based on the legal regulated rent, not the market rent or any inflated amount. If the landlord charged a deposit based on a rent that exceeds the legal rent, the deposit itself may exceed the one-month cap when measured against what the law actually allows.

When a rent-stabilized tenant renews a lease at a higher rent (due to an RGB increase), the landlord may request an increase in the security deposit to match the new rent. However, the deposit may never exceed one month's rent, and the landlord must return the difference if the deposit exceeds the current rent for any reason.

In overcharge cases where the legal rent is reduced retroactively, the security deposit may also be affected. If the deposit was based on an illegal rent, the excess may be recoverable as part of the overcharge claim.

These interactions are worth noting because they can increase the total amount a rent-stabilized tenant recovers when multiple violations are present. An overcharge claim, a deposit claim, and a claim for illegal fees can sometimes be pursued together, compounding the landlord's exposure.

Real-World Example: The Clock That Cost the Landlord

A tenant moved out of a one-bedroom apartment in Astoria after a two-year tenancy. The security deposit was $1,700, equal to one month's rent. The tenant cleaned the apartment, took photographs and video of every room, emailed the landlord a forwarding address, and returned the keys in person, documented by a text exchange confirming the handoff.

Three weeks passed. No deposit was returned. No itemized statement was received.

On day 25, the landlord mailed a letter listing deductions for "repainting: $600," "deep cleaning: $400," and "general repairs: $300." The landlord enclosed a check for $400, representing the deposit minus $1,300 in claimed deductions.

The tenant examined the letter. The deductions were vague ("general repairs" with no specifics). The repainting charge was for routine turnover painting, not damage. The cleaning charge was for standard apartment cleaning, not extraordinary conditions. And the letter arrived 11 days after the 14-day deadline had passed.

The tenant filed a case in small claims court. At the hearing, the judge examined three issues: whether the deductions were legitimate, whether the itemization was proper, and whether the deadline was met.

The judge found that the repainting and cleaning charges were normal wear and tear, not chargeable to the tenant. The "general repairs" charge was not sufficiently itemized. And the 14-day deadline had been missed by 11 days.

The court ordered the landlord to return the full $1,700 deposit and awarded additional damages for the improper withholding. The total judgment exceeded $3,000.

The outcome had nothing to do with the alleged damage. It turned entirely on the calendar and the paperwork. The landlord might have had a defensible position on some minor damage, but by missing the deadline and failing to itemize properly, they lost the right to claim any of it.

What to Take From This Chapter

Security deposits in New York are capped at one month's rent, with no exceptions. Any charge that functions as a deposit counts toward the cap, regardless of what it is called.

The deposit covers only damage beyond normal wear and tear. Routine painting, ordinary cleaning, and aging fixtures are the landlord's responsibility, not the tenant's.

Landlords must hold deposits in interest-bearing accounts (in buildings with six or more units) and may not commingle deposit funds with operating accounts.

If the landlord withholds any portion of the deposit, they must provide an itemized statement listing each deduction, describing the specific damage, and stating the cost. Vague or lump-sum descriptions are insufficient.

The 14-day deadline is strict and consequential. Landlords who miss it may lose the right to claim any deductions, may be required to return the full deposit, and may face additional penalties.

Document everything at move-out. Photographs, video, a forwarding address in writing, and written confirmation of key return create a record that protects you in any dispute.

If your landlord is holding your deposit, the most important question is not "Did I cause damage?" It's "Did the landlord meet every legal requirement, on time?"

In the next chapter, we'll go deeper into deposit disputes, examining illegal deductions, cleaning scams, and when courts award triple damages against landlords who treat the deposit as free money.

15

Illegal Deductions and Triple-Damage Penalties

Most security deposit disputes in New York aren't about broken windows or smashed appliances. They're about routine turnover costs that landlords try to shift onto tenants, quietly, confidently, and illegally.

The law is clear about what a security deposit can be used for. It is equally clear about what happens when a landlord withholds money in bad faith. In serious cases, courts don't just order the deposit returned. They impose treble damages, tripling the amount the landlord must pay as punishment for misconduct.

This chapter explains what counts as an illegal deduction, identifies the most common scams landlords use, and explains when improper withholding crosses the line from wrong to punishable. Chapter 14 covered the rules governing collection, holding, and return. This chapter covers what happens when landlords break those rules and how tenants recover more than they lost.

Normal Wear and Tear: The Line Landlords Ignore

The single most important concept in any security deposit dispute is the distinction between normal wear and tear and actual damage.

Normal wear and tear is the natural, expected deterioration of an apartment that results from ordinary, reasonable living over time. It is the inevitable consequence of a human being inhabiting a space. It is not chargeable to the tenant.

Normal wear and tear includes faded or slightly discolored paint, small nail holes from hanging pictures or shelves, worn carpet from everyday foot traffic, minor scuffs and scratches on walls or woodwork, dust and grime accumulation in areas that are difficult to reach, slightly worn finish on countertops or fixtures, and minor marks around light switches and door handles from regular use.

Damage, by contrast, involves negligence, misuse, or abuse. It is something beyond what would result from ordinary living, something that a reasonable tenant exercising reasonable care would have prevented.

Damage includes large holes in walls from impacts or removed hardware, broken windows or doors caused by the tenant, burn marks on floors or countertops, significant staining from spills that were not cleaned, pet damage to flooring, molding, or doors, water damage caused by tenant neglect (such as leaving a window open during a storm), and unauthorized alterations that cannot be easily reversed.

The distinction is contextual. A carpet that is worn thin after seven years of normal use is wear and tear. The same carpet soaked with pet urine after two years is damage. A wall with three small nail holes is wear and tear. A wall with a fist-sized hole is damage. Context, duration of tenancy, and the nature of the condition all factor into the analysis.

Courts understand this distinction even when landlords pretend not to. The burden of proving that a deduction reflects actual damage, not normal wear and tear, falls on the landlord. If the landlord cannot make that showing, the deduction fails.

The Painting Scam

Painting is one of the most frequent illegal deductions, and it is one of the easiest to challenge.

Landlords routinely charge departing tenants for full repainting, touch-ups, or what they describe as "restoring" the apartment's paint to its original condition. These charges appear on itemized statements as line items of several hundred dollars, often supported by invoices from painting contractors.

The problem is that repainting between tenants is a normal landlord expense, not a tenant liability.

Paint fades over time. It yellows near windows. It discolors around radiators and stove vents. It shows scuff marks near furniture. These are all the natural result of someone living in the apartment. They are normal wear and tear.

In New York City, the Housing Maintenance Code historically required landlords to repaint apartments every three years. While enforcement of this specific provision has varied, the underlying principle is clear: painting is a maintenance obligation, not something the tenant pays for at move-out.

A landlord who repaints after every tenancy, regardless of condition, and charges the outgoing tenant for it, is treating the deposit as a painting fund. That is not what the deposit is for.

There are limited circumstances where a painting charge might be legitimate. If the tenant painted the walls an unusual color without permission and the landlord must repaint to restore a neutral finish, a deduction may be defensible. If the tenant caused actual damage to walls (large holes, graffiti, extensive gouging) that requires priming and painting as part of the repair, the painting cost associated with the repair may be chargeable. But routine repainting after a normal tenancy is the landlord's expense, period.

When you see "painting" on an itemized statement, the first question is whether the apartment needed painting because of something you did beyond normal living, or whether it needed painting because paint ages and the landlord repaints between tenants as a matter of course. If it is the latter, the charge is illegal.

The Cleaning Scam

After painting, cleaning is the second most common illegal deduction.

Landlords frequently charge departing tenants for professional cleaning, deep cleaning, carpet shampooing, appliance cleaning, and similar services.

The charges often come with invoices from cleaning companies, lending them an air of legitimacy.

The invoice does not make the charge legal. Purpose determines legality.

If the tenant left the apartment in a condition that a reasonable person would consider acceptably clean, cleaning charges are the landlord's expense. Turnover cleaning, the cleaning a landlord does to prepare the apartment for the next tenant, is a cost of doing business. It is not a tenant penalty.

The standard is reasonableness, not perfection. A departing tenant is not required to leave the apartment in the condition it was in on move-in day. Some dust, some residue in the oven, some minor grime in the bathroom, these are normal conditions at the end of a tenancy. They are not grounds for a cleaning deduction.

A cleaning deduction may be legitimate only if the apartment was left in a condition that goes significantly beyond what any reasonable person would consider normal. An apartment with garbage left in every room, a kitchen with grease coating every surface, a bathroom with severe mold caused by the tenant's failure to ventilate, these conditions might justify a cleaning charge. But the charge must reflect the cost of addressing the extraordinary condition, not the cost of routine turnover cleaning.

When evaluating a cleaning deduction, ask two questions. First, was the apartment left in a condition that goes beyond normal end-of-tenancy mess? Second, would the landlord have hired cleaners anyway before the next tenant moved in? If the answer to the second question is yes, the charge is almost certainly the landlord's expense, not yours.

Bogus Repair Claims and Inflated Costs

Some landlords go beyond painting and cleaning and into territory that is difficult to characterize as anything other than fabrication.

Common tactics include exaggerating minor damage into major repairs, replacing items that could have been repaired at far lower cost, charging retail prices for materials while using discount suppliers, using related-party contractors (the landlord's cousin, the super's brother-in-law) who charge inflated rates, billing for upgrades and improvements rather than repairs (installing a new premium faucet to replace a functioning basic one), and charging for repairs to conditions that existed before the tenant moved in.

Each of these practices is problematic, but the last one is particularly insidious. A landlord who never fixed a cracked bathroom tile during the tenancy and then deducts the repair cost from the departing tenant's deposit is not recovering from damage. They are using the tenant's money to make an improvement they should have made years ago.

Courts look skeptically at repair claims that lack supporting documentation. Receipts, photographs of the alleged damage, before-and-after comparisons, and contractor invoices with specific descriptions of the work performed are all relevant evidence. A landlord who claims $500 in repairs but cannot produce a single receipt, photograph, or written estimate faces a credibility problem that is difficult to overcome.

The more padded the claim, the more likely it is to backfire. Courts that find a pattern of inflated or unsupported deductions may conclude that the entire withholding was in bad faith, which opens the door to treble damages.

Pre-Existing Conditions: Damage That Was Already There

One of the most effective defenses against a security deposit deduction is proof that the condition the landlord is charging for existed before the tenant moved in.

This is where move-in documentation becomes critical. Tenants who took photographs or video of the apartment at the beginning of their tenancy have a powerful tool for rebutting deduction claims. A landlord who charges for a scratched floor can be defeated by a move-in photo showing the same scratches. A landlord who charges for a stained countertop can be defeated by a move-in video showing the stain already present.

Even without move-in documentation, tenants can sometimes establish pre-existing conditions through other evidence. Maintenance requests submitted during the tenancy that reference the condition, communications with the landlord about existing problems, and testimony from visitors or roommates who observed the condition early in the tenancy can all serve this purpose.

The burden of proof in a deposit dispute ultimately falls on the landlord. The landlord must prove that the damage occurred during the tenancy and was caused by the tenant. If the tenant can raise a reasonable question about whether the condition was pre-existing, the landlord's deduction becomes much harder to sustain.

This is one of the strongest arguments for documenting the apartment's condition on move-in day. Five minutes of photographs at the start of a tenancy can save hundreds or thousands of dollars at the end of it.

When Illegal Becomes Bad Faith

Not every improper deduction triggers additional penalties. The line that matters is bad faith.

An honest mistake, a good-faith disagreement about what constitutes normal wear and tear, a genuine but incorrect belief that a charge is justified, these may result in the return of the deposit but are unlikely to produce treble damages.

Bad faith is different. Bad faith means the landlord knew or should have known that the withholding was improper, and did it anyway.

Courts may find bad faith when deductions are obviously improper on their face (charging for routine painting after a multi-year tenancy), when charges are unsupported by any documentation (no receipts, no photos, no estimates), when the landlord fabricated damage claims (charging for conditions that did not exist), when the landlord ignored the 14-day deadline and offered no explanation, when the landlord kept the entire deposit without any itemization, and when there is a pattern of similar conduct with other tenants (suggesting a business practice rather than an isolated error).

Bad faith is a factual determination made by the court based on the totality of the circumstances. There is no bright-line rule. But the more egregious the conduct, the more likely the court is to find it.

When bad faith is found, the consequences escalate significantly.

Why Treble Damages Exist

When a court determines that a landlord withheld a security deposit in bad faith, it may award treble damages, meaning three times the amount improperly withheld.

If the landlord withheld $1,500 improperly and the court finds bad faith, the tenant may receive $4,500 ($1,500 times three). If the landlord withheld the entire $2,000 deposit and the court finds bad faith, the tenant may receive $6,000.

Treble damages are not compensation. They are punishment. They exist because the legislature concluded that without meaningful penalties, landlords would routinely gamble with tenant deposits. The calculus for a landlord without penalty exposure is simple: keep the deposit, hope the tenant doesn't fight, and return it only if forced. The worst-case scenario is returning what was owed in the first place, which is the same as complying with the law voluntarily. There is no downside to cheating.

Treble damages change that calculus. They make bad-faith withholding expensive. They create a financial risk that exceeds the potential gain. And they give tenants a meaningful incentive to pursue claims, because the recovery can be substantial enough to justify the effort.

Treble damages are not automatic. They require a finding of bad faith, which means the tenant must present evidence of the landlord's intent or recklessness. But in cases where the evidence is clear, courts impose them regularly.

How Treble Damages Work in Practice

The mechanics of treble damages are straightforward but worth understanding precisely.

The court first determines the amount that was improperly withheld. This is the difference between the deposit and the amount the landlord was entitled to keep (if any). If the entire deposit was withheld without justification, the improper amount is the full deposit. If some deductions were legitimate but others were not, the improper amount is the total of the illegitimate deductions.

The court then determines whether the withholding was in bad faith. If it was, the improper amount is multiplied by three.

The tenant receives the trebled amount plus any legitimate portion of the deposit that was not returned. Interest may also be awarded.

A simplified example: the deposit was $2,000. The landlord deducted $800 for painting, $500 for cleaning, and $400 for "general repairs," returning $300 to the tenant. The court finds the painting and cleaning charges are normal wear and tear and the "general repairs" charge is unsupported. The total improper deduction is $1,700. The court finds bad faith based on the vague itemization, the lack of documentation, and the fact that the landlord charged for routine turnover costs. The treble damages award is $1,700 times three, which equals $5,100. The tenant receives $5,100 plus the $300 already returned, for a total recovery of $5,400 on a $2,000 deposit.

These numbers are real. They happen in small claims courts across New York City with regularity. Treble damages transform deposit disputes from nuisances into meaningful financial events for landlords who treat tenant money carelessly.

Pursuing a Deposit Claim

Security deposit claims are among the most accessible legal actions available to tenants.

Small claims court is the most common venue. The filing fee is modest (typically under $30). No attorney is required. Cases are usually heard within a few weeks of filing. And judges who sit in small claims court are familiar with security deposit law and apply it consistently.

To bring a small claims case, you need to know the landlord's legal name and address (available through property records or HPD's building registration data), have documentation of the deposit (canceled checks, bank statements, the lease, or any receipt), have documentation of the move-out date and condition (photographs, video, forwarding address correspondence), and have a copy of the itemized statement (or evidence that no statement was received).

Present your case clearly and chronologically. Explain the amount of the deposit, the date you moved out, the condition of the apartment when you left, the deadline for return, what the landlord sent (or didn't send), and why the deductions are improper. Let the photographs and documents do the heavy lifting.

If the landlord does not appear in court, you may be entitled to a default judgment. If the landlord appears and disputes your account, the judge will evaluate the evidence and make a determination.

Many tenants do not pursue deposit claims because they believe the amount is too small to justify the effort. Treble damages change that calculation. A $1,000 improper deduction becomes a $3,000 claim. A $2,000 improper deduction becomes a $6,000 claim. These are amounts worth an afternoon in small claims court.

The Move-Out Checklist: Protecting Yourself Before You Leave

Everything in this chapter and the previous one depends on what you do at the end of your tenancy. The strongest legal position in the world is weakened by poor documentation. The following steps, taken at move-out, create the evidentiary foundation for any deposit claim you may need to bring.

Photograph and video every room. Capture walls, floors, ceilings, windows, fixtures, appliances, closets, and bathrooms. Open cabinets and photograph inside. Photograph the stove, refrigerator, and any built-in features. Use natural light where possible. Include wide shots and close-ups. Make sure the timestamp feature on your phone is enabled, or include a dated newspaper or printed page in several frames.

Do the walkthrough with a witness. Ask a friend, family member, or neighbor to be present during your final walkthrough. Have them take their own photographs or video independently. If a dispute arises, their testimony corroborates your account.

Clean the apartment thoroughly. You are not required to make it perfect, but leaving it in reasonably clean condition eliminates the landlord's best argument. Sweep, mop, wipe down surfaces, clean the stove and oven, scrub the bathroom, and remove all personal belongings and trash. If the apartment is visibly clean in your move-out photos, the landlord's cleaning deduction has nowhere to stand.

Provide your forwarding address in writing. Send it by email, text, and certified mail. Keep copies of all three. The forwarding address is where the landlord must send the deposit or itemized statement. If you provide it in writing and the landlord claims they didn't know where to send the money, your documentation defeats that claim.

Return all keys and access devices, and document the return. A text message or email confirming the date and method of return is sufficient. If you return keys in person, ask the landlord or super to sign a receipt or send a confirming text. If you mail them, use certified mail.

Keep copies of your lease, all rent payment records, your move-in photographs (if you took them), your move-out photographs, and all correspondence with the landlord about the deposit or the apartment's condition. Store these digitally where they cannot be lost.

Note the exact date you vacate. This is the date the 14-day clock starts. Mark your calendar for day 15. If you have not received the deposit or an itemized statement by then, the landlord has missed the deadline.

These steps take less than an hour. They can be worth thousands of dollars.

Real-World Example: The Invoice That Backfired

A tenant moved out of a rent-stabilized apartment in the East Village after three years. The landlord kept the entire $1,800 security deposit and mailed an itemized statement listing three charges: "full apartment repainting: $900," "professional deep cleaning: $500," and "miscellaneous repairs: $400." An invoice from a painting company was attached. No photographs of the alleged damage were included. No description of the "miscellaneous repairs" was provided.

The tenant had taken detailed move-out photographs showing the apartment in clean, good condition. Small nail holes were visible in two rooms. The paint was slightly faded near the windows. The bathroom showed normal wear. Nothing in the photographs suggested damage beyond ordinary use.

The tenant filed a claim in small claims court. At the hearing, the tenant presented the move-out photographs and testified that the apartment was left clean, that no damage beyond normal wear existed, and that the "miscellaneous repairs" were never described specifically enough to evaluate.

The landlord presented the painting invoice and argued that the apartment required repainting. The judge asked whether the landlord repaints between every tenancy. The landlord said yes. The judge asked whether the repainting was necessitated by specific damage the tenant caused. The landlord could not identify any specific damage beyond "normal use."

The judge found that the repainting was routine turnover maintenance, not chargeable to the tenant. The cleaning charge was found to be standard turnover cleaning, not extraordinary. The "miscellaneous repairs" charge was found to be insufficiently itemized, with no receipts, no photographs, and no description of the work performed.

The judge further found that the withholding was in bad faith, noting the vague itemization, the lack of documentation, and the landlord's admission that repainting was a standard practice unrelated to tenant-caused damage.

The court awarded treble damages. The tenant recovered $5,400 on an $1,800 deposit.

The landlord didn't lose because of a technical error. They lost because they treated the deposit as money they were entitled to keep, and the law says otherwise.

What to Take From This Chapter

Normal wear and tear is the landlord's responsibility. Painting, routine cleaning, and aging fixtures are not chargeable to the tenant.

Common illegal deductions include routine repainting, standard turnover cleaning, inflated or unsupported repair charges, and charges for pre-existing conditions.

The itemization must be specific. Vague or lump-sum descriptions do not satisfy the legal requirement and may result in forfeiture of all deductions.

Bad-faith withholding triggers treble damages, tripling the amount the landlord must pay. Bad faith is determined by looking at the totality of the circumstances, including the nature of the deductions, the quality of the documentation, and the landlord's compliance with deadlines.

Document the apartment at move-out with photographs, video, and a witness. Provide a forwarding address in writing. Return keys with documentation. Note the exact vacate date. These steps take less than an hour and can be worth thousands of dollars.

If your landlord deducted money from your deposit, the key question is not "Did they give a reason?" It's "Was that reason legally valid, honestly applied, and properly documented within 14 days?"

In the next chapter, we'll look at another source of quiet overcharging: application fees, move-in fees, and the creative ways landlords try to collect more than the law allows before you even get your keys.

16

Application Fees, Move-In Fees and Illegal Charges

Some of the most common violations of New York tenant law happen before a tenant ever moves in.

Because renters are competing for housing, often under intense time pressure, landlords and brokers push fees quickly, label them vaguely, and rely on urgency to prevent questions. The apartment is available now. Other people are looking. You need to move fast. Sign here. Pay here. Don't overthink it.

New York law responded to this dynamic by putting hard limits on what can be charged up front. Those limits are clear, specific, and frequently violated. And since the passage of the FARE Act in 2025, the landscape has shifted again, this time on the single largest upfront cost most tenants faced: the broker fee.

This chapter explains what landlords and brokers can and cannot charge before you get the keys, how the FARE Act changed the rules on broker fees, and how tenants recover money that never should have been collected.

Application Fee Caps: The Number That Doesn't Change

New York law strictly limits what a landlord or broker may charge a tenant for processing a rental application.

Under Real Property Law Section 238-a, the total amount a landlord or broker may charge for application-related costs, including background checks and credit reports, is capped at $20. That is the maximum. It covers the actual cost of running a background check and obtaining a credit report. It does not cover anything else.

The cap does not increase based on demand for the apartment, the tenant's income, the number of applicants, whether a guarantor is involved, or any other factor. It is $20, period.

Before this cap was established as part of the HSTPA in 2019, application fees varied wildly. Charges of $50, $100, or even $200 were common, particularly in competitive markets where tenants felt they had no leverage to push back. The HSTPA eliminated that practice by setting a firm ceiling.

The $20 cap covers only the actual, reasonable cost of the background check and credit report. It does not cover administrative overhead, staff time, document review, or lease preparation. If a landlord or broker charges more than $20 for "application processing" or "screening," the excess is illegal and recoverable.

If you paid more than $20 in application fees, you are entitled to a refund of the excess. If the landlord or broker refuses to refund, you may file a complaint with the New York State Attorney General's office or pursue the claim in small claims court.

What Application Fees Cannot Cover

The $20 cap is not just a price limit. It is a scope limit. The fee may only be used for specific screening-related expenses.

Application fees cannot lawfully cover general administrative overhead associated with processing applications. They cannot cover the landlord's time spent reviewing documents or meeting with prospective tenants. They cannot cover lease preparation, document drafting, or contract review. They cannot cover "convenience" charges for online applications or digital platforms. And they cannot cover any cost that is not directly related to the background check and credit report.

If a landlord itemizes the application fee and the items include anything beyond screening costs, the charges above $20 are illegal regardless of how they are described.

Some landlords attempt to circumvent the cap by splitting the charges. They charge $20 as an "application fee" and then add a separate "processing fee," "review fee," or "administrative fee." The labels do not matter. If the total exceeds $20 and the charges relate to the application process, the excess violates the law.

Holding Deposits: Where the Line Gets Crossed

Holding deposits are often presented as refundable payments to "take the apartment off the market" while the application is being processed or the lease is being prepared.

In theory, a holding deposit is a good-faith payment that demonstrates the tenant's commitment. In practice, holding deposits are frequently misused in ways that violate New York law.

A holding deposit may become illegal if it exceeds the one-month security deposit cap. As Chapter 14 explained, total security deposits in New York are limited to one month's rent. If a holding deposit is refundable and tied to the rental of the apartment, courts may treat it as a security deposit, and any amount collected in addition to the security deposit exceeds the legal cap.

A holding deposit may also be illegal if it is automatically forfeited. Some landlords structure holding deposits as non-refundable if the tenant decides not to proceed. But a non-refundable charge collected before move-in that is tied to the rental of the apartment raises serious questions about whether it is a disguised fee, a penalty, or an illegal deposit, none of which are permissible under current law.

A holding deposit may further be illegal if the landlord keeps it after the tenant fulfills all conditions. If the tenant completes the application, passes the screening, and is ready to sign the lease, the holding deposit should be applied to the security deposit or first month's rent. A landlord who keeps the holding deposit on top of these charges has collected more than the law allows.

The safest approach as a tenant is to get any holding deposit arrangement in writing before paying. The writing should specify the amount, the conditions under which it will be refunded, and how it will be applied if the lease is signed. If the landlord is unwilling to put these terms in writing, that is itself a warning sign.

"Administrative" Fees: The Most Common Workaround

When application fee caps took effect in 2019, a new category of charges appeared almost overnight across the New York rental market: administrative fees.

Landlords and management companies began charging fees under names that sounded distinct from application fees but served the same function. These charges appeared under labels including processing fees, move-in fees, onboarding fees, documentation fees, lease preparation fees, amenity fees, and registration fees.

The labels are creative. The law is not impressed by creativity.

If a charge is required to rent the apartment, is paid before or at move-in, and is not clearly tied to a specific, lawful expense (like the $20 screening cap or the one-month security deposit), it is likely illegal. The substance of the charge determines its legality, not the name the landlord gives it.

New York law does not recognize a general category of "administrative fees" that landlords may impose on tenants at will. Every charge must have a legal basis. Security deposits are capped at one month's rent. Application fees are capped at $20. Broker fees are now governed by the FARE Act. And beyond those categories, the universe of lawful pre-move-in charges is extremely narrow.

When you encounter a fee that doesn't fit neatly into one of the legally recognized categories, ask two questions. First, is this charge required to rent the apartment? If yes, it is functionally part of the move-in cost, and it must comply with the applicable caps. Second, what specific legal authority permits this charge? If the landlord cannot cite one, the charge is likely illegal.

Broker Fees: The FARE Act and the End of Tenant-Paid Landlord Brokers

For decades, broker fees were the single largest upfront cost for New York City renters, and one of the most widely resented.

The traditional arrangement worked like this. A landlord hired a broker to market and lease an apartment. The broker listed the apartment, showed it to prospective tenants, and facilitated the lease signing. And then the tenant, not the landlord who hired the broker, paid the broker's fee. That fee typically ranged from one month's rent to 15 percent of the annual rent, adding thousands or even tens of thousands of dollars to the cost of moving.

The arrangement was unusual by national standards. In most American cities, the party who hires the broker pays the broker. In New York, the cost was routinely shifted to the tenant, even though the tenant had no role in selecting, directing, or contracting with the broker. The tenant paid for a service they didn't request, provided by someone who represented the landlord's interests, as a non-negotiable condition of renting the apartment.

The Fairness in Apartment Rental Expenses (FARE) Act, which took effect on June 11, 2025, changed this arrangement fundamentally.

Under the FARE Act, a broker who represents the landlord, including any listing agent who publishes an apartment listing with the landlord's permission, cannot charge a fee to the tenant. The fee is the landlord's responsibility. The core rule is straightforward: whoever hires the broker pays the broker.

The law creates a rebuttable presumption that any broker who publishes a listing for a rental apartment does so with the landlord's permission or authorization. This means that if you found the apartment through a listing, the default legal assumption is that the broker represents the landlord, and you should not be paying that broker a fee.

The FARE Act does not prohibit tenants from hiring their own brokers. If you independently retain a broker to help you search for apartments, negotiate lease terms, or represent your interests, you may pay that broker's fee. But the relationship must be genuinely initiated by you, not imposed by the landlord as a condition of renting the apartment.

The FARE Act also includes important disclosure and transparency requirements. Landlords or their agents must disclose all fees that tenants are required to pay in a clear and conspicuous manner. Before the tenant signs a lease, the landlord must provide an itemized written disclosure of every fee the tenant will pay, including a written description of each charge.

The tenant must sign this disclosure, and the landlord must keep a copy for three years.

No one, landlord, broker, or otherwise, may condition the rental of an apartment on the tenant retaining a particular broker, including a "dual agent" who purports to represent both the landlord and the tenant simultaneously.

Violations of the FARE Act are enforceable through multiple channels. The Department of Consumer and Worker Protection (DCWP) can investigate complaints, issue summonses, and pursue penalties through OATH (the Office of Administrative Trials and Hearings). Penalties for violations can reach $2,000, and violators may be required to refund illegally collected fees. The FARE Act also creates a private right of action, meaning tenants can sue in civil court to recover broker fees that were charged in violation of the law.

FARE Act Workarounds: What to Watch For

Since the FARE Act took effect, some landlords and brokers have attempted creative workarounds to continue shifting broker costs to tenants. The DCWP received over 1,100 complaints in the first several months of the law's implementation, suggesting that noncompliance is a significant and ongoing problem.

The most common workaround involves relabeling. A broker who represents the landlord claims to be acting as a "tenant's broker" and charges the tenant accordingly. This is a direct violation of the FARE Act. A broker who publishes a listing with the landlord's permission is legally presumed to be the landlord's agent. Relabeling the relationship does not change the legal reality.

Another common workaround involves requiring the tenant to hire a specific broker as a condition of renting the apartment. This is also prohibited. The FARE Act explicitly bars landlords from conditioning a rental on the tenant retaining a particular agent.

Some landlords have introduced new fees described as "leasing services fees," "move-in coordination fees," or "tenant services charges" that bear a suspicious resemblance to broker fees in everything but name. These charges should be scrutinized carefully. If a fee is hundreds or thousands of dollars, is imposed as a condition of renting the apartment, and is paid to a broker or agent associated with the landlord, it is likely an illegal broker fee regardless of what it is called.

Some landlords have raised rents to absorb the cost of paying their own brokers. Early data suggests that landlords who switched from tenant-paid to landlord-paid broker fees raised rents by an average of roughly 5 percent, which is less than the full cost of the typical broker fee spread over a lease term. This suggests that the market is absorbing much of the cost rather than passing it through entirely. Rent increases are lawful (subject to stabilization and Good Cause limits where applicable), but they are different from illegal fee-shifting.

If you encounter any of these practices, take the following steps. Save screenshots of all listings and communications about fees. Ask directly who hired the broker and whether the fee is being charged to you or the landlord. Do not sign any document stating that you hired a broker you did not actually hire. Review the itemized fee disclosure before signing the lease. And if you believe a broker fee was charged in violation of the FARE Act, file a complaint with DCWP and consider consulting an attorney about a private cause of action.

Non-Refundable Move-In Fees: When "Non-Refundable" Means Illegal

Some landlords impose fees at move-in that they describe as non-refundable. These may be called move-in fees, elevator reservation fees, key fees, amenity access fees, or similar charges.

The legality of these charges depends on what they actually cover. A fee for a specific, documented service (such as the actual cost of replacing locks and providing new keys) may be defensible if the amount is reasonable and the service is real. But many so-called move-in fees are simply additional charges imposed on tenants with no legal basis, designed to extract more money at a moment when the tenant is least likely to push back.

A non-refundable fee that functions as a condition of renting the apartment, that is not tied to any specific service, and that exceeds the legally permitted charges (security deposit, screening fee, lawful broker fee) is likely illegal.

The test is always the same: what is this charge for, and what legal authority permits it? If the landlord cannot answer both questions clearly, the charge is suspect.

Why These Fees Are Collected So Aggressively

Illegal upfront fees persist because the conditions under which they are collected are ideal for landlords and terrible for tenants.

Tenants are under time pressure. They need an apartment now. Questioning fees feels risky when other applicants are waiting.

The amounts, taken individually, often feel too small to fight over. A $100 fee, a $200 fee, a $500 fee. Each one feels like an annoyance rather than a legal violation.

Enforcement is usually retrospective. The fee is collected before the tenant moves in. Challenging it requires effort after the fact. Many tenants assume the effort is not worth the recovery.

And social pressure works in the landlord's favor. Tenants worry about starting a relationship with conflict. They fear that challenging a fee will mark them as difficult and cost them the apartment.

Landlords know all of this. It is why illegal fees are collected with such confidence and so rarely refunded voluntarily. The business model depends on tenants deciding not to fight.

But the legal framework has shifted significantly. The HSTPA capped deposits and application fees. The FARE Act eliminated tenant-paid landlord broker fees. And courts consistently treat disguised fees as what they actually are, regardless of the label. The gap between what landlords charge and what the law allows has never been more clearly defined.

How Tenants Get Their Money Back

Tenants who paid illegal fees may pursue recovery through several channels.

For fees paid in violation of the FARE Act, file a complaint with DCWP through their online portal. DCWP will investigate, and violations can result in fines, summonses, and mandatory refunds. Tenants also have a private right of action, meaning they can sue the landlord or broker directly in civil court.

For application fees exceeding the $20 cap, file a complaint with the New York State Attorney General's office or pursue the claim in small claims court.

For excessive security deposits or illegal move-in charges, small claims court is the most accessible venue. The filing fee is minimal, no attorney is required, and judges are familiar with the applicable rules.

In all cases, documentation is essential. Save receipts, canceled checks, bank statements, emails, text messages, listing screenshots, fee disclosures (or evidence that no disclosure was provided), and any other evidence of what was charged and how. The stronger your documentation, the more straightforward the recovery.

Some tenants discover illegal fees only after the tenancy has ended. The passage of time does not necessarily prevent recovery. Statutes of limitations vary by the type of claim, but many fee recovery actions can be brought for several years after the fee was paid.

Real-World Example: The Fee That Wasn't Optional

A renter applied for an apartment in a prewar building in Prospect Heights in early 2026. The listing appeared on a major rental platform. The broker, whose name appeared on the listing, showed the apartment and facilitated the application.

The tenant paid the $20 application fee. The application was approved. Then the broker informed the tenant that there would be a "tenant broker fee" equal to one month's rent, approximately $2,800, payable before the lease would be issued.

The tenant asked who had hired the broker. The broker said that under the current arrangement, the broker represented the tenant. The tenant pointed out that the broker had published the listing, which under the FARE Act creates a presumption that the broker represents the landlord.

The broker insisted the fee was standard. The tenant declined to pay.

The tenant filed a complaint with DCWP, attaching screenshots of the listing, the broker's communications, and the fee demand. DCWP investigated. The broker was found to be the landlord's agent, not the tenant's. The fee demand violated the FARE Act.

The tenant was not charged the fee. The landlord ultimately leased the apartment directly with no broker fee to the tenant. DCWP pursued penalties against the broker.

The tenant didn't need a lawyer. They needed a screenshot and the knowledge that the law had changed.

What to Take From This Chapter

Application fees are capped at $20, covering only the actual cost of background and credit checks. Any amount above that is illegal and recoverable.

Holding deposits may function as security deposits under the law. If refundable and tied to the rental, they count toward the one-month cap.

"Administrative" fees, "processing" fees, and similar charges are common disguises for illegal costs. Labels do not override substance.

The FARE Act, effective June 11, 2025, prohibits landlord-hired brokers from charging fees to tenants. Whoever hires the broker pays the broker. Violations are enforceable through DCWP complaints, penalties, and private lawsuits.

Landlords must provide an itemized written fee disclosure before the tenant signs a lease. Failure to provide this disclosure is itself a violation.

All upfront charges must have a specific legal basis. If the landlord cannot identify the authority that permits the fee, the fee is suspect.

If you're being asked to pay money before moving in, the right question is not "Is this common?" It's "Is this actually legal under New York law?"

In the next chapter, we turn to life inside the apartment, starting with repairs, habitability, and when withholding rent helps or hurts your case.

Part VI: Your Rights While Living In The Unit

17

Repairs, Habitability and Rent Withholding

When something breaks in your apartment, the legal question isn't whether it's annoying. It's whether the apartment remains habitable.

New York law imposes a powerful, ongoing obligation on landlords to keep rental units safe, livable, and in good repair. That obligation exists independently of the lease, cannot be waived, and applies to every residential rental in the state. But how tenants enforce that obligation, and whether they withhold rent or pursue other remedies, can determine whether a repair dispute turns into leverage or into an eviction case.

This chapter explains the warranty of habitability, the enforcement tools available to tenants, how to trigger city inspections that create official records, and why the choice between withholding rent and filing an HP action is one of the most important strategic decisions a tenant can make.

The Warranty of Habitability: A Non-Negotiable Duty

Every residential lease in New York includes a warranty of habitability, whether it is written in the lease or not.

This warranty is implied by operation of law under Real Property Law Section 235-b. It exists in every lease, for every apartment, in every building, regardless of what the lease says. It cannot be waived by agreement. It cannot be disclaimed by a clause stating the tenant accepts the apartment "as is." It cannot be eliminated by a provision making the tenant responsible for all repairs. Any lease language that purports to shift the habitability obligation from the landlord to the tenant is unenforceable.

The warranty requires landlords to maintain conditions that do not endanger health or safety, that are fit for human habitation, and that comply with applicable housing and building codes.

The scope of the warranty is broad. It covers conditions that affect the basic livability of the apartment and the building as a whole. Violations of the warranty can include lack of heat during the heating season (October 1 through May 31 in New York City), lack of hot water at any time of year, persistent water leaks that cause damage or create mold, mold growth that poses health risks, pest infestations including roaches, mice, rats, and bedbugs, electrical hazards including faulty wiring, exposed wires, and non-functioning outlets, broken or inadequate locks on doors and windows, lead paint hazards (particularly in apartments where children under six reside), structural deficiencies including cracked walls, sagging ceilings, and unstable flooring, lack of adequate ventilation, broken or missing smoke and carbon monoxide detectors, and chronic elevator outages in buildings where elevators are required.

This list is illustrative, not exhaustive. Any condition that renders the apartment unsafe, unsanitary, or unfit for reasonable habitation may violate the warranty. The standard is not perfection. It is livability.

The warranty applies to individual apartments and to building-wide conditions. A landlord who maintains common areas in a dangerous state (broken stairs, non-functioning lighting in hallways, unsecured entry doors) is violating the warranty for every tenant in the building, not just those who happen to use the specific area.

What Landlords Must Do, and What They Often Don't

The warranty of habitability creates an affirmative obligation. Landlords must make repairs within a reasonable time after receiving notice of a condition that violates the warranty. They must respond to serious conditions promptly. They must maintain building-wide systems (heating, plumbing, electrical, elevator) in working order. And they must correct code violations identified by city inspectors.

What often happens instead is that repairs are delayed repeatedly, with landlords promising action that never materializes. Complaints are ignored entirely, especially when they come from tenants the landlord views as difficult or expendable. Temporary fixes replace permanent ones, with the same problem recurring month after month. Tenants are told to "live with it" or are blamed for conditions the landlord is responsible for addressing. And serious conditions are left unaddressed until they create health hazards or structural damage.

At some point, patience stops being practical. The question becomes how to force the landlord to act, and which enforcement tool gives the tenant the most leverage with the least risk.

Documenting Conditions: The Foundation of Every Enforcement Action

Before choosing an enforcement path, tenants must build a documentation record. Every tool described in this chapter, 311 complaints, HPD inspections, HP actions, and rent withholding, depends on evidence. Without documentation, enforcement is fragile. With it, enforcement is powerful.

The documentation process should begin the moment a problem appears and continue until it is fully resolved.

Notify the landlord in writing. Every repair request should be made in writing, whether by email, text message, or letter. Verbal requests are difficult to prove. Written requests create a timestamped record showing when the landlord was notified and what was reported. If you make a verbal request, follow it up immediately with a written confirmation: "As I mentioned on the phone today, the bathroom ceiling is leaking and there is visible mold growth around the leak. Please arrange for repair as soon as possible."

Take photographs and video. Document the condition from multiple angles. Include wide shots showing the room and close-ups showing the specific problem. Use your phone's timestamp feature or include a dated reference in the frame. Photograph the same condition repeatedly over time to show that it persists or worsens.

Keep a log. Maintain a simple written record of each occurrence: the date, a description of the condition, what you reported, how you reported it, who you spoke with, and what response (if any) you received. A chronological log transforms scattered complaints into a clear narrative of landlord neglect.

Save all correspondence. Every email, text message, letter, voicemail, and work order related to the condition should be preserved. If the landlord sends a contractor who performs a temporary fix, document the visit, the work done, and whether the problem recurred.

Request inspections. As described in the next section, you can request HPD inspections through 311, which create official violation records that carry significant legal weight.

The goal of documentation is to create a record that is clear, chronological, and difficult to dispute. If the case reaches court, your evidence will be compared to the landlord's. Tenants with organized documentation consistently outperform tenants who rely on memory and oral testimony.

311 Complaints and HPD Inspections: Creating an Official Record

Many tenants do not realize that they can trigger an official city inspection of their apartment by making a single phone call or submitting a complaint online.

In New York City, the Department of Housing Preservation and Development (HPD) is the agency responsible for enforcing the Housing Maintenance Code. HPD has the authority to inspect residential buildings, identify violations, and order landlords to make repairs. Tenants can initiate this process by filing a complaint through 311.

You can file a 311 complaint by calling 311 from any phone in New York City, by visiting the 311 website at nyc.gov/311, by using the NYC 311 mobile app, or by texting 311-692. When filing the complaint, describe the condition as specifically as possible: the location within the apartment, the nature of the problem, how long it has persisted, and any health or safety concerns. You do not need to identify yourself to the landlord (the complaint can be anonymous to the building owner), and you do not need the landlord's permission.

After a complaint is filed, HPD will schedule an inspection. An HPD inspector will visit the apartment, examine the reported condition, and determine whether it constitutes a violation of the Housing Maintenance Code. If a violation is found, the inspector issues a formal notice of violation to the landlord, specifying the condition and the timeframe for correction.

HPD violations are categorized by severity. Class A violations are non-hazardous conditions that must be corrected within 90 days. Class B violations are hazardous conditions that must be corrected within 30 days. Class C violations are immediately hazardous conditions that must be corrected within 24 hours. A Class C violation for no heat in winter, a gas leak, or a lead paint hazard creates immediate legal pressure on the landlord.

The violation record is public and becomes part of the building's official history. It is accessible through HPD's online Building Information Search tool, and it can be cited in court proceedings, HP actions, rent abatement claims, and harassment complaints.

This is why 311 complaints are so valuable. They do three things simultaneously. They put the landlord on official notice that a problem exists, eliminating any future claim that the landlord didn't know. They create an independent, government-generated record of the condition, which carries more evidentiary weight than the tenant's own photographs (though both are important). And they start a compliance clock, giving the landlord a specific deadline to correct the violation, with penalties for failure.

Tenants should file 311 complaints for every significant condition that the landlord has failed to address after reasonable written notice. There is no limit to the number of complaints you can file. Each complaint generates a separate inspection and, if warranted, a separate violation. A building with a long list of open HPD violations is a building where the landlord's credibility is diminished in every future proceeding.

One practical note: HPD inspections require access to the apartment. If the inspector arrives and cannot gain entry, the complaint may be closed without a violation being issued. When you file a 311 complaint, be prepared to provide access during the inspection window. If you work during the day, mention that in your complaint so the inspection can be scheduled accordingly. If the landlord interferes with the inspection (by denying the inspector access to the building), document that interference, as it may constitute a separate violation.

HP Actions: The Most Underused Tenant Tool

An HP action is a court proceeding that tenants can file in Housing Court to compel repairs. It is one of the most powerful enforcement tools available to New York tenants, and it is dramatically underused because most tenants don't know it exists.

The letters "HP" stand for "Housing Part," which is the division of Housing Court that handles code enforcement cases. An HP action is not an eviction case. It is not a rent dispute. It is a case brought by the tenant (or by HPD, or by another interested party) asking the court to order the landlord to fix conditions that violate the housing code.

Through an HP action, a tenant can ask the court to order the landlord to correct specific violations within a set timeframe, impose civil penalties on the landlord for failure to comply, direct HPD to conduct inspections and issue violations, appoint an administrator to oversee repairs if the landlord is unresponsive, and, in cases involving harassment, impose additional sanctions.

The HP action is initiated by filing a petition in Housing Court, which is called an Order to Show Cause. The filing fee is modest, and the forms are available at the Housing Court clerk's office and through court-affiliated help centers. Many tenants file HP actions without an attorney, though legal assistance can strengthen the case significantly.

After the petition is filed, the court schedules a hearing, typically within a few days for emergency conditions and within a few weeks for non-emergency conditions. At the hearing, the judge reviews the evidence (including HPD violation records, tenant photographs, and testimony), and if the court finds violations, it issues an order directing the landlord to make repairs by a specific date.

If the landlord fails to comply with the court's order, the tenant can return to court and ask for enforcement. The court may impose fines, hold the landlord in contempt, or appoint an outside party to oversee the repairs. The escalating consequences create pressure that informal complaints cannot match.

HP actions are particularly effective for several reasons.

They do not create rent arrears. Unlike rent withholding, an HP action does not put the tenant at risk of a nonpayment proceeding. The tenant continues paying rent while the court addresses the repair issue.

They focus on conditions, not money. The court's attention is directed at the physical state of the apartment, not at the landlord-tenant financial relationship. This keeps the dispute on terrain where the tenant's position is strongest.

They create judicial oversight. Once the court issues an order, the landlord is answerable to a judge, not just to the tenant. Noncompliance is contempt of court, which carries consequences that a landlord's indifference to tenant complaints does not.

They build a legal record. Every HP action creates a court file that documents the conditions, the landlord's response (or lack of response), and the court's findings. This record can be used in future proceedings, including rent abatement claims, harassment cases, and defenses to eviction.

For many tenants, the HP action is the safest and most effective enforcement tool available. It forces repairs without the risks associated with rent withholding, and it creates accountability that 311 complaints alone cannot achieve.

Rent Withholding: Powerful but Risky

Withholding rent is the enforcement tool tenants think of first, and it is the one most likely to backfire if used incorrectly.

In New York, tenants may have the right to withhold rent when the landlord has breached the warranty of habitability and the conditions are serious enough to justify the withholding. The legal theory is that the landlord's obligation to maintain habitable conditions and the tenant's obligation to pay rent are interdependent. When the landlord fails to maintain the apartment, the tenant's obligation to pay full rent is reduced or suspended.

Rent withholding may be effective when the conditions are serious and well-documented, when the landlord has been given written notice of the conditions, when repairs have been unreasonably delayed despite the notice, when the tenant is prepared to defend the withholding in court if the landlord files a nonpayment case, and when the tenant has set aside the withheld rent in a separate account to demonstrate good faith.

Rent withholding can create serious problems when the conditions are minor or poorly documented, when the landlord was not given adequate notice, when the tenant cannot prove the severity of the problem, when the landlord responds by filing a nonpayment case and the tenant is unprepared, and when the tenant has spent the withheld rent and cannot produce it if ordered to pay by the court.

The fundamental risk of rent withholding is that it invites a nonpayment proceeding. Once the landlord files, the tenant is in Housing Court defending against eviction. The tenant can raise the warranty of habitability as a defense (and courts will consider it), but the burden shifts in uncomfortable ways. Instead of being the party demanding repairs, the tenant is now the party defending against removal. The framing changes, and the stakes rise.

Courts may grant a rent abatement, reducing the amount of rent owed to reflect the diminished value of the apartment during the period when conditions were substandard. But the abatement is rarely 100 percent. A court might find that conditions warranted a 25 percent or 50 percent reduction, meaning the tenant still owes the balance. If the tenant has spent the withheld rent, they may not be able to pay.

For these reasons, rent withholding should generally be treated as a last resort rather than a first response. It is most effective when combined with other enforcement tools (311 complaints, HPD violations, HP actions) and when the tenant has created a thorough documentation record that supports the withholding.

Why HP Actions Usually Work Better Than Rent Withholding

The comparison between HP actions and rent withholding comes down to risk and framing.

HP actions do not create rent arrears. The tenant keeps paying rent, which eliminates the risk of a nonpayment case. The landlord cannot retaliate by filing for eviction based on unpaid rent, because the rent is being paid.

HP actions keep the focus on the landlord's failure. In an HP action, the central question is whether the landlord has maintained the apartment in compliance with the housing code. The landlord is the respondent, answering to the court for their own conduct. In a nonpayment case triggered by rent withholding, the central question shifts to whether the tenant owes money. The framing favors the landlord.

HP actions create court orders with teeth. A court order directing repairs is enforceable through contempt proceedings, fines, and judicial oversight.

A tenant's decision to withhold rent creates pressure, but it is pressure the landlord can redirect through a nonpayment filing.

HP actions build a record that supports future claims. The court file from an HP action is evidence that can be used in rent abatement claims, overcharge cases (if the landlord failed to maintain conditions that justify the rent being charged), harassment claims, and defenses to eviction.

Many tenants withhold rent hoping it will force repairs. Many landlords respond by filing eviction cases. HP actions flip that dynamic. The tenant is the one bringing the case. The landlord is the one answering for their conduct. And the court is the one setting deadlines and enforcing compliance.

This does not mean rent withholding is never appropriate. In extreme cases, where conditions are so severe that paying full rent while the apartment is uninhabitable feels unjust, withholding may be the right choice. But it should be made with eyes open, with legal advice if possible, and with the withheld rent set aside in a separate account.

Rent Abatement: Getting Money Back for Bad Conditions

Even if you don't withhold rent, you may be entitled to a retroactive rent reduction for the period during which your apartment was uninhabitable or substandard.

A rent abatement is a court-ordered reduction in the rent you owed during the period when the warranty of habitability was breached. The amount of the abatement depends on the severity of the conditions and the duration of the breach.

Courts calculate abatements as a percentage of the rent. The percentage reflects how much the conditions reduced the apartment's habitability. A complete loss of heat in winter might warrant an abatement of 50 percent or more. A persistent leak in the bathroom that the landlord ignored for months might warrant 15 to 25 percent. A bedbug infestation that renders the apartment partially unusable might warrant 25 to 50 percent. The percentages vary by case and by judge, but the principle is consistent: you should not pay full rent for a substandard apartment.

Rent abatements can be awarded in HP actions, in nonpayment cases (as a defense), and in affirmative claims brought by the tenant. If you paid full rent during a period when conditions were seriously deficient, you may be able to recover the difference between what you paid and what the apartment was worth in its impaired state.

To support a rent abatement claim, you need the same documentation described earlier in this chapter: written complaints to the landlord, photographs and video, HPD violations, repair logs, and any other evidence showing the conditions and their duration.

Escalation: When Conditions Become Emergencies

Some conditions are so serious that they require immediate action beyond standard enforcement tools.

If you have no heat during the heating season and the temperature inside your apartment falls below 68 degrees during the day or 62 degrees at night (the minimums set by the Housing Maintenance Code), this is an emergency. File a 311 complaint immediately. HPD treats heat complaints as high priority during the heating season and will schedule inspections rapidly. In extreme cases, HPD can issue emergency repair orders or arrange for emergency heat restoration.

If you have no hot water, this is also treated as an emergency regardless of the season. Hot water must be provided 24 hours a day, 365 days a year, at a minimum temperature of 120 degrees Fahrenheit at the tap.

If you have a gas leak, leave the apartment immediately, call 911, and then call Con Edison's emergency line. Do not use any electrical switches or open flames. A gas leak is a life-threatening emergency that requires immediate professional response, not a repair request to the landlord.

If you have a structural emergency (ceiling collapse, wall failure, floor instability), contact 311 and the Department of Buildings (DOB). DOB handles structural safety issues and can order emergency evacuations or repairs.

If the landlord has shut off essential services (heat, water, electricity) deliberately, this may constitute illegal eviction or harassment. Contact 311, HPD, and, if necessary, the police. Deliberate service interruptions are criminal acts under New York City law and are enforceable through the courts.

In all emergency situations, document what you can safely document, but prioritize your safety. Photographs of dangerous conditions are valuable evidence, but they are not worth personal injury. Get to safety first, then build the record.

Real-World Example: Choosing the Right Tool

A tenant in a rent-stabilized apartment in Crown Heights had persistent leaks in the kitchen ceiling and visible mold growth around the leak area. The landlord had been notified in writing three times over four months. Each time, the landlord sent a handyman who applied sealant to the ceiling. Each time, the leak returned within weeks. The mold grew worse.

Friends and family advised the tenant to stop paying rent. The logic seemed straightforward: why pay for an apartment the landlord won't fix?

Instead of withholding rent, the tenant took a different approach. She filed a 311 complaint. An HPD inspector visited the apartment and issued a Class B violation for the leak and a Class C violation for the mold (which was in an area where food was prepared). The violations were placed on the building's record.

The tenant then filed an HP action in Housing Court. She attached the HPD violations, her photographs (timestamped over four months), and copies of her three written complaints to the landlord.

The court ordered an inspection, found multiple violations, and set a 30-day deadline for repairs. The landlord, now facing court oversight, judicial deadlines, and the prospect of fines for noncompliance, completed the repairs within three weeks.

The tenant then filed a motion for rent abatement, seeking a reduction in the rent she had paid during the four months when the apartment was substandard. The court awarded a 20 percent abatement for the affected period, refunding a meaningful portion of the rent the tenant had overpaid relative to the apartment's actual condition.

The tenant never withheld a dollar of rent. She never faced a nonpayment case. She never had to defend herself in court. Instead, she used the system offensively, putting the landlord in the position of having to answer to a judge for failing to maintain the apartment.

She didn't win by escalating conflict. She won by choosing the right enforcement path.

What to Take From This Chapter

The warranty of habitability is guaranteed by law and cannot be waived. Landlords must maintain conditions that are safe, sanitary, and fit for human habitation.

Document everything. Written complaints, photographs, video, and repair logs create the evidentiary foundation for every enforcement tool.

File 311 complaints to trigger HPD inspections. HPD violations create official records that carry significant weight in court proceedings and put the landlord on a compliance clock.

HP actions are the most effective enforcement tool for most tenants. They compel repairs through court orders without creating rent arrears or triggering nonpayment proceedings.

Rent withholding is legal in some circumstances but carries significant risks. It should generally be treated as a last resort, used only when conditions are serious, documentation is strong, and the tenant is prepared to defend the withholding in court.

Rent abatements allow tenants to recover money for periods when the apartment was substandard, even if rent was paid in full during that period.

If your apartment is unlivable, the key question is not "Should I stop paying rent?" It's "What enforcement tool gives me the most leverage with the least risk?"

In the next chapter, we'll look at privacy, landlord entry, and when "access" crosses the line into harassment.

18

Landlord Entry, Privacy and Harassment

Renting an apartment does not mean giving up your right to privacy.

In New York, landlords have limited rights to enter a tenant's home, and those limits exist because unauthorized entry is one of the most common ways landlords pressure tenants into compliance or move-outs. What is framed as "access" or "inspection" can quickly become harassment, especially when tenants don't know where the legal line is.

This chapter explains when landlords may enter, when they may not, how to recognize when lawful access has crossed into unlawful harassment, and how tenants stop the conduct through the courts.

Your Right to Quiet Enjoyment

Before examining the specific rules around entry, it helps to understand the legal principle that underlies all of them.

Every residential tenant in New York has the right to "quiet enjoyment" of their apartment. This is a legal term of art, and it means more than silence. Quiet enjoyment means the tenant's right to use and occupy the apartment without unreasonable interference from the landlord. It encompasses privacy, peace, physical security, and the ability to live in your home without being subjected to intrusions, disruptions, or pressure that undermines your tenancy.

The right to quiet enjoyment is implied in every residential lease in New York, whether or not the lease mentions it. It cannot be waived. It exists alongside the warranty of habitability as one of the two foundational tenant protections that shape the entire landlord-tenant relationship.

When a landlord enters your apartment without proper notice or without a legitimate reason, they are not just being rude. They are violating a legal right. And when that violation becomes a pattern, it may constitute harassment, which carries its own set of consequences.

Notice Requirements: Entry Is Not On-Demand

Landlords do not have a general right to enter your apartment whenever they want. Outside of genuine emergencies, a landlord must provide reasonable advance notice and have a legitimate purpose before entering.

Legitimate purposes for landlord entry include making necessary repairs or performing maintenance that the tenant has requested or that is required by code, showing the apartment to prospective tenants or buyers (typically only near the end of the lease term or when the apartment is being sold), performing inspections required by law or by a government agency, and addressing conditions that affect the safety of the building or other tenants.

Notice should include the proposed date of entry, the approximate time, and the reason for the visit. New York law does not specify a precise number of hours or days for advance notice in most residential contexts, but courts have consistently interpreted "reasonable" to mean at least 24 hours for non-emergency situations. Some leases specify a notice period, and if the lease provides for more notice than the law requires, the longer period may apply.

The manner of notice matters as well. A phone call, an email, a text message, or a written note slipped under the door can all serve as notice, depending on the circumstances and what is reasonable for the specific landlord-tenant relationship. But notice must actually reach the tenant or be delivered in a manner reasonably calculated to reach them. A landlord who claims to have "tried to call" but left no message, sent no email, and posted no written notice has not provided reasonable notice.

Entry must occur at a reasonable time. Courts have generally interpreted this to mean normal business hours or hours that the tenant and landlord have agreed upon. A landlord who shows up at 7 a.m. on a Sunday or at 10 p.m. on a weeknight without prior arrangement is not acting reasonably, regardless of the purpose.

"Stopping by," "checking something," and letting oneself in without warning are not lawful access. A landlord who enters your apartment while you are away, without notice and without an emergency, has committed an unauthorized entry. The fact that they have a key does not give them the right to use it whenever they choose.

Emergencies: Narrowly Defined

Emergencies are the one exception to the notice requirement. In a genuine emergency, a landlord may enter the apartment without advance notice and without the tenant's consent.

But the definition of emergency is narrow. True emergencies include fire or evidence of fire (smoke, the smell of burning), active flooding or a burst pipe that threatens the apartment or other units, a gas leak or suspected gas leak, and structural failure or a condition posing immediate danger to life or safety.

Routine issues do not qualify as emergencies, regardless of how the landlord characterizes them. A slow leak that has been developing for weeks is not an emergency. A repair that the landlord wants to complete on their own schedule is not an emergency. Curiosity about the apartment's condition is not an emergency. A desire to show the apartment to a contractor or prospective buyer without notice is not an emergency.

Landlords sometimes stretch the definition of emergency to justify unannounced entry. Courts do not accept these expansions. If the condition could have been addressed with advance notice and there was no immediate risk to life or property, it was not an emergency.

If your landlord enters your apartment without notice and claims it was an emergency, ask what the emergency was. Document the landlord's explanation, the condition of the apartment when you return, and any evidence that the claimed emergency did or did not exist. If the explanation doesn't hold up, the entry was unauthorized.

What Unauthorized Entry Looks Like in Practice

Unauthorized entry takes many forms, and not all of them involve the landlord walking through the front door while the tenant watches.

The most obvious form is the landlord entering while the tenant is home without prior notice or consent. This is confrontational and easy to document.

A more common form is the landlord entering while the tenant is away. The tenant returns to find evidence that someone was in the apartment: items moved, lights on that were left off, a smell of paint or cleaning products, evidence of work done without the tenant's knowledge. Sometimes the evidence is subtle. Sometimes it is unmistakable.

Another form involves the landlord sending workers, contractors, or building staff into the apartment without notice. The landlord may argue that the super needed to check on something or that a contractor was in the building and the landlord wanted to take advantage of the opportunity. Neither explanation satisfies the notice requirement.

Still another form involves the landlord changing locks or installing cameras in or around the apartment without the tenant's consent. Changing locks on a tenant's apartment without providing a key is a violation of the Unlawful Eviction Law. Installing surveillance equipment directed at a tenant's private space raises serious privacy and harassment concerns.

In all cases, the question is the same: did the landlord have a legitimate purpose, did they provide reasonable notice, and did the tenant consent? If any of those elements is missing, the entry is unauthorized.

When Access Becomes Harassment

Harassment is not about a single entry. It is about patterns and purpose.

New York City defines landlord harassment broadly under the Housing Maintenance Code (NYC Administrative Code Section 27-2004(a)(48)). Harassment includes any conduct by a landlord that is intended to cause a tenant to vacate or to surrender or waive any rights to which the tenant is entitled.

Repeated, unwanted entry into a tenant's apartment can constitute harassment when it is part of a pattern designed to pressure the tenant. But harassment extends well beyond entry issues. Under the city's definition, harassment can include repeated or prolonged interruption of essential services (heat, hot water, electricity, water), filing repeated, baseless court proceedings against a tenant, removing the tenant's possessions from the apartment, engaging in threatening or intimidating behavior, making false statements to a tenant about their legal rights or the legal status of the apartment, offering repeated buyout offers after the tenant has declined (when coupled with other harassing conduct), failing to make repairs as a means of pressuring the tenant, interfering with the tenant's privacy or quiet enjoyment, and engaging in construction or renovation work designed to make the apartment uninhabitable or to pressure the tenant.

The critical element is intent. Harassment requires that the landlord's conduct be directed at causing the tenant to leave or to surrender rights. A landlord who genuinely needs access for a legitimate repair, follows proper notice procedures, and respects the tenant's schedule is not harassing. A landlord who shows up repeatedly without notice, enters the apartment while the tenant is at work, ignores objections, and escalates the intrusions over time is engaged in a pattern that courts will scrutinize carefully.

Harassment claims often involve the accumulation of individually minor acts that, taken together, reveal a campaign of pressure. No single act may seem extreme. But when the pattern is laid out chronologically, the purpose becomes clear.

Why Harassment Claims Matter

Harassment is not just improper behavior. It is illegal conduct that carries serious consequences under New York law.

Tenants who document harassment may be entitled to court orders (injunctions) barring the landlord from continuing the conduct, civil penalties against the landlord, damages for the harm caused by the harassment, enhanced protections in related proceedings (such as eviction cases, where harassment may be raised as a defense), and leverage in buyout negotiations or other disputes.

In New York City, the Housing Maintenance Code allows HPD to bring harassment cases against landlords on behalf of tenants. Tenants can also bring harassment claims directly in Housing Court, either as standalone proceedings or as part of HP actions.

The consequences for landlords found to have engaged in harassment are significant. Courts can impose substantial civil penalties per violation, and in cases involving a pattern of harassment, the penalties can accumulate rapidly. In buildings where the landlord is found to have harassed multiple tenants, the building may be subject to enhanced monitoring and enforcement by city agencies.

Ignoring harassment does not make it stop. In most cases, it escalates. Tenants who tolerate unauthorized entry, service interruptions, or pressure tactics without objection send a signal that the conduct will not be challenged. Landlords who face no consequences have no reason to change their behavior.

Enforcement Through Housing Court

Tenants can enforce their privacy rights and stop harassment through Housing Court proceedings.

An HP action (described in Chapter 17) can include harassment claims. If the landlord's conduct includes both maintenance failures and harassment (which often go together, since landlords sometimes allow conditions to deteriorate as a form of pressure), the HP action can address both issues simultaneously.

Tenants can also bring standalone harassment petitions in Housing Court, asking the court to find that the landlord has engaged in harassment and to issue orders stopping the conduct.

Courts have broad authority in harassment cases. They can issue injunctions barring specific conduct (such as unauthorized entry, service interruptions, or repeated buyout offers). They can set access protocols specifying when and how the landlord may enter the apartment. They can impose civil penalties for each act of harassment. They can order the landlord to restore services that were interrupted. And they can create enforceable orders that, if violated, expose the landlord to contempt proceedings.

Housing Court is not just for eviction cases. It is also where tenants stop misconduct. Tenants who view Housing Court solely as a threat (the place where you get evicted) are missing the fact that it is also a tool (the place where you compel compliance and hold landlords accountable).

Building Your Harassment Case

Harassment cases are built on patterns, and patterns require documentation.

Keep a log of every unauthorized entry, every attempted entry, every intrusion, and every incident of landlord conduct that feels designed to pressure you. Record the date, the time, what happened, who was involved, and how you responded. Save this log digitally and in a format that is timestamped and difficult to alter.

Save all communications. Emails, text messages, letters, voicemails, notes slipped under the door, and any other communications from the landlord or building staff should be preserved. These communications often reveal the landlord's intent, especially when they contain threats, misleading statements about legal rights, or escalating demands.

Photograph evidence of unauthorized entry. If you come home and believe someone has been in your apartment, photograph anything that appears to have been moved, disturbed, or changed. Note the condition of the locks. Check whether any work was done that you did not authorize.

Identify witnesses. Neighbors who have observed the landlord's conduct, building staff who can testify about the landlord's instructions, and anyone who has been present during incidents of harassment can provide corroborating testimony. Ask whether they are willing to provide a written statement or appear in court.

File 311 complaints. If the harassment includes service interruptions (loss of heat, hot water, or water), file 311 complaints for each incident. HPD violations created by these complaints become official records that support the harassment claim.

Consider whether the conduct is retaliatory. If the harassment began after you filed a complaint, requested repairs, reported code violations, or asserted your legal rights, the timing may establish a retaliatory motive, which strengthens both the harassment claim and any defense to eviction. Chapter 19 covers retaliation in detail.

The key to a successful harassment case is making the invisible visible. Harassment often works precisely because it happens behind closed doors, in moments that feel too small to report. Documentation turns those moments into evidence, and evidence turns a feeling of helplessness into a court case.

Real-World Example: Drawing the Line

A tenant in a rent-stabilized apartment in the East Village noticed that her landlord was entering the apartment frequently. At first, it was once a month, supposedly for "inspections." The landlord would give one or two days' notice, and the visits lasted 15 to 20 minutes. The tenant found the visits intrusive but tolerated them.

Over time, the frequency increased. The landlord began visiting every two weeks, then weekly. The stated reasons became vague: "checking on things," "making sure everything is okay," "looking at the pipes." Sometimes the landlord arrived with a contractor who measured walls and took notes. Sometimes the landlord came alone. On two occasions, the tenant came home to find evidence that someone had been in the apartment while she was at work. The landlord did not deny entering but said it was to "check on a potential leak."

The tenant began documenting. She logged every entry and every attempted entry. She photographed the condition of the apartment before and after each visit. She saved every text message and email from the landlord, including ones that were vague about the purpose of the visits.

After three months of documentation, the tenant filed a harassment petition in Housing Court, attaching her log, her photographs, and the communications showing the escalating pattern. She also filed a 311 complaint regarding the unauthorized entries.

The court issued an injunction requiring the landlord to provide at least 48 hours' written notice before any non-emergency entry, limiting entries to once per month unless the tenant requested repairs, and prohibiting entry when the tenant was not home except in documented emergencies.

The landlord's behavior stopped.

The tenant didn't win by arguing. She didn't win by withholding rent or escalating the conflict. She won by documenting the pattern, filing in court, and letting the judge set boundaries that the landlord had refused to respect voluntarily.

What to Take From This Chapter

Tenants have the right to quiet enjoyment of their apartments, including the right to privacy and freedom from unreasonable interference.

Landlords must provide reasonable advance notice (generally at least 24 hours) and have a legitimate purpose before entering a tenant's apartment. The only exception is a genuine emergency, which is narrowly defined.

Unauthorized entry is a legal violation, not just a nuisance. Repeated unauthorized entry may constitute harassment.

Harassment includes any landlord conduct intended to cause a tenant to vacate or surrender their rights. It encompasses not just entry issues but also service interruptions, threats, baseless court filings, and other pressure tactics.

Documentation is essential. Logs, photographs, saved communications, and witness statements transform individual incidents into a provable pattern.

Housing Court can issue injunctions, set access protocols, and impose civil penalties for harassment. Tenants can bring harassment claims through HP actions or standalone petitions.

If your landlord keeps showing up, the key question is not "Can they do this?" It's "Is this lawful access, or is it a pattern meant to pressure me?"

In the next chapter, we'll examine one of the most common fears tenants have: that asserting their rights will lead to retaliation, and what the law says about landlords who punish tenants for pushing back.

19

Retaliation

What It Is and How to Prove It

This chapter addresses the fear that keeps more tenants silent than any other.

Not the fear of losing in court. Not the fear of paperwork or process. The fear that if you assert your rights, your landlord will make your life worse. That if you complain about conditions, the landlord will find a reason to evict you. That if you file a complaint with a city agency, the rent will go up. That if you organize with your neighbors, you'll be singled out for punishment.

That fear is not irrational. Landlord retaliation is real, it is common, and it is one of the most effective tools for suppressing tenant rights. But it is also illegal. New York law specifically prohibits retaliatory conduct by landlords and gives tenants both defensive and offensive tools to challenge it.

This chapter explains what legally constitutes retaliation, what triggers the statutory presumption that shifts the burden to the landlord, how to document a retaliation claim, and when retaliation functions as a defense to eviction versus an affirmative claim for damages. If you have been afraid to assert your rights because of what your landlord might do in response, this is the chapter that tells you what the law does about it.

What Retaliation Means Under New York Law

Retaliatory conduct is any action by a landlord that is motivated by the tenant's exercise of a legal right.

New York Real Property Law Section 223-b defines retaliation and prohibits landlords from taking adverse action against tenants who engage in protected activities. The statute was designed to ensure that tenants can exercise their rights without fear that doing so will cost them their housing.

Retaliatory actions can take many forms. The most common include commencing eviction proceedings against the tenant (whether nonpayment or holdover), refusing to renew a lease, substantially increasing the rent (in situations where the increase is discretionary, not regulated), decreasing or eliminating housing services (reducing heat, hot water, maintenance, or building amenities), interfering with the tenant's privacy or quiet enjoyment, filing baseless court proceedings designed to pressure the tenant, refusing to make repairs, and engaging in a pattern of harassment.

The critical element is not the action itself but the motivation behind it. A landlord who files a legitimate nonpayment case because the tenant genuinely owes rent is not retaliating, even if the tenant recently filed a complaint. A landlord who files a nonpayment case with inflated charges one week after the tenant reported code violations to HPD is engaging in conduct that looks very different.

Retaliation does not require proof of malice or explicit statements of intent. Courts infer motivation from circumstance, primarily from the timing between the protected activity and the adverse action. The closer in time the landlord's action follows the tenant's protected activity, the stronger the inference of retaliation.

Protected Activities: What Tenants Can Do Without Fear

The anti-retaliation statute protects tenants who engage in a specific set of activities. These are the actions that trigger protection, meaning that any adverse landlord conduct following these activities may be presumed retaliatory.

Filing a complaint with a government agency is the most clearly protected activity. This includes complaints to HPD, complaints through 311, complaints to the Department of Buildings, complaints to the New York State Attorney

General, complaints to DHCR or HCR, and complaints to any other governmental body with authority over housing conditions, rent regulation, or landlord conduct.

Requesting repairs is protected. A tenant who asks the landlord, in writing or verbally, to fix conditions that violate the warranty of habitability or the housing code is exercising a legal right. A landlord who responds to that request with adverse action is retaliating.

Reporting code violations is protected. Tenants who report violations of the Housing Maintenance Code, the Building Code, or the Multiple Dwelling Law to any enforcement agency are engaging in protected activity.

Organizing with other tenants is protected. Tenants who form or participate in tenant associations, who meet with other tenants to discuss building conditions, who collectively request repairs, or who engage in collective bargaining with the landlord are exercising rights protected by law.

Filing legal proceedings is protected. Tenants who file HP actions, overcharge complaints, fair housing complaints, or any other legal proceeding against the landlord are engaging in protected activity.

Exercising any other legal right is protected. The statute is broad enough to cover any situation where the tenant acts in accordance with the law. Requesting a renewal lease, demanding a rent stabilization rider, asserting Good Cause Eviction protections, challenging an illegal fee, and declining a buyout offer are all exercises of legal rights that trigger anti-retaliation protection.

The breadth of the protection is deliberate. The legislature understood that tenant rights are meaningless if landlords can punish tenants for using them. The anti-retaliation statute exists to break the connection between knowledge and punishment, ensuring that informed tenants are not worse off than ignorant ones.

The Statutory Presumption: How Timing Shifts the Burden

The most powerful feature of New York's anti-retaliation law is the statutory presumption of retaliation.

Under RPL Section 223-b, if a landlord takes adverse action against a tenant within a specified period after the tenant engages in a protected activity, the law presumes that the landlord's action is retaliatory. The burden then shifts to the landlord to prove, by a preponderance of the evidence, that the action was taken for a legitimate, non-retaliatory reason.

The protected window varies depending on the type of adverse action, but the general framework is as follows. If a landlord commences an eviction proceeding, refuses to renew a lease, or substantially increases the rent within six months after the tenant has filed a complaint with a governmental agency or taken other protected action, the landlord's conduct is presumed retaliatory.

This presumption does not mean the tenant automatically wins. It means the landlord must come forward with a credible, non-retaliatory justification for the action. If the landlord cannot do so, the presumption controls and the action is deemed retaliatory. If the landlord provides a credible justification, the court weighs the evidence and makes a determination.

The presumption is powerful because it reverses the normal burden of proof. In most legal disputes, the party making the claim bears the burden. In retaliation cases within the protected window, the tenant establishes the timeline (protected activity followed by adverse action within the statutory period), and the landlord must explain why the action was not retaliatory. The tenant does not need to prove the landlord's state of mind. The timeline creates the inference, and the landlord must rebut it.

Outside the protected window, the presumption does not apply automatically. But retaliation claims are not limited to the statutory period. A tenant can still prove retaliation outside the window by presenting circumstantial evidence of retaliatory motive. The claim is simply harder to establish because the tenant bears the full burden of proof.

What Retaliation Looks Like in Practice

Retaliation rarely announces itself. Landlords do not typically say "I'm evicting you because you called HPD." Instead, retaliation is disguised as routine business decisions, justified by pretextual reasons, or executed through incremental pressure that is difficult to attribute to any single cause.

Understanding the common patterns helps tenants recognize retaliation when it happens.

The most recognizable pattern is the eviction filing that follows a complaint. A tenant files a 311 complaint about persistent leaks. HPD inspects and issues violations. Within weeks, the landlord serves a rent demand for an amount the tenant disputes, or serves a termination notice citing a minor lease violation that was never previously enforced. The timing is the tell.

Another common pattern is the sudden service reduction. A tenant organizes a meeting with neighbors to discuss building conditions. Shortly afterward, the hallway lights stop working, the hot water becomes intermittent, and the super becomes unreachable. No single event is dramatic enough to seem deliberate. But the cumulative effect, and the timing, suggests a response to the organizing activity.

Selective enforcement is another hallmark of retaliation. A landlord who has tolerated a tenant's pet for two years suddenly serves a notice to cure the "no pets" lease violation after the tenant files an overcharge complaint with DHCR. The lease violation may be technically real, but the timing suggests the enforcement is motivated by the complaint, not the pet.

Increased scrutiny is a subtler form. After a tenant asserts their right to a renewal lease, the landlord begins visiting the apartment frequently, sending notices about minor issues that were never previously mentioned, and documenting everything the tenant does. The message is clear: you are being watched. The legal term is harassment, and when it follows a protected activity, it is also retaliation.

Rent increases in unregulated or partially regulated apartments can be retaliatory if they follow a protected activity and exceed what the market or the law would support. A landlord who raises the rent by 20 percent after the tenant complained about conditions may be retaliating, particularly if comparable apartments in the building or neighborhood are not seeing similar increases. Under Good Cause Eviction, rent increases above the local standard are presumptively unreasonable, which creates an additional layer of protection against retaliatory hikes.

In each of these patterns, the individual action might be defensible in isolation. What makes it retaliation is the context: the protected activity that preceded it, the timing, the departure from the landlord's normal practice, and the absence of any credible non-retaliatory explanation.

Retaliation as a Defense to Eviction

One of the most important applications of anti-retaliation law is as a defense in eviction proceedings.

If a landlord files an eviction case and the tenant can show that the case was motivated by retaliation for a protected activity, the court may dismiss the case entirely. Retaliation is an affirmative defense, meaning the tenant raises it in their answer to the petition, and the court evaluates it as part of the case.

The defense works as follows. The tenant establishes that they engaged in a protected activity (filed a complaint, requested repairs, organized with neighbors, or exercised another legal right). The tenant shows that the landlord took adverse action (filed the eviction case) within the protected window or in circumstances that suggest retaliatory motive. If the statutory presumption applies, the burden shifts to the landlord to prove a legitimate, non-retaliatory reason for the case. If the landlord cannot meet that burden, the case is dismissed.

Even outside the statutory window, retaliation can be raised as a defense. The tenant would need to present enough evidence of retaliatory motive to persuade the court that the case was filed for an improper purpose. This might include evidence of the timeline, the landlord's failure to take similar action against other tenants in comparable situations, statements by the landlord or building staff suggesting retaliatory intent, a pattern of escalating harassment following the protected activity, and the absence of any legitimate basis for the eviction claim.

The retaliation defense is particularly powerful in holdover cases based on minor lease violations. If the landlord never enforced the provision before, and the enforcement began only after the tenant asserted a right, the timing creates a strong inference of retaliation. Courts are skeptical of landlords who suddenly discover lease violations they tolerated for months or years.

In nonpayment cases, the retaliation defense works differently. The tenant may still owe rent, and the defense does not eliminate the obligation to pay. But if the court finds that the nonpayment case was filed in retaliation (for example, by inflating the amount owed, including illegal charges, or filing prematurely), the case may be dismissed on those grounds, giving the tenant time and leverage to resolve the underlying dispute.

Retaliation as an Affirmative Claim

Retaliation is not only a shield. It is also a sword.

Tenants who have been subjected to retaliatory conduct can bring affirmative claims seeking damages, injunctive relief, and attorney's fees.

These claims can be brought in Housing Court (often as part of an HP action), in Civil Court, or in Supreme Court, depending on the type and amount of damages sought.

An affirmative retaliation claim does not require the landlord to have filed an eviction case. It can be based on any retaliatory adverse action, including service reductions, harassment, rent increases, refusal to make repairs, or any other conduct that harms the tenant in response to the exercise of a legal right.

If the claim is successful, the tenant may be entitled to compensatory damages (for harm caused by the retaliatory conduct, such as the cost of alternative heating if heat was reduced, the cost of temporary housing if conditions became uninhabitable, or emotional distress in severe cases), injunctive relief (a court order directing the landlord to stop the retaliatory conduct and restore services or conditions), attorney's fees and costs (in some circumstances, particularly when the retaliation involved eviction proceedings), and civil penalties (in cases involving harassment, which may overlap with retaliation claims).

The availability of affirmative claims means that tenants are not limited to waiting for the landlord to file an eviction case and then raising retaliation as a defense. Tenants can go on offense, bringing the claim proactively and seeking both relief and accountability.

How to Document a Retaliation Claim

Retaliation cases are won on timelines. The evidence that matters most is the sequence of events: what the tenant did, when they did it, and what the landlord did in response.

Build the timeline immediately. The moment you engage in a protected activity, begin documenting everything the landlord does in response. Start a log. Record dates, times, and specific actions. Note any communications from the landlord, any changes in service, any unusual visits, any notices received, and any departures from the landlord's previous behavior.

Preserve evidence of the protected activity. Keep copies of every complaint you filed, every repair request you submitted, every letter you sent, and every legal proceeding you initiated. If you filed a 311 complaint, save the confirmation number and any follow-up communications. If you attended a tenant meeting, note the date, who was present, and what was discussed.

Preserve evidence of the adverse action. Keep copies of every notice, every eviction filing, every rent increase letter, and every communication from the landlord that reflects the adverse action. If the retaliation involves service reductions, document the conditions with photographs, video, and 311 complaints.

Note any changes in the landlord's pattern. If the landlord previously tolerated a condition (a pet, a roommate, a minor lease variation) and suddenly begins enforcing against it after your protected activity, document both the prior tolerance and the sudden change. This before-and-after comparison is often the strongest evidence of retaliatory motive.

Talk to neighbors. If other tenants in the building have been subjected to similar treatment after engaging in protected activities, their experiences corroborate your claim and may establish a pattern of retaliatory behavior by the landlord. Patterns are more persuasive than isolated incidents.

Consult an attorney early. Retaliation claims involve nuanced questions of timing, burden of proof, and strategy. A tenant attorney can help you assess the strength of the claim, preserve your rights, and determine whether to pursue the claim defensively (as part of an eviction defense) or offensively (as an affirmative action).

The Fear Problem: Why Retaliation Works Even When It's Illegal

The anti-retaliation statute exists because the legislature understood that the threat of retaliation suppresses rights as effectively as retaliation itself.

A tenant who believes their landlord will punish them for filing a complaint does not file the complaint. A tenant who believes that requesting repairs will lead to eviction does not request repairs. A tenant who believes that organizing with neighbors will result in harassment does not organize. In each case, the tenant's rights exist on paper but are never exercised.

This is the landlord's ideal outcome. Not a court victory. Not a legal argument. Just silence.

Landlord retaliation works because of the asymmetry of consequences. The landlord who retaliates may eventually face legal consequences, but those consequences are delayed, uncertain, and require the tenant to take the very action they fear. The tenant who is retaliated against faces immediate harm: loss of services, loss of housing, loss of stability. The immediate harm outweighs the distant remedy, and the tenant stays silent.

The anti-retaliation statute is designed to break this cycle. The statutory presumption, the burden shift, the defensive and affirmative remedies, the availability of injunctions and damages, all of these tools exist to change the calculus. They exist to make retaliation costly for landlords and recoverable for tenants.

But the tools only work if tenants use them. And tenants will only use them if they know they exist.

That is why this chapter is in the book. The fear is real. The law addresses it. And the difference between a tenant who knows about anti-retaliation protections and one who doesn't is often the difference between silence and action.

Real-World Example: The Complaint That Triggered a Case

A tenant in a rent-stabilized apartment in Washington Heights filed a 311 complaint about a persistent cockroach infestation. HPD inspected the apartment and issued a Class B violation. The landlord was given 30 days to address the infestation.

Twenty-two days later, the tenant received a notice to cure for having a small dog in the apartment. The lease contained a no-pet clause. The tenant had kept the dog openly for over two years. The landlord had seen the dog multiple times. The super had greeted the dog by name. No one had ever raised the issue.

Three weeks after the notice to cure, the landlord served a notice of termination based on the tenant's alleged failure to cure the pet violation. The landlord then filed a holdover proceeding seeking to evict the tenant.

The tenant's attorney raised retaliation as a defense. The timeline was straightforward: the tenant filed a complaint, HPD issued a violation, and the landlord initiated enforcement of a lease provision that had been openly and knowingly tolerated for two years. The adverse action (the eviction case) fell within six months of the protected activity (the 311 complaint), triggering the statutory presumption of retaliation.

The landlord argued that the pet clause was a legitimate lease provision and that enforcement was not retaliatory. The court asked why the landlord had never enforced the clause during the two years the pet had been in the apartment. The landlord could not provide a credible explanation unrelated to the HPD complaint.

The court found the eviction was retaliatory and dismissed the case. The tenant stayed. The dog stayed.

The landlord had waited for a pretext. The law saw through it.

What to Take From This Chapter

Retaliation is any adverse action by a landlord motivated by the tenant's exercise of a legal right. It includes eviction filings, rent increases, service reductions, harassment, and refusal to make repairs.

Protected activities include filing government complaints, requesting repairs, reporting code violations, organizing with other tenants, filing legal proceedings, and exercising any other right under the law.

The statutory presumption of retaliation applies when adverse action occurs within the protected window (generally six months) after a protected activity. The presumption shifts the burden to the landlord to prove a legitimate, non-retaliatory reason.

Retaliation is both a defense to eviction and an affirmative claim for damages. Tenants can raise it defensively to defeat eviction cases and offensively to seek compensation, injunctions, and penalties.

Documentation is critical. Build a timeline showing the protected activity, the adverse action, the timing between them, and any changes in the landlord's pattern of behavior.

The fear of retaliation keeps tenants silent. The law of retaliation protects tenants who speak up. The difference between the two is knowledge.

If you have asserted a legal right and your landlord's behavior changed for the worse, the key question is not "Was this a coincidence?" It's "Can I document the timeline, and does the law presume this was retaliatory?"

In the next chapter, we'll return to the issue of money, examining nonpayment of rent, late fees, and why many rent demands are legally defective before court ever begins.

20

Nonpayment of Rent and Late Fees

Nonpayment of rent is the most common reason landlords go to Housing Court, and one of the most misunderstood by tenants.

Many tenants assume that falling behind on rent means automatic eviction. That the landlord sends a notice, files a case, and the tenant is out. That there is nothing to argue, nothing to challenge, and no defense worth raising.

None of that is accurate. In New York, nonpayment does not mean automatic eviction. It triggers a highly regulated process with built-in protections, strict notice requirements, and limits on what landlords can charge. Many nonpayment cases fail not because rent wasn't owed, but because the landlord demanded the wrong amount, at the wrong time, in the wrong way. And many tenants who do owe rent have defenses, procedural and substantive, that can change the outcome entirely.

This chapter explains grace periods, late fee limits, rent demand requirements, and the reasons inflated or defective demands routinely sink eviction cases. It also explains what to do if you fall behind, how to protect yourself before a case is filed, and why the math on a rent demand matters more than most tenants realize.

When Rent Is Actually Late

Rent in New York is not late the instant it is due.

New York law provides a statutory grace period before landlords can impose penalties or begin the eviction process. For monthly rent, the grace period is generally five days after the due date.

If your rent is due on the first of the month, it is not legally late until the sixth. During those five days, the landlord cannot charge a late fee, cannot impose a penalty, and cannot begin nonpayment proceedings. The grace period is a legal right, not a landlord courtesy. It cannot be shortened by the lease, waived by agreement, or eliminated by landlord policy.

The grace period matters for several reasons beyond the obvious.

Late fees charged during the grace period are illegal. A landlord who imposes a late fee on the second of the month, or who automatically assesses fees on any payment received after the first, is violating the law. The fee is unenforceable and, if included in a rent demand, may render the demand defective.

The grace period affects the timing of notices. A landlord who serves a rent demand on the second of the month, before the grace period has expired, has served the demand prematurely. Prematurely served demands create procedural problems that can affect the entire case.

The grace period is not extendable by payment method. If you pay by check and the check takes three days to arrive but was mailed before the due date, the question is when the rent was tendered, not when it was received. Electronic payments that are initiated within the grace period are generally timely.

If your landlord treats rent as late before the grace period expires, they are wrong. Document the date you were charged a late fee, compare it to the due date plus the grace period, and preserve the evidence. It may matter later.

Limits on Late Fees

Late fees in New York are strictly regulated, and the limits are lower than many landlords claim.

A landlord may charge a late fee only when the rent is past the grace period, the fee is authorized by the lease, and the fee is within the legal cap. All three conditions must be met. A late fee that fails any one of them is unenforceable.

New York law caps late fees at the lesser of $50 or 5 percent of the monthly rent. For an apartment renting at $2,000 per month, the maximum late fee is $50 (because $50 is less than 5 percent of $2,000, which would be $100). For an apartment renting at $800, the maximum is $40 (5 percent of $800).

Late fees cannot exceed this cap regardless of what the lease says. A lease that imposes a $200 late fee on a $2,000 apartment contains an unenforceable provision. The landlord may collect $50 at most, and only after the grace period has expired.

Late fees cannot compound. A landlord cannot charge a new late fee each month on the same unpaid rent. The fee applies once, when the payment becomes late, and does not grow over time.

Late fees cannot be disguised as other charges. Some landlords impose "administrative fees," "processing charges," or "service fees" that function identically to late fees. If the charge is triggered by late payment and is collected on top of the rent, it is a late fee and is subject to the same cap.

Late fees cannot be charged retroactively. A landlord who never charged late fees during the tenancy cannot suddenly assess them for past months. Fees must be imposed contemporaneously with the late payment, in accordance with the lease terms and the statutory cap.

Late fees that violate these rules are not just unenforceable in isolation. When included in a rent demand, they can render the entire demand defective, which can cause the nonpayment case to be dismissed. This is why the details matter: an illegal $150 late fee doesn't just cost the tenant $150. It can cost the landlord the entire eviction proceeding.

What a Rent Demand Must Get Right

Before filing a nonpayment eviction, the landlord must serve the tenant with a written rent demand. As Chapter 12 explained, this demand is a mandatory predicate to the nonpayment case. Without a valid demand, the court lacks jurisdiction. With a defective demand, the result is the same.

The requirements bear repeating here because they are so frequently violated and because the consequences of violation are so significant.

The demand must state the correct amount of rent owed. This means the legal regulated rent (in stabilized apartments), not the landlord's preferred rent, not an inflated figure, and not an amount that includes illegal charges. If the tenant pays $1,800 per month and owes three months, the demand should state $5,400. A demand for $5,950 that includes late fees, utility charges, or other add-ons is overstating the amount, and overstated demands are defective.

The demand must identify the specific rental periods covered. The tenant has the right to know exactly which months are being claimed. A demand that says "you owe $7,200" without specifying the months does not give the tenant enough information to verify the claim. The demand should list each month individually and the amount owed for each.

The demand must exclude illegal fees and charges. Late fees that exceed the cap, fees imposed during the grace period, charges for services the tenant did not agree to, attorney's fees that are not yet owed, and any other amount that is not lawfully collectible as rent must be excluded. Including them does not just inflate the total. It contaminates the demand.

The demand must reflect the legal rent, not just the lease rent. In rent-stabilized apartments, the legal rent may be lower than what the lease states. If the tenant has an overcharge claim pending, or if the landlord has been collecting more than the legal rent, the demand should reflect the lawful amount. A demand based on an illegal rent is a demand for an illegal amount, and it is defective.

The demand must be served at least 14 days before the landlord files the nonpayment petition. This 14-day period gives the tenant the opportunity to pay the arrears or dispute the amount before the case reaches court. The period begins when the demand is properly served, not when the landlord decides to send it. Filing the petition before the 14 days have elapsed makes the case premature and subject to dismissal.

The demand must include the Good Cause Eviction notice, if applicable. Since August 2024, landlords must attach the Good Cause disclosure to any 14-day rent demand, stating whether the apartment is covered by Good Cause protections. Failure to include the notice may provide grounds to challenge the proceeding.

Each of these requirements is independently enforceable. A demand that satisfies four out of five is still defective. Courts do not grade on a curve.

Why Inflated Demands Are So Common

Landlords inflate rent demands for several reasons, and understanding those reasons helps tenants spot the problem.

The most common reason is the inclusion of illegal late fees. Landlords who routinely assess late fees above the statutory cap, or who charge fees during the grace period, carry those amounts onto their internal ledgers. When the ledger is used to generate a rent demand, the illegal fees are included automatically. The landlord may not even realize the fees are improper, because the system has been generating them for years without challenge.

Another common reason is the inclusion of non-rent charges. Landlords sometimes include utility charges, repair costs billed to the tenant, legal fees, or other amounts that are not lawfully collectible as rent. These charges may be the subject of legitimate disputes, but they do not belong in a rent demand. A rent demand is a demand for rent. Other obligations, even if valid, must be pursued through other means.

In rent-stabilized apartments, inflated demands often result from the landlord charging more than the legal rent. If the tenant has been paying $2,100 but the legal rent is $1,750, the demand based on $2,100 overstates the amount owed. The tenant may owe back rent, but they owe back rent at the legal rate, not the illegal one.

Copying amounts directly from internal ledgers without verifying them against the law is the most common mechanical cause of inflated demands. Landlords and management companies treat their accounting records as authoritative. But accounting records reflect what was charged, not what was lawfully chargeable. The two are not always the same.

In every case, the tenant's defense is the same: compare the demand to the law. If the amount exceeds what is legally owed, the demand is defective, and the case built on it is vulnerable.

The Difference Between Owing Rent and Losing Your Case

A principle that surprises many tenants is worth stating plainly: a landlord can lose a nonpayment case even when rent is owed.

This happens because nonpayment cases in New York are about process as much as substance. The landlord must prove not just that rent is owed, but that every procedural step was followed correctly. If the demand is defective, the case fails. If the demand was served too early, the case fails. If the petition was filed before the 14-day period elapsed, the case fails. If the wrong amount was demanded, the case fails.

The tenant may still owe money after the case is dismissed. The dismissal does not eliminate the debt. But it forces the landlord to start the process over, with a new demand, properly prepared and properly served, and a new waiting period. That process takes time, and time often changes the dynamic. The tenant may use the additional time to pay the arrears, apply for rental assistance, negotiate a payment plan, consult an attorney, or prepare defenses to the next case.

This is why procedural precision matters in nonpayment law. The rules are not there to protect tenants from paying rent. They are there to ensure that the process for removing someone from their home is followed exactly, because the consequences of getting it wrong are too severe to tolerate shortcuts.

What to Do When You Fall Behind

Falling behind on rent is stressful, and the natural response is often to avoid the problem. Don't. The earlier you act, the more options you have.

Communicate with the landlord. Many landlords will negotiate a payment plan if approached before the situation escalates. A tenant who contacts the landlord, explains the situation, and proposes a specific plan (with dates and amounts) is in a stronger position than a tenant who goes silent. Put any agreement in writing.

Apply for rental assistance. New York has multiple programs that provide emergency rental assistance to tenants facing arrears. The specific programs change over time, but 311 can direct you to current resources. HRA (the Human Resources Administration) administers several assistance programs, and community-based organizations may have emergency funds available. Apply as early as possible, because processing takes time.

Consult a legal services organization. If you are facing arrears and anticipate a nonpayment case, contact a tenant legal services organization early. Legal Aid Society, Legal Services NYC, and other organizations provide free representation to eligible tenants and can advise on defenses, negotiate with the landlord, and help you navigate the process. Early consultation often prevents cases from being filed at all.

Continue paying whatever you can. Partial payments demonstrate good faith and reduce the total arrears. They also affect the dynamics of any court proceeding. A tenant who has been making partial payments is in a different position than a tenant who has paid nothing. Courts consider the tenant's efforts, and landlords are more willing to negotiate with tenants who are visibly trying.

Do not ignore a rent demand. If you receive a 14-day rent demand, read it carefully. Check the amount against what you actually owe. Check for illegal fees. Check the dates. If the demand is defective, that defect is a defense. If the demand is accurate, you have 14 days to pay before a case can be filed. Use that time.

Set aside whatever rent you are withholding. If you are withholding rent for any reason (habitability issues, a dispute about the amount, or financial hardship), keep the money in a separate account. Do not spend it. If the case reaches court, the judge will ask whether you have the rent available. A tenant who has set aside the rent demonstrates good faith and may be offered a more favorable outcome than a tenant who has spent it.

Defenses in Nonpayment Cases

Even when rent is genuinely owed, tenants in nonpayment cases may have defenses that reduce the amount owed, delay the proceedings, or result in dismissal.

Defective rent demand is the most powerful procedural defense. As discussed throughout this chapter, any error in the amount, timing, content, or service of the rent demand can be grounds for dismissal.

Breach of the warranty of habitability is the most common substantive defense. If the landlord has failed to maintain the apartment in habitable condition, the tenant may be entitled to a rent abatement, reducing the amount owed for the period when conditions were substandard. The abatement is calculated as a percentage of the rent, reflecting the degree to which the apartment's livability was impaired. Chapter 17 covers habitability in detail.

Retaliation is a defense if the nonpayment case was filed in response to the tenant's exercise of a protected right. If the tenant recently filed a complaint, requested repairs, or organized with neighbors, and the landlord responded by filing a nonpayment case with inflated charges, the case may be retaliatory. Chapter 19 covers retaliation in detail.

Payment is a defense. If the tenant paid the rent and has proof (canceled checks, bank statements, electronic payment confirmations), the landlord's claim fails as to the amounts that were paid.

Overcharge is a defense in rent-stabilized apartments. If the landlord has been charging more than the legal rent, the tenant may owe less than the demand claims. The demand, based on the illegal rent, is defective.

Improper service is a defense. If the rent demand or the petition was not served in accordance with the rules described in Chapter 12, the court lacks jurisdiction.

Each of these defenses must be raised in the tenant's answer to the petition. A defense that is not pleaded may be waived. This is why legal representation, even if limited to preparing the answer, is critically important.

Late Fees and the Nonpayment Trap

The interaction between late fees and nonpayment cases creates a trap that catches many tenants.

Here is how it works. A landlord charges illegal late fees (fees that exceed the cap or are imposed during the grace period). The tenant, not knowing the fees are illegal, pays them. Over time, the illegal fees accumulate on the landlord's ledger. When the tenant falls behind on rent, the landlord generates a demand that includes both the unpaid rent and the accumulated illegal fees. The total is inflated.

The tenant sees a large number and panics. They may assume they owe more than they actually do. They may make partial payments that the landlord applies to fees first, leaving rent arrears on the books even though the tenant has paid enough to cover the actual rent.

When the landlord files a nonpayment case, the petition states the inflated amount. The tenant, overwhelmed by the number, may not realize that a significant portion of the claimed amount consists of illegal fees. If the tenant doesn't raise the issue, the court may enter a judgment based on the inflated amount.

The defense is straightforward: compare the demand to the legal rent, subtract any illegal fees, and challenge the demand as defective if the total includes amounts that are not lawfully collectible. But the defense works only if the tenant recognizes the problem.

This is why understanding late fee rules is not abstract. Late fees are the most common source of demand inflation, and demand inflation is the most common landlord mistake in nonpayment cases. The tenant who knows the rules catches the error. The tenant who doesn't may pay money they never owed.

Real-World Example: The Math That Ended the Case

A tenant in a rent-stabilized apartment in Harlem fell behind on rent after a temporary job loss. The landlord served a rent demand claiming $8,200 in arrears. The tenant, afraid and behind on payments, assumed the number was correct and began preparing for the worst.

Before the court date, the tenant spoke with a legal services attorney through the Right to Counsel program. The attorney reviewed the rent demand line by line.

The demand included three months of unpaid rent at $2,200 per month ($6,600 total). It also included $1,600 in late fees: $200 per month for eight months, assessed from the first day after the rent due date without regard for the five-day grace period.

The attorney identified two problems. First, the late fees exceeded the statutory cap of $50 per instance. The landlord had been charging $200, four times the legal maximum. Second, the fees had been assessed during the grace period, before the rent was legally late.

The total amount of illegal late fees included in the demand was $1,600. Because the demand overstated the amount owed by including unlawful charges, it was defective.

The attorney moved to dismiss the case based on the defective demand. The judge granted the motion. The case was dismissed.

The tenant still owed three months' rent. But the landlord had to start the process over, with a new demand that accurately stated the amount owed. That process took weeks, during which the tenant secured a new job and negotiated a payment plan for the arrears.

The case didn't turn on hardship. It turned on math. The landlord demanded $8,200. The law allowed $6,750 ($6,600 in rent plus $150 in lawful late fees). The difference was an error, and the error was fatal.

What to Take From This Chapter

Rent is not late until the grace period expires. In New York, the grace period is generally five days for monthly rent. Late fees charged during the grace period are illegal.

Late fees are capped at $50 or 5 percent of the monthly rent, whichever is less. Fees above the cap are unenforceable and, if included in a rent demand, may render the demand defective.

Rent demands must state the correct amount, identify the specific periods covered, exclude illegal charges, and be served at least 14 days before the landlord files a nonpayment petition. Defective demands are grounds for dismissal.

A landlord can lose a nonpayment case even when rent is owed. Procedural errors in the demand, service, or filing are independently sufficient to end the case.

Tenants who fall behind should act early: communicate with the landlord, apply for rental assistance, consult legal services, and continue paying whatever they can.

Defenses in nonpayment cases include defective demands, breach of the warranty of habitability, retaliation, payment, overcharge, and improper service. Each must be raised in the answer.

If your landlord says you're being evicted for nonpayment, the most important question is not "Do I owe money?" It's "Did they demand it in a way the law allows?"

In the next chapter, we move to one of the most common and most misunderstood areas of New York tenant law: roommates, sublets, unauthorized occupants, and how tenants accidentally evict themselves by doing the wrong thing informally.

Part VII: Special Rental Situations

21

Roommates, Sublets and Unauthorized Occupants

Sharing an apartment in New York is normal. Getting threatened with eviction over it is also normal, usually because tenants don't realize how precise New York's occupancy rules are, or how aggressively landlords use the phrase "unauthorized occupant" to regain control.

Roommates, subtenants, and long-term guests are treated differently under the law. Each category has its own rules, its own procedures, and its own consequences for getting it wrong. Mixing the categories up, or handling any of them informally, can hand landlords leverage they wouldn't otherwise have.

This chapter explains how primary residence rules work, what roommate rights actually protect, what subletting requires in rent-stabilized apartments, how the "unauthorized occupant" label is used as a weapon, and how tenants accidentally lose their apartments by doing the wrong thing for the right reasons.

Primary Residence: The Legal Anchor

For many New York apartments, especially rent-stabilized units, the tenant must maintain the apartment as their primary residence. This is the foundational requirement that controls nearly every occupancy question in this chapter.

Primary residence generally means the apartment is your main home, you live there for the majority of the year, and your personal, legal, and financial life is centered there. The Rent Stabilization Code uses 183 days as the threshold: you must occupy the apartment for at least 183 days out of the year for it to qualify as your primary residence.

Primary residence is established through the totality of your life, not any single factor. Courts and DHCR look at where you receive mail, where you file taxes, where your driver's license is registered, where you vote, where your bank accounts are maintained, where your children attend school (if applicable), and where you spend most of your nights. No single factor is decisive. The analysis considers the overall picture.

Primary residence does not mean you can never leave. You can travel for work. You can visit family for extended periods. You can spend weekends at a partner's apartment. You can take a temporary assignment in another city. What you cannot do is permanently relocate somewhere else while maintaining the apartment as a secondary residence, an investment, or a rental asset.

Landlords often raise primary residence challenges not because the tenant has actually abandoned the apartment, but because the rent is low. A rent-stabilized apartment with below-market rent creates an ongoing financial incentive for the landlord to find any basis for removal. Primary residence challenges are one of the most common methods.

The challenge typically begins with a Golub Notice (described in Chapter 11) stating that the landlord believes the tenant is not using the apartment as a primary residence and citing evidence such as an alternative address, utility usage patterns, or the presence of another person in the apartment. The landlord must then prove the claim in court, and the tenant has the opportunity to present evidence of continued primary residence.

The best defense against a primary residence challenge is a well-maintained paper trail. Keep your address current on government documents. File taxes from the apartment's address. Maintain utility accounts in your name. Vote from the apartment. Receive mail there. If you are temporarily away, maintain visible connections to the apartment that demonstrate your intent to return.

Roommates: Stronger Rights Than Most Tenants Realize

New York law gives tenants broad rights to have roommates, and those rights exist regardless of what the lease says.

Under Real Property Law Section 235-f, known as the "Roommate Law," tenants in apartments with buildings of any size have the right to share their apartment with at least one additional occupant and the occupant's dependent children, provided the tenant or the tenant's spouse occupies the apartment as their primary residence.

This right exists even if the lease prohibits roommates. It exists even if the lease says only the named tenant may occupy the apartment. It exists even if the landlord has a policy against additional occupants. The Roommate Law overrides contrary lease provisions because the legislature determined that tenants should have the right to make basic decisions about who lives with them.

The practical implications are significant. A tenant may live with immediate family members without landlord approval. A tenant may add a roommate within legal occupancy limits without landlord approval. A tenant may share rent with a roommate without creating a separate landlord-tenant relationship between the roommate and the landlord.

The landlord's rights in this context are limited. The landlord may request the name of the roommate within 30 days of a written request by the landlord, and the tenant must provide the name within 30 days of receiving that request. The landlord may verify that the apartment is not overcrowded beyond legal occupancy standards (which are determined by square footage and room count, not by the landlord's preference).

The landlord may not demand a new lease adding the roommate as a named tenant. The landlord may not charge an additional security deposit for the roommate. The landlord may not impose a fee for having a roommate. The landlord may not refuse to renew the lease because of the roommate. And the landlord may not evict the tenant solely because an additional person lives in the apartment, as long as occupancy limits are not exceeded.

These protections are among the strongest and most frequently violated tenant rights in New York. Landlords routinely tell tenants they cannot have roommates, that having a roommate violates the lease, or that the tenant must pay extra for an additional occupant. Each of these statements is wrong.

If your landlord is pressuring you about a roommate, your first step is to verify that your apartment is not overcrowded under the applicable occupancy standards (which are based on floor area and number of rooms, not the landlord's rules). If you are within the legal limits, the Roommate Law protects your arrangement, and the landlord cannot force the roommate out or use the roommate's presence as a ground for eviction.

One important limitation: the Roommate Law gives the primary tenant the right to have a roommate, but the roommate does not acquire independent rights to the apartment. If the primary tenant moves out, the roommate generally does not have the right to remain. The roommate's right to occupy derives from the primary tenant's right, not from an independent landlord-tenant relationship.

Subletting in Rent-Stabilized Apartments: Allowed, But Formal

Subletting is different from having a roommate, and the distinction matters enormously.

In a sublet, the tenant temporarily vacates the apartment and another person (the subtenant) occupies it during the tenant's absence. The tenant intends to return. The sublease is for a defined period. And the arrangement is governed by specific rules that the tenant must follow.

In rent-stabilized apartments, tenants generally have the right to sublet. But the right comes with procedural requirements that must be followed exactly. Informality is the enemy.

The process begins with a written request to the landlord. The tenant must send the landlord a written request for permission to sublet, sent by certified mail, return receipt requested. The request must include the term of the proposed sublease, the name of the proposed subtenant, the business and permanent home address of the proposed subtenant, the tenant's reason for subletting, the tenant's address during the sublet period, the written consent of any cotenant or guarantor, a copy of the proposed sublease, and a copy of the tenant's own lease (if available).

After receiving this information, the landlord has 30 days to request additional information that is reasonably related to the proposed sublease. If the landlord requests additional information, the 30-day clock for responding to the sublet request does not start until the tenant provides it.

Once the landlord has all required information, they have 30 days to consent or reasonably withhold consent. If the landlord does not respond within 30 days, consent is deemed granted. The tenant may proceed with the sublet.

If the landlord unreasonably withholds consent, the tenant may sublet anyway. The standard is reasonableness, not absolute discretion. A landlord who refuses without a legitimate reason has unreasonably withheld consent, and the tenant's recourse is to proceed and defend the sublet if challenged.

The subtenant may not be charged more than the tenant's stabilized rent. If the apartment is furnished, the tenant may add a surcharge of up to 10 percent. Charging the subtenant more than the regulated rent (plus the furniture surcharge, if applicable) is a violation that can expose the tenant to penalties, including the loss of the right to sublet.

The tenant must maintain the apartment as their primary residence over the course of the tenancy, even while subletting. Subletting is a temporary arrangement. A tenant who sublets indefinitely, never returns, and treats the apartment as a passive income source is not subletting. They have abandoned primary residence, and the landlord may challenge the tenancy on that basis.

Rent-stabilized tenants may generally sublet for up to two years out of any four-year period, though the specific rules and timeframes should be verified against current law.

The formality of this process frustrates many tenants, who feel it should be simpler to let someone stay in their apartment while they are temporarily away. But the formality exists for a reason: it protects the tenant. A tenant who follows the procedure has documentation proving that the sublet was lawful, that the landlord was notified, and that consent was given or deemed granted. A tenant who sublets informally has none of that, and is vulnerable to a holdover case alleging unauthorized subletting.

Subletting in Unregulated Apartments

In unregulated apartments in buildings with four or more units, tenants also have the right to sublet under Real Property Law Section 226-b.

The process is similar in structure: the tenant must request permission in writing, the landlord may request additional information, and the landlord must respond within 30 days. Unreasonable refusal of consent entitles the tenant to sublet anyway or, alternatively, to be released from the lease.

The key difference is that unregulated tenants do not have the same rent limitations. The subtenant's rent in an unregulated apartment is governed by the sublease agreement between the tenant and subtenant, not by a regulatory cap. However, profiteering (charging substantially more than the tenant pays) may raise issues if the landlord challenges the arrangement.

In unregulated apartments not covered by Good Cause, subletting rights are more limited, and the landlord has broader discretion. The lease terms matter more, and the Roommate Law provides the primary protection for sharing arrangements.

"Unauthorized Occupants": The Label That Gets Abused

"Unauthorized occupant" is one of the most powerful phrases in a landlord's vocabulary. It carries an implication of wrongdoing, suggests that the tenant has violated the lease, and creates a sense of urgency that pressures tenants into conceding before they investigate.

In many cases, the label is strategically applied rather than factually accurate.

A landlord may describe someone as an unauthorized occupant when the person is a lawful roommate under the Roommate Law, when the person is a family member living with the tenant, when the person is a guest who has stayed for an extended period, when the person is a subtenant whose sublet the tenant handled informally, or when the person is a caretaker or companion of an elderly or disabled tenant.

In each case, the question is not whether the landlord applied a label. The question is whether the law supports the label. Courts look at facts, not characterizations.

When evaluating an "unauthorized occupant" claim, courts consider who pays rent (the primary tenant, the alleged occupant, or both), who actually lives in the apartment on a day-to-day basis, whether the primary tenant maintains the apartment as their primary residence, whether the arrangement falls within the Roommate Law's protections, whether the tenant followed subletting procedures (if the arrangement is a sublet), and whether the landlord previously knew about and tolerated the occupant.

A long-term guest is not automatically unauthorized. A roommate is not automatically unauthorized. A subtenant is not automatically unauthorized. And the presence of another person in the apartment is not, by itself, grounds for eviction.

The most important thing a tenant can do when confronted with an "unauthorized occupant" claim is to slow down and investigate. Do not concede the claim. Do not agree to remove the person without understanding whether the law actually requires it. And do not panic, because panic is what the label is designed to produce.

How Tenants Accidentally Self-Evict

The most dangerous occupancy mistakes are not the ones tenants make intentionally. They are the ones tenants make through informality, good intentions, and a failure to follow procedures that feel unnecessarily bureaucratic.

Moving out without following the sublet approval process is the most common form of self-eviction. A tenant takes a job in another city, asks a friend to stay in the apartment and pay rent, and assumes everything will be fine. The friend pays rent directly to the landlord. The landlord accepts the payments. Months pass.

Then the landlord files a holdover case, alleging that the tenant abandoned the apartment and that the "occupant" is unauthorized. The tenant, now living elsewhere, has no documentation of a sublet request, no evidence of consent, and no proof of intent to return. The landlord argues that the tenant forfeited primary residence. The court agrees.

The tenant didn't intend to give up the apartment. But by handling the arrangement informally, they handed the landlord every argument needed to take it.

Overcharging subtenants is another form of self-eviction. In rent-stabilized apartments, the tenant may not charge the subtenant more than the regulated rent (plus a 10 percent surcharge for furnished apartments). A tenant who charges $2,500 for an apartment with a legal rent of $1,800 is violating the Rent Stabilization Code. If the landlord discovers the overcharge, it can be used as grounds to challenge the tenancy and potentially terminate the tenant's right to the apartment.

Failing to respond to landlord notices is a quieter form of self-eviction. A landlord who suspects unauthorized occupancy may send the tenant a letter requesting the names of all occupants, as permitted by the Roommate Law. If the tenant fails to respond within 30 days, the landlord may argue noncompliance with the statute, which weakens the tenant's position even if the underlying arrangement is lawful.

Leaving no proof of intent to return is the thread connecting all of these scenarios. A tenant who sublets without documentation, who does not maintain utility accounts, who changes their address on official documents, and who has no evidence of regular return visits has created a record that looks indistinguishable from abandonment. Courts interpret ambiguous records against the tenant.

Documentation Protects Occupancy

The solution to every occupancy risk described in this chapter is documentation.

If you have a roommate, respond to any landlord inquiry about the roommate's identity within 30 days. Keep a copy of your response. Confirm that occupancy limits are not exceeded.

If you are subletting, follow the written request process exactly. Send the request by certified mail. Keep copies of everything you send and everything the landlord sends in response. If the landlord does not respond within 30 days, document the date you sent the request, the date the 30 days expired, and your reliance on deemed consent. Do not charge more than the legal rent.

If you are temporarily away, maintain your primary residence documentation. Keep utility accounts in your name. Continue receiving mail at the apartment. File taxes from the apartment's address. Return regularly and keep evidence of your returns (transit records, receipts, photographs).

If you are living with a family member, partner, or companion, ensure that your own primary residence is documented. The other person's presence does not, by itself, create a problem as long as you are living there too and occupancy limits are not exceeded.

In all cases, keep records. Occupancy disputes are decided on paper, and the tenant who has a paper trail wins. The tenant who has nothing but an oral explanation of what was supposed to happen is at risk.

Real-World Example: Proving the Apartment Was Still Home

A tenant in a rent-stabilized apartment in Inwood accepted a temporary work assignment in Philadelphia that was expected to last 18 months. She asked a close friend to sublet the apartment but did not follow the formal sublet request procedure. She did not send a written request to the landlord. She did not disclose the subtenant's information. She simply told the friend to pay rent and take care of the apartment.

The landlord, noticing a different name on utility accounts and different patterns of building entry, began an investigation. After several months, the landlord served a Golub Notice alleging that the tenant had abandoned the apartment and allowed an unauthorized occupant.

The tenant was alarmed. She had not abandoned the apartment. She intended to return when the assignment ended. The apartment still contained her furniture, her personal belongings, and items that clearly identified it as her home.

The tenant consulted an attorney, who helped her assemble evidence of continued primary residence. She showed that she had maintained her voter registration at the apartment's address. She had filed taxes from the apartment. She had kept a bank account at a branch near the apartment. She had returned to the apartment approximately once per month, with Metro-North tickets and transit records documenting each visit. Her driver's license still listed the apartment's address.

The attorney also helped the tenant retroactively document the sublet arrangement by sending the landlord a written notice of the arrangement and the subtenant's information.

In court, the landlord argued abandonment. The tenant presented her documentation. The court found that the tenant had maintained primary residence, that the arrangement was a temporary sublet, and that the landlord's claim failed.

The tenant didn't win because the arrangement was invisible. She won because it was provable, even though the initial steps had been done informally.

The lesson is not that informal arrangements always work out. It is that this tenant was lucky enough to have maintained enough documentation to survive the challenge. Many tenants in the same situation would not. The formal procedures exist to prevent exactly this kind of dispute.

What to Take From This Chapter

Primary residence is the legal anchor for occupancy rights in New York, especially in rent-stabilized apartments. Maintain documentation of your primary residence at all times.

Roommates are broadly protected by the Roommate Law. Tenants may have at least one additional occupant (plus dependent children) regardless of what the lease says. Landlords may request the roommate's name but may not charge fees, demand lease changes, or evict based on a lawful roommate.

Subletting in rent-stabilized apartments requires a formal written process. Tenants must request permission, provide specific information, and comply with rent limitations. Informality creates legal risk that formal procedures eliminate.

"Unauthorized occupant" is often a strategic label rather than a legal conclusion. Courts evaluate the facts, not the landlord's characterization. Slow down and investigate before conceding the claim.

Self-eviction happens through informality. Moving out without following sublet procedures, overcharging subtenants, failing to respond to landlord inquiries, and leaving no proof of intent to return are the most common ways tenants lose apartments they had every right to keep.

Documentation is the difference between a defensible arrangement and a vulnerable one. Follow procedures, keep records, and maintain your paper trail.

If your landlord says someone in your apartment doesn't belong there, the real question is not "Did I ask for permission?" It's "What does New York law actually allow?"

In the next chapter, we'll cover one of the most emotionally charged and practically important topics in rent-stabilized housing: succession rights, and what happens when the tenant of record dies or permanently leaves.

22

Succession Rights

When a Tenant Leaves or Dies

When the tenant of record in a rent-stabilized apartment dies or permanently moves out, the apartment does not automatically revert to the landlord.

If a qualifying family member has been living in the apartment as their primary residence for the required period, that person has the legal right to take over the tenancy. The lease continues. The rent stays regulated. The protections remain. The apartment passes not through the landlord's generosity but through a right established by law.

Succession rights are among the most valuable and most contested protections in New York tenant law. For families who have lived in the same apartment for decades, succession can mean the difference between staying in a neighborhood and being priced out of it permanently. For landlords, succession represents the continuation of a below-market tenancy that may cost them thousands of dollars per year in unrealized rent. The financial stakes on both sides are enormous, and landlord challenges to succession claims are aggressive, well-funded, and procedurally demanding.

This chapter explains who qualifies to succeed, what the co-residency requirements are, how "family member" is defined (more broadly than most people expect), how to assert a succession claim, how landlords challenge those claims, and what documentation you need to build now, even if the primary tenant is alive and healthy.

What Succession Rights Are

Succession rights allow a qualifying family member to inherit a rent-regulated tenancy when the tenant of record either dies or permanently vacates the apartment.

The successor does not receive a new lease at a new rent. They step into the existing tenancy. The rent remains the regulated amount. The stabilization protections continue. The successor becomes the new tenant of record, entitled to renewal leases, RGB increases, and all other rights of a rent-stabilized tenant.

For the first succession (the first time a family member takes over the tenancy from the original tenant of record), the landlord is not entitled to any vacancy increase. The successor pays the same rent the departing tenant was paying, plus any lawful RGB increase at the next renewal. For subsequent successions (a second family member succeeding after the first successor departs), the landlord may be entitled to a vacancy allowance, depending on the circumstances.

Succession can happen multiple times. An apartment can pass from parent to child, and then from that child to their own child, as long as the co-residency requirements are met each time. There is no limit on the number of successions, though each one must independently satisfy the requirements.

Succession rights apply to both rent-stabilized and rent-controlled apartments, though the procedures differ slightly. This chapter focuses primarily on rent-stabilized succession, which is the more common scenario.

Who Qualifies: The Definition of "Family Member"

The definition of "family member" for succession purposes is broader than most people assume, and understanding that breadth is critical.

The Rent Stabilization Code defines family member in two categories.

The first category includes traditional family relationships. A spouse, son, daughter, stepson, stepdaughter, father, mother, stepfather, stepmother, brother, sister, grandfather, grandmother, grandson, granddaughter, father-in-law, mother-in-law, son-in-law, or daughter-in-law of the tenant of record qualifies as a family member. These relationships are established by blood, marriage, or legal adoption, and they are straightforward to prove.

The second category is where the definition becomes unusually expansive. Any other person residing with the tenant as a primary resident who can demonstrate emotional and financial commitment and interdependence with the tenant also qualifies as a family member.

This second category exists because the legislature and the courts recognized that families take many forms. A long-term romantic partner who is not married to the tenant may qualify. A close friend who has shared the household for many years and has built an interdependent life with the tenant may qualify. A caretaker who has devoted years to supporting the tenant and has merged their life with the tenant's household may qualify.

The landmark case that established this principle, *Braschi v. Stahl* Assocs. Co., 74 N.Y.2d 201, 543 N.E.2d 49, 544 N.Y.S.2d 784 (1989), involved a same-sex partner who sought succession rights after his partner died of AIDS. The Court of Appeals held that the surviving partner qualified as a family member based on the couple's emotional and financial interdependence, even though same-sex marriage was not legal at the time. The decision established that "family" for succession purposes is defined by the reality of the relationship, not by formal legal status.

Courts and DHCR evaluate non-traditional family claims by looking at a range of factors. These include the longevity of the relationship, the sharing of expenses and financial obligations, whether the parties have intermingled their finances (joint bank accounts, shared credit cards, co-signed loans), whether they have formalized their relationship through legal documents (wills, powers of attorney, health care proxies, domestic partnership declarations), whether they have held themselves out publicly as a family unit (attending events together, being introduced as family, being treated as family by others), whether they have performed family functions (caring for each other during illness, supporting each other financially, sharing holidays and daily life), and the nature of the emotional bond between them.

No single factor is decisive. The analysis considers the totality of the relationship. But the more factors that are present, the stronger the claim.

One critical limitation: nieces, nephews, cousins, and other extended relatives who are not listed in the first category do not automatically qualify as family members. They must prove emotional and financial interdependence under the second category, which requires more than simply being related. The biological relationship alone is not sufficient.

The Co-Residency Requirement: How Long You Must Have Lived There

Qualifying as a family member is necessary but not sufficient. The family member must also satisfy the co-residency requirement.

The general rule is that the family member must have resided in the apartment with the tenant of record, as a primary resident, for at least two years immediately prior to the tenant's death or permanent departure.

There are two exceptions that shorten this period. If the family member is a senior citizen (62 years of age or older), the co-residency requirement is reduced to one year. If the family member is a disabled person (as defined under applicable law), the co-residency requirement is also reduced to one year.

There is also a circumstance that eliminates the time requirement entirely. If the family member has resided with the tenant from the inception of the tenancy (from the day the tenant first moved into the apartment) or from the commencement of the family relationship, there is no minimum co-residency period. This exception is most commonly relevant when a couple moves into the apartment together, or when a child is born into the household.

The co-residency period is measured backward from the date the tenant of record dies or permanently vacates the apartment. If the tenant died on March 1, 2026, the two-year period runs from March 1, 2024 to March 1, 2026. The family member must have lived in the apartment as a primary resident during that entire period.

Certain temporary absences do not interrupt the co-residency period. The Rent Stabilization Code excuses absences for active military duty, enrollment as a full-time student, court-ordered relocation (not involving the lease or grounds for eviction), temporary relocation due to employment, hospitalization, and other reasonable grounds as determined by DHCR.

This means that a family member who left the apartment for two semesters to attend college did not break the co-residency period. A family member who was hospitalized for several months did not break it. A family member who took a temporary work assignment in another city did not break it, provided the absence was temporary and the intent to return was genuine.

The critical distinction is between temporary absences (which are excused) and permanent departures (which break the chain). A family member who moved out, established a household elsewhere, and then moved back in must satisfy the co-residency requirement from the date they returned, not from the date they originally moved in.

How to Assert a Succession Claim

Succession rights become active at the moment the tenant of record dies or permanently vacates the apartment. The family member asserting succession should act promptly.

The first step is to notify the landlord in writing. Send a letter by certified mail, return receipt requested, stating that the tenant of record has died or permanently departed, that you are a qualifying family member who has resided in the apartment as a primary resident for the required period, and that you are asserting your right to succeed to the tenancy.

If the tenant died, include a copy of the death certificate with the letter.

If the apartment is rent-stabilized, your letter should request that the next renewal lease be issued in your name. Succession in a stabilized apartment is effectuated through the renewal lease process. When the current lease expires and the landlord offers a renewal, the renewal should be offered to the successor, not to the departed or deceased tenant.

The landlord may respond in one of several ways. The landlord may accept the claim, issue a renewal lease in the successor's name, and continue the tenancy. This is the simplest outcome and occurs most often when the relationship and co-residency are obvious and well-documented.

The landlord may request documentation supporting the claim. The landlord is entitled to ask for evidence that you qualify as a family member and that you meet the co-residency requirement. Provide documentation promptly and thoroughly. The documentation section later in this chapter describes what you should prepare.

The landlord may reject the claim and attempt to evict you. This is the outcome that leads to court. The landlord files a holdover proceeding, and the tenant asserts succession rights as a defense. The court evaluates the evidence and determines whether the succession claim is valid.

The landlord may also try to offer a new lease at a higher rent, claiming that the successor is a "new tenant" not entitled to the prior tenant's rent. This is wrong. A valid successor inherits the existing rent. The landlord may not impose a vacancy increase on the first succession.

Do not sign a lease in the deceased or departed tenant's name. This is one of the most common and most damaging mistakes successors make. If a renewal lease arrives addressed to the former tenant, do not sign it. Contact the landlord and request that the lease be issued in your name. If the landlord refuses, file a complaint with DHCR using Form RA-90.

How Landlords Challenge Succession Claims

Landlords challenge succession claims because every successful succession means the continuation of a regulated tenancy at a below-market rent. The financial incentive to defeat succession claims is substantial, and landlords pursue these challenges aggressively.

The most common challenge is to the co-residency requirement. The landlord argues that the family member did not actually live in the apartment for the required period, or did not use it as a primary residence. Landlords investigate this claim using the same tools they use in primary residence challenges: voter registration records, tax filings, driver's license addresses, utility accounts, credit card statements, bank records, and any other documentation that might suggest the family member's primary residence was somewhere else.

Another common challenge is to the family relationship itself. For traditional family members, this challenge is usually straightforward to resolve with birth certificates, marriage certificates, or other official documents. For non-traditional family members, the challenge is more complex and requires the extensive documentation of emotional and financial interdependence described earlier.

Landlords may also challenge the timing of the departure. If the tenant of record left the apartment gradually (spending increasing time elsewhere over months or years), the landlord may argue about when the "permanent departure" actually occurred, which affects when the two-year co-residency clock is measured.

In some cases, landlords conduct surveillance. They may hire investigators to monitor the building's entrance, track the family member's movements, photograph the family member entering or leaving other locations, and review social media for evidence that the family member's life is centered elsewhere.

These tactics are legal, and they can be effective if the family member's documentation is weak. The defense against them is the same as the defense against any primary residence challenge: maintain a thorough, consistent paper trail showing that the apartment is your primary home.

Since the passage of the HSTPA, some practitioners have noted that landlords are somewhat less likely to challenge succession claims than they were previously. Before 2019, defeating a succession claim meant the landlord could potentially deregulate the apartment and charge market rent. After the HSTPA eliminated vacancy decontrol, the apartment remains stabilized regardless of the outcome, which reduces (though does not eliminate) the financial incentive to litigate.

Documentation: Building the Record Before You Need It

The most important advice in this chapter is also the simplest: start documenting now, before the tenant of record leaves or passes away.

Succession claims are won or lost on documentation. The family member who has a two-year paper trail showing continuous primary residence in the apartment is in a fundamentally different position than the family member who has to reconstruct their history after the fact.

To establish primary residence, maintain your voter registration at the apartment's address. File your state and federal taxes using the apartment as your home address. Keep your driver's license or state ID registered to the apartment. Maintain a bank account at a branch near the apartment. Receive mail at the apartment, including official correspondence from government agencies, financial institutions, and medical providers. Keep utility accounts in your name (or jointly with the tenant of record) at the apartment. If you have children, enroll them in schools near the apartment.

To establish the family relationship (for non-traditional family members), create and maintain joint financial accounts. Execute wills, powers of attorney, and health care proxies naming each other. File domestic partnership declarations if available. Maintain joint insurance policies or name each other as beneficiaries. Document shared expenses, shared holidays, and shared daily life. Collect photographs, correspondence, and other evidence of your relationship over time.

To protect against challenges, avoid maintaining ties to other residences that could be interpreted as your primary home. Do not register a car at another address. Do not co-sign a mortgage or lease at another address. Do not file taxes from another address. Do not vote from another address. Any of these actions can be used by a landlord to argue that the apartment is not your primary residence.

Keep all of this documentation organized and accessible. A folder (physical or digital) containing your succession evidence should be updated regularly and should be available on short notice if the tenant of record's departure is sudden or unexpected.

What Happens to the Rent After Succession

For the first succession, the successor inherits the existing legal regulated rent. The landlord may not impose a vacancy increase. The next rental increase is the RGB increase at the next lease renewal, calculated on the inherited rent.

For subsequent successions (a second family member succeeding after the first successor departs), the landlord may be entitled to collect the vacancy allowance then in effect. Before the HSTPA eliminated vacancy bonuses, this could result in a significant rent jump. Under current law, the available increases are more limited, but the rules are technical and depend on the specific circumstances.

In rent-controlled apartments, succession can result in a change in regulatory status. When a rent-controlled tenant dies or permanently vacates the apartment and a family member succeeds, the apartment may transition from rent control to rent stabilization (if the building qualifies for stabilization). The rent would be adjusted according to the applicable rules, which may include a vacancy allowance.

In all cases, the successor's rent should be verified against the apartment's rent history and the applicable regulatory framework. If the landlord attempts to charge the successor a rent that exceeds what the law allows, the successor has the same overcharge remedies available to any rent-stabilized tenant.

Pre-Succession Planning: The Form That Helps

DHCR provides a form, RA-23.5, titled "Notice to Owner of Family Members Residing With The Named Tenant In The Apartment Who May Be Entitled To Succession Rights/Protection From Eviction."

This form allows the current tenant of record to formally notify the landlord that specific family members are living in the apartment and may be entitled to succession rights in the future. The form does not prove succession rights. It does not begin the succession process. And it does not grant any rights that the family member does not already have.

What the form does is create a contemporaneous record of the family member's residence. If the landlord later challenges succession, the form establishes that the landlord was notified of the family member's presence at a specific point in time. This can be valuable in disputes about whether the family member actually lived in the apartment during the co-residency period.

However, filing this form is a strategic decision, not an automatic one. Notifying the landlord of a potential successor can invite scrutiny and, in some cases, trigger the landlord to begin building a case against the succession claim while the primary tenant is still in residence. Some tenant advocates recommend filing the form, while others recommend simply maintaining documentation without alerting the landlord.

The right approach depends on your specific circumstances. If your landlord is cooperative and the family relationship is obvious, filing the form creates a helpful record. If your landlord is adversarial and the relationship is non-traditional, alerting the landlord may provoke a challenge that could have been avoided. Consult a tenant attorney if you are uncertain.

Real-World Example: The Partner Who Stayed

A tenant in a rent-stabilized apartment on the Upper West Side had lived in the apartment for 28 years. Her partner, a woman she had been in a committed relationship with for 15 years, had lived with her for the last 12 of those years. They were not married. They were not domestic partners under any formal registration. But they shared every aspect of their lives.

They had a joint bank account. They had named each other in their wills. They had executed health care proxies designating each other as decision-makers.

They shared household expenses. They attended family events together. They were known to neighbors, friends, and the building's staff as a couple.

When the tenant of record died, her partner sent a certified letter to the landlord asserting succession rights, enclosing the death certificate and requesting that the next renewal lease be issued in her name.

The landlord rejected the claim, arguing that the partner was not a "family member" under the Rent Stabilization Code because the couple was not married and had no formal legal relationship.

The partner retained an attorney. The attorney assembled the documentation: the joint bank account statements, the wills, the health care proxies, photographs spanning more than a decade, letters from friends and family attesting to the relationship, and affidavits from neighbors and building staff who had known the couple for years.

When the landlord filed a holdover proceeding, the partner raised succession rights as a defense. The court evaluated the evidence under the non-traditional family member standard, looking at the totality of the emotional and financial interdependence between the two women.

The court found that the partner qualified as a family member. The co-residency requirement was satisfied many times over. The succession claim was valid.

The partner stayed. The rent remained regulated. The apartment that two people had shared as a home for 12 years remained a home.

The landlord had relied on a narrow definition of family. The law uses a broader one.

What to Take From This Chapter

Succession rights allow qualifying family members to inherit a rent-regulated tenancy when the tenant of record dies or permanently vacates the apartment. The successor takes over the existing rent and all stabilization protections.

"Family member" is defined broadly. It includes traditional family relationships (spouse, parent, child, sibling, grandparent, grandchild, in-law) and any person who can demonstrate emotional and financial commitment and interdependence with the tenant.

The co-residency requirement is two years of primary residence in the apartment immediately before the tenant's departure or death. The period is reduced to one year for senior citizens (62 and older) and disabled persons. There is no time requirement if the family member lived in the apartment from the inception of the tenancy or the relationship.

Assert succession rights promptly by notifying the landlord in writing by certified mail. Request that the renewal lease be issued in your name.

Landlords challenge succession claims aggressively. The most common attacks target co-residency and primary residence. Build your documentation now, before you need it.

Documentation is everything. Voter registration, tax filings, driver's license, bank accounts, utility accounts, mail delivery, joint financial documents, and evidence of the family relationship should all consistently reflect the apartment as your primary residence.

If you live with a family member in a rent-stabilized apartment and may one day need to assert succession rights, the most important thing you can do is create and maintain a paper trail that proves you live there. Start now. Update regularly. And keep the records somewhere safe.

In the next chapter, we'll examine what happens when tenants live in spaces that aren't legally classified as residential: illegal apartments, certificate of occupancy issues, and the protections that may or may not apply.

23

Illegal Apartments and Certificate of Occupancy Problems

Hundreds of thousands of New Yorkers live in spaces that are not legally classified as residential.

Basement apartments in two-family houses. Converted attics above bodegas. Former commercial spaces subdivided into bedrooms. Buildings where the certificate of occupancy says one thing and the reality says something else entirely. These apartments are often affordable, often the only option a tenant could find, and often completely invisible to the regulatory system that is supposed to protect tenants.

Living in an illegal apartment creates a unique and uncomfortable legal position. You have some protections. You lack others. Your landlord is violating the law by renting to you, but you may face consequences too, including the possibility of a government-ordered vacate that forces you out on short notice with nowhere to go.

This chapter explains what makes an apartment "illegal," which tenant protections still apply regardless of legality, which protections become complicated, what the landlord's liability is for renting a non-compliant unit, and how to evaluate the tension between your safety and your legal position.

What Makes an Apartment Illegal

An apartment is generally considered illegal when it is used for residential purposes in a manner that does not comply with the building's certificate of occupancy, the zoning code, or the housing maintenance code.

The certificate of occupancy (commonly called the CO) is the document issued by the Department of Buildings that specifies how a building may legally be used. It states how many dwelling units the building contains, what each floor may be used for, and what type of occupancy is permitted. Buildings constructed after April 18, 1929 are required to have a certificate of occupancy. Buildings built before that date may not have one, but are still subject to housing and building code requirements.

An apartment is illegal when it exists in a space the CO does not designate as residential. The most common example is a basement apartment in a one- or two-family house where the CO does not authorize residential use in the basement. Other examples include attic conversions, garage conversions, commercial-to-residential conversions without proper permits, and subdivisions of existing apartments into additional units without building department approval.

An apartment may also be functionally illegal when it exists in a space designated as residential but does not meet the minimum standards required for legal occupancy. These standards include minimum ceiling height (at least seven feet in New York City), adequate natural light and ventilation (at least one window in every habitable room), sufficient means of egress (exits that allow escape in an emergency), fire safety compliance (smoke detectors, carbon monoxide detectors, sprinklers where required), and sanitation requirements (functioning plumbing, hot and cold water, proper waste disposal).

A space can look like a perfectly reasonable apartment and still be illegal. A finished basement with a full kitchen, a bathroom, and a separate entrance may feel like a home, but if the CO does not authorize residential use in that space, the apartment is illegal regardless of how comfortable it is.

The distinction between basements and cellars matters in this context. A basement has at least half of its height above the curb level. A cellar has less than half of its height above curb level. Under New York City law, cellars in one- and two-family homes can never be lawfully rented for residential use. Basements can be lawfully rented only if they meet specific requirements for ceiling height, light, ventilation, egress, dampproofing, and occupancy, and only if the CO reflects the residential use.

How to Check Whether Your Apartment Is Legal

If you are unsure whether your apartment is legal, you can check through publicly available records.

The certificate of occupancy for any building in New York City can be searched through the Department of Buildings' BIS (Building Information System) or the DOB NOW portal at the DOB website. Enter the building's address and look for the CO. The document will list the authorized use for each floor and each unit. If your apartment does not appear on the CO, or if the space you occupy is designated for a non-residential use (storage, commercial, cellar), the apartment may be illegal.

You can also check HPD's Building Information Search, which provides information about building registrations, open violations, and complaints. If the building contains three or more apartments (counting all units, including any illegal ones), it must be registered with HPD as a multiple dwelling. If it is not registered, that itself may indicate noncompliance.

These searches do not require the landlord's permission, and they are free.

If you discover that your apartment does not appear on the CO, or that the building's configuration does not match the CO, that is important information, but it does not necessarily mean you must leave immediately. It does mean you should understand your rights and risks, which is what the rest of this chapter addresses.

Protections That Still Apply

The most important thing tenants in illegal apartments need to know is that illegality does not strip away all tenant protections. Many fundamental rights apply regardless of whether the apartment is legal.

You are still protected against illegal eviction. A landlord cannot lock you out, remove your belongings, shut off utilities, or use physical force to remove you, even if the apartment is illegal. The Unlawful Eviction Law (NYC Administrative Code Section 26-521) protects any person who has lawfully occupied a dwelling unit for 30 days or more, regardless of the unit's legal status. Self-help eviction is a crime, and tenants who are illegally locked out can call the police and obtain a court order restoring them to possession.

You are still protected by security deposit rules. The one-month cap on security deposits, the 14-day return requirement, and the prohibition on illegal deductions apply to all residential rentals, whether the apartment is legal or not. A landlord who collected a deposit on an illegal apartment must return it under the same rules that apply to any other apartment.

You still have the right to a safe living environment. While the Housing Maintenance Code technically applies to legal dwelling units, courts have consistently held that landlords who rent illegal apartments cannot escape basic safety obligations. A landlord who creates a residential tenancy, even in an illegal space, assumes some responsibility for the conditions. This principle is especially strong when the landlord knowingly rented the illegal unit and collected rent from it.

You are still protected by anti-discrimination laws. Fair housing protections apply to all housing transactions, including rentals of illegal units. A landlord who discriminates in renting, maintaining, or terminating a tenancy in an illegal apartment is still violating the law.

You may still be protected by Good Cause Eviction, depending on the circumstances. The Good Cause law applies to residential tenancies in covered buildings, and its applicability does not depend on whether the unit has a valid CO. If the building and the tenancy otherwise meet the criteria for Good Cause coverage, the protections may apply. This is an evolving area of law, and tenants in illegal units who face eviction should consult an attorney about whether Good Cause provides a defense.

Protections That Become Complicated

While basic rights survive, other protections become more difficult to enforce when the apartment is illegal.

Rent stabilization eligibility is complicated by illegality. Rent stabilization generally applies to buildings with six or more units built before 1974, or buildings receiving certain tax benefits. If the building's CO shows fewer units than actually exist (because some units are illegal and unauthorized), the question of whether the building meets the six-unit threshold becomes contested. Some courts have counted illegal units toward the threshold, reasoning that the landlord should not benefit from their own noncompliance. Others have taken a narrower view. The answer may depend on the specific facts of the building and the jurisdiction.

The warranty of habitability is technically tied to legal dwelling units. A landlord who rents an illegal apartment may argue that the warranty does not apply because the space is not a lawful dwelling. Courts have generally rejected this argument, holding that a landlord who creates a residential tenancy and collects rent cannot then deny the tenant the basic protections of that tenancy. But the issue is not as cleanly settled as it is for legal apartments, and tenants in illegal units may face additional hurdles in enforcing habitability claims.

Renewal rights may be affected. In a rent-stabilized apartment, the tenant has a statutory right to a renewal lease. But if the apartment is not recognized as a legal unit, the stabilization framework may not clearly apply. The tenant's right to remain depends on which protections are found to cover the unit, which can vary.

HP actions (housing code enforcement proceedings) are generally available only for legal dwelling units. A tenant in an illegal apartment who files an HP action may encounter the argument that Housing Court lacks jurisdiction because the space is not a lawful residence. Some judges have entertained HP actions for illegal units, particularly when conditions pose immediate health or safety risks. Others have declined jurisdiction. The outcome is unpredictable.

These complications do not mean tenants in illegal apartments have no options. They mean the options are less certain and more dependent on the specific facts. Legal advice is especially valuable in these situations.

The Landlord's Liability for Renting an Illegal Unit

A landlord who rents an illegal apartment is not an innocent participant. They are violating the law.

The Multiple Dwelling Law requires buildings with three or more residential units to be registered as multiple dwellings. A landlord who creates additional units without authorization (by converting a basement, an attic, or a commercial space) and rents those units without obtaining a proper

CO is operating an unregistered and illegal multiple dwelling. This carries significant consequences.

A landlord generally cannot collect rent on an illegal apartment. New York courts have held in multiple cases that a landlord who rents an apartment that is illegal under the Multiple Dwelling Law may be barred from collecting rent for that unit. The reasoning is that the law should not reward a landlord for profiting from their own illegal conduct. If the landlord sues for nonpayment of rent and the tenant raises the defense that the apartment is illegal, the landlord may lose the case even though rent was genuinely unpaid.

This principle is powerful but nuanced. It generally applies when the apartment's illegality is established (not just alleged), when the building qualifies as an unregistered multiple dwelling (typically three or more units including the illegal one), and when the landlord, not the tenant, created the illegal condition. The defense does not necessarily apply in every case involving an illegal apartment, and the specific facts matter.

The landlord may also face penalties from city agencies. The Department of Buildings can issue violations and fines for unauthorized construction, lack of a proper CO, and failure to comply with building codes. HPD can issue violations for failure to register a multiple dwelling and for housing maintenance code violations. And in extreme cases, the city can issue a vacate order requiring all occupants to leave the building.

The landlord's liability extends to any damages the tenant suffers as a result of the illegality. If the tenant is forced to relocate because of a vacate order issued due to the landlord's noncompliance, the tenant may have a claim against the landlord for moving costs, temporary housing expenses, and other damages arising from the displacement.

The Vacate Order: The Risk Tenants Fear Most

The most serious risk for tenants in illegal apartments is a vacate order.

A vacate order is an official directive from a city agency (usually HPD or the Department of Buildings) requiring all occupants to leave a space that is unsafe or illegal. Vacate orders can be issued after an inspection reveals that the space violates fire safety, structural, or occupancy standards, and that continued occupancy poses a risk to health or safety.

Vacate orders can be triggered by complaints from neighbors or other occupants, by inspections conducted as part of routine enforcement, by investigations following fires, floods, or other emergencies, and by referrals from other agencies (including building permit applications that reveal unauthorized units).

When a vacate order is issued, the tenant must leave. The order is not negotiable. Failure to comply can result in penalties and, in extreme cases, forced removal.

This creates the tension that makes illegal apartment situations so difficult. Tenants may know or suspect that their apartment is illegal, but they also know that reporting conditions or requesting inspections could trigger the very investigation that leads to a vacate order. The fear of losing their home keeps tenants silent about safety problems, which allows dangerous conditions to persist.

There is no clean resolution to this tension. But understanding the landscape helps tenants make informed decisions.

If conditions in the apartment are genuinely dangerous (gas leaks, structural instability, fire hazards, carbon monoxide risks), the safety concern outweighs the housing concern. Reporting those conditions may result in displacement, but the alternative is continued exposure to a life-threatening hazard. In these situations, your safety comes first.

If conditions are unpleasant but not immediately dangerous (minor leaks, cosmetic issues, inadequate maintenance), the calculus is different. Reporting may still trigger an investigation, but the risk of a vacate order is lower for conditions that do not pose immediate hazards. Filing a 311 complaint for a minor leak is less likely to result in a full building inspection than reporting a gas leak.

If you are considering reporting conditions, consult a tenant attorney first. An attorney can help you evaluate the risk, identify which enforcement tools are available without triggering a full building investigation, and prepare for the possibility of displacement if it occurs.

The Basement Legalization Pilot Program

New York City has begun addressing the illegal apartment crisis through a pilot program designed to legalize existing basement and cellar apartments in certain neighborhoods.

The Accessory Dwelling Unit (ADU) program, established under Local Law 126 of 2024 and part of the "City of Yes" housing initiative, allows eligible homeowners to legalize existing illegal basement and cellar apartments in one- and two-family homes in designated community districts. Property owners who are accepted into the program can legalize their units without penalty, provided they follow a series of steps to bring the units into full compliance with safety and building codes over a 10-year period.

The program includes important tenant protections. Tenants who occupied a qualifying basement or cellar apartment on April 20, 2024 have a right of first return if they must temporarily vacate while legalization work is performed. Owners must provide written notice to tenants about the work, including the scope, timeline, and the tenant's right to return. After the work is completed and a new certificate of occupancy is issued, the tenant has the right to return to the legalized apartment.

The program is currently limited in geographic scope and applies only to one- and two-family homes. It does not cover basement apartments in larger buildings, commercial-to-residential conversions, or other types of illegal units. But it represents a significant step toward addressing a problem that affects hundreds of thousands of New Yorkers.

If you live in a basement apartment and want to know whether the legalization program applies to your building, check with the Department of Buildings or HPD. The program may offer a path to legalization that benefits both you and the property owner.

Safety First: When to Prioritize Getting Out

Legal rights matter. But they do not matter as much as your life.

If your apartment has conditions that pose an immediate threat to your safety, the priority is getting safe, not preserving your tenancy.

Carbon monoxide risks are among the most dangerous conditions in illegal apartments, particularly basement units. Without proper ventilation, gas appliances (stoves, water heaters, furnaces) can produce carbon monoxide that accumulates in enclosed below-grade spaces. Carbon monoxide is odorless and colorless, and exposure can be fatal. If you live in a basement apartment with gas appliances and no carbon monoxide detector, install one immediately. If the detector alarms, leave the apartment and call 911.

Fire safety is another critical concern. Illegal apartments often lack the egress (exit routes) required by code. A basement apartment with one exit that leads through the main house may trap occupants in a fire. Check whether your apartment has at least two means of egress, including a window large enough for an adult to escape through.

Flooding is a persistent risk in below-grade apartments. Basement and cellar units are vulnerable to flooding during heavy rain, and the consequences can be fatal. Several tenants in illegal basement apartments in New York City have died during severe storms when their apartments flooded rapidly and they could not escape. If your apartment floods during heavy rain, or if you notice water intrusion during storms, take the risk seriously. Do not stay in a below-grade apartment during severe weather warnings if the unit has a history of flooding.

Structural issues (cracked foundations, sagging ceilings, unstable walls) may indicate that the space was not designed to support residential use. If you notice structural changes (new cracks, doors that no longer close properly, floors that feel uneven), have the conditions evaluated. These may be signs of structural failure that could worsen suddenly.

The hardest decision a tenant in an illegal apartment faces is whether to leave a home they can afford for a safer situation they may not be able to find. There is no legal framework that makes that decision easy. But the law provides remedies for displacement (claims against the landlord, emergency housing assistance, relocation support) that do not exist for injury or death. Safety first, always.

Real-World Example: The Apartment That Wasn't on the Books

A tenant rented a basement apartment in a two-family house in East Flatbush. The apartment had a full kitchen, a bathroom, a bedroom, and a separate entrance. The rent was affordable. The landlord was friendly. Everything seemed normal.

Two years into the tenancy, the city received a complaint about the building (filed by a neighbor, not the tenant). An HPD inspector visited and discovered that the basement apartment did not appear on the building's certificate of occupancy. The CO authorized a two-family dwelling with no basement unit. The basement apartment was an illegal third unit, making the building an unregistered multiple dwelling.

HPD issued violations to the landlord. The Department of Buildings followed up with an inspection of its own and found that the basement ceiling height was six feet eight inches, below the seven-foot minimum. The apartment also lacked a second means of egress.

A vacate order was issued. The tenant had 30 days to leave.

The tenant was devastated. The apartment had been her home for two years. She had paid rent reliably, maintained the apartment well, and had no other housing options lined up.

She consulted a legal services attorney. The attorney helped her pursue two remedies. First, she filed a claim against the landlord for her security deposit, relocation costs, and the difference between her rent and the cost of temporary housing. Because the landlord had knowingly rented an illegal apartment, the landlord bore liability for the tenant's displacement. Second, the attorney connected her with emergency housing resources through the city's shelter and rehousing system.

The tenant recovered her security deposit, a portion of her relocation costs, and found a new apartment within six weeks. The outcome was not what she wanted, but it was better than it would have been if she had not known her rights.

The landlord, meanwhile, faced fines from both DOB and HPD, and could not legally re-rent the basement until it was brought into compliance with the building code and a new certificate of occupancy was issued.

The tenant had done nothing wrong. She rented what looked like a normal apartment. The landlord had rented a space the law did not authorize for residential use. When the system caught up with the landlord, the tenant bore the immediate burden, but the law provided tools to shift that burden back.

What to Take From This Chapter

An apartment is illegal when it does not comply with the building's certificate of occupancy, the zoning code, or the housing maintenance code. The most common illegal apartments are basement and cellar units, attic conversions, and unauthorized subdivisions.

Many tenant protections still apply to illegal apartments, including protection against illegal eviction, security deposit rules, and anti-discrimination protections. The landlord cannot use the apartment's illegality as a license to violate the tenant's basic rights.

Some protections become complicated in illegal apartments, including rent stabilization eligibility, the warranty of habitability, renewal rights, and access to HP actions. Legal advice is especially valuable in these situations.

Landlords who rent illegal apartments may be barred from collecting rent, may face fines and violations from city agencies, and may be liable for damages if the tenant is displaced.

Vacate orders are the most serious risk for tenants in illegal apartments. They require immediate departure and cannot be negotiated.

Safety concerns in illegal apartments, particularly carbon monoxide, fire egress, flooding, and structural issues, can be life-threatening. When safety is at risk, getting out is more important than preserving the tenancy.

If you live in an apartment that may be illegal, check the certificate of occupancy, understand your rights, and consult a tenant attorney if you face enforcement action, displacement, or unsafe conditions.

In the next chapter, we'll examine landlord claims of exemption, including small landlord status and owner-occupied buildings, and why "exempt" rarely means what landlords say it means.

Part VIII: The Endgame: Buyouts, Negotiation & Strategy

Buyouts, Negotiation & Strategy

24

Small Landlords, Owner-Occupied Buildings and Exemptions

One of the most effective landlord arguments in New York housing disputes is also one of the vaguest: "I'm exempt."

Tenants hear variations constantly. Small landlord. Owner-occupied. Family building. Not regulated. These labels are presented as conversation-enders, implying that tenant protections simply don't apply and that the tenant has no recourse, no leverage, and no choice but to accept whatever the landlord demands.

In reality, exemptions in New York are narrow, fact-specific, and frequently misapplied. Being a small landlord does not erase tenant rights. Owner-occupied does not mean unregulated. And claiming an exemption without proof is not the same as having one.

This chapter explains when exemptions actually apply, how landlords misclassify buildings, how tenants investigate and challenge exemption claims, and why "exempt" almost never means "no tenant rights."

Why Exemptions Exist

Exemptions exist because the legislature recognized that not all landlord-tenant relationships are the same.

A corporation that owns 500 apartments across ten buildings operates differently than an individual who rents out the second floor of a house they live in. The regulatory burden that is appropriate for the first may be disproportionate for the second. Exemptions attempt to draw lines between these situations, reducing obligations for certain categories of landlords or buildings while preserving protections for the broader tenant population.

The problem is that exemptions are frequently over-claimed. Landlords assert exemptions they don't qualify for, mischaracterize their buildings to avoid regulation, and present partial exemptions as blanket immunity. Tenants, lacking the tools to verify the claim, accept it.

Understanding what exemptions actually do, and what they don't do, is the first step toward knowing whether the landlord's claim holds up.

Rent Stabilization Exemptions

Rent stabilization is the most common regulatory system from which landlords claim exemption. As Chapter 4 explained, stabilization generally applies to buildings with six or more units constructed before 1974, and to buildings that received certain tax benefits regardless of age.

An apartment may be genuinely exempt from rent stabilization if the building was constructed in 1974 or later and did not receive tax benefits that triggered stabilization, if the building contains fewer than six residential units and did not receive tax benefits, if the building is a co-op or condominium (with exceptions for certain tenants in place at the time of conversion), if the apartment is in a building where a tax benefit (such as 421-a) has expired and the conditions for continued stabilization have been lawfully met, or if the apartment was lawfully deregulated before the HSTPA eliminated vacancy decontrol (though many pre-HSTPA deregulations are now being challenged as improper).

Each of these exemptions depends on specific facts about the building, its history, and its regulatory status. None of them is established by the landlord's assertion alone. They must be demonstrated with evidence.

An important principle applies to all stabilization exemptions: the HSTPA eliminated vacancy decontrol. Since June 2019, apartments can no longer be deregulated by reaching a high-rent threshold. Any stabilization exemption based solely on the rent exceeding a former deregulation threshold should be scrutinized carefully, because the mechanism that created the exemption no longer exists for units that were still stabilized when the HSTPA took effect.

If your landlord claims the apartment is exempt from rent stabilization, request the rent history from DHCR. The records will show whether the apartment was ever registered as stabilized and, if so, whether it was lawfully deregulated. Chapter 5 explains this process in detail.

Good Cause Eviction Exemptions

The Good Cause Eviction Law, effective since April 2024, introduced its own set of exemptions that are now among the most frequently asserted and most frequently misunderstood.

An apartment may be exempt from Good Cause if it was built after 2009 (specifically, if the temporary or permanent certificate of occupancy was issued on or after January 1, 2009). This exemption lasts for 30 years from the date the CO was issued. After 30 years, the apartment becomes subject to Good Cause.

An apartment may be exempt if it is in an owner-occupied building with 10 or fewer units (or fewer than 5 units in some opt-in municipalities outside New York City). This is the exemption that generates the most confusion and the most abuse, and it is discussed in detail later in this chapter.

An apartment may be exempt if the landlord is a "small landlord," defined as someone who owns no more than 10 residential units total in New York State. This definition applies to individual natural persons, not to entities. If the building is owned by an LLC, the 10-unit threshold applies to any individual person who holds an ownership interest in the LLC. A person who owns a 20-unit building through an LLC is not a small landlord, regardless of how the ownership is structured.

An apartment may be exempt if the rent exceeds 245 percent of the Fair Market Rent for the unit size in the applicable area. In New York City, this threshold currently exceeds $6,000 per month for a one-bedroom apartment, meaning the vast majority of apartments are below the threshold and are covered.

An apartment may be exempt if it is already subject to rent stabilization, rent control, or another form of government-mandated rent or income restriction. These apartments are exempt from Good Cause because they already have protections that are generally stronger than what Good Cause provides.

An apartment may be exempt if it is in a co-op, a condo, a manufactured home, a school dormitory, or public housing.

An apartment may be exempt if it was provided to the tenant as part of an employment arrangement.

Each of these exemptions is defined by specific criteria, and the landlord bears the burden of proving them. Since August 2024, landlords have been required to provide tenants with a written Good Cause notice stating whether the apartment is covered and, if not, explaining the basis for the claimed exemption. If the landlord has not provided this notice, that is itself a violation that may be raised in court.

The Owner-Occupied Exemption: Not a Blank Check

The owner-occupied exemption is the most commonly asserted and most commonly misunderstood exemption in New York tenant law.

Under the Good Cause law, buildings with 10 or fewer units where the owner lives in the building are exempt from Good Cause protections. This means the landlord does not need to prove good cause to terminate a tenancy or to impose a rent increase.

But the exemption is narrower than it sounds, and it does not eliminate all tenant protections.

First, the owner must actually live in the building. This means primary residence, not occasional visits, not a mailing address, not an intention to move in someday. An owner who claims to live in the building but actually lives elsewhere does not qualify for the exemption.

Second, the unit count matters. The building must contain 10 or fewer residential units (or fewer in some municipalities). If the building has 11 or more units, the exemption does not apply regardless of whether the owner lives there.

Third, the exemption applies to Good Cause only. It does not exempt the building from rent stabilization (which has its own, separate criteria). It does not exempt the landlord from security deposit rules, the warranty of habitability, anti-discrimination protections, notice period requirements under RPL 226-c, anti-retaliation protections, or the prohibition on self-help eviction. The owner-occupied exemption removes one layer of protection. It does not remove all of them.

Fourth, the exemption must be proved, not just asserted. In court, the landlord bears the burden of demonstrating that they live in the building and that the building has 10 or fewer units. If the landlord cannot meet this burden, the exemption fails and Good Cause protections apply.

Landlords frequently overstate the owner-occupied exemption. They say "I live in the building, so tenant protections don't apply." In fact, tenant protections do apply. Good Cause may not, but the dozens of other protections described throughout this book remain fully in effect.

The "Small Landlord" Misnomer

"Small landlord" is not a universal legal category that reduces all tenant protections. It is a specific defined term under the Good Cause Eviction Law, and its scope is limited to that law.

Under Good Cause, a small landlord is a natural person who owns no more than 10 residential units in total across New York State. This includes units in all buildings the person owns, not just the building where the tenant lives. A person who owns one four-unit building and one seven-unit building owns 11 units and is not a small landlord.

If the building is owned by an entity (an LLC, a corporation, a partnership, or a trust), the small landlord exemption applies only if every individual person with an ownership interest in the entity owns no more than 10 units total. This is designed to prevent landlords from structuring ownership through entities to artificially reduce their unit count.

When a landlord claims the small landlord exemption in court, they may be required to disclose the name of every owner behind the LLC and the addresses of all buildings they own. This disclosure requirement was built into the Good Cause law specifically because LLC ownership structures make it easy for landlords to obscure how many units they actually control.

The small landlord exemption, like the owner-occupied exemption, applies only to Good Cause. It does not exempt the landlord from any other tenant protection: not rent stabilization, not security deposit rules, not notice requirements, not habitability obligations, not anti-retaliation protections, and not the prohibition on illegal eviction.

A landlord who says "I'm a small landlord, so the law doesn't apply to me" is making a claim that is, at best, partially true. The Good Cause law may not apply. Everything else still does.

What Exemptions Do Not Eliminate

This point cannot be overemphasized: even when an exemption is valid, it usually applies to a single regulatory framework, not to the entire body of tenant law.

A tenant in an apartment that is exempt from both rent stabilization and Good Cause still has the right to a security deposit no greater than one month's rent, with a 14-day return deadline and itemization requirements. They still have the warranty of habitability. They still have the right to reasonable notice before the landlord enters the apartment. They still have protection against illegal eviction (lockouts, utility shutoffs, removal of belongings). They still have the right to the 30/60/90-day notice before non-renewal or a rent increase of 5 percent or more, based on length of tenancy. They still have protection against retaliation for exercising their legal rights. They still have protection against discrimination under federal, state, and city human rights laws. And they still have the right to file complaints with HPD, the Attorney General's office, and other enforcement agencies.

An exempt apartment is not a lawless apartment. The exemption removes specific protections from specific regulatory systems. The baseline protections that apply to all residential tenancies in New York remain in full effect.

How Landlords Misclassify Buildings

Landlords misclassify buildings for the same reason they selectively quote the law: because tenants are unlikely to verify the claim.

Common misclassifications include the following patterns.

A landlord claims the building has fewer than six units to avoid rent stabilization, when in fact the building contains six or more units (sometimes because the landlord has not counted basement apartments, superintendent apartments, or units that were previously combined but still exist as separate units on the CO). A proper count of all residential units, including those that may not be currently rented, determines whether the stabilization threshold is met.

A landlord claims owner occupancy when the owner does not actually live in the building. The owner may have lived there at one time and moved out. The owner may have a mailing address at the building but a primary residence elsewhere. The owner may be a corporate entity that cannot "live" in a building at all.

A landlord claims small landlord status when the total unit count across all properties exceeds 10. This is particularly common with LLC-owned buildings, where the landlord assumes the unit count applies only to the specific building rather than to all units owned by any individual with an ownership interest.

A landlord claims the building was constructed after 2009 when it was actually built earlier and renovated. The post-2009 exemption applies to buildings that received their certificate of occupancy on or after January 1, 2009. A building constructed in 1960 and renovated in 2015 is not a post-2009 building, even if a new CO was issued for the renovation. The exemption is based on when the building was originally constructed for the purpose of residential use.

A landlord claims deregulation based on pre-HSTPA rules that no longer apply. Before 2019, high-rent vacancy decontrol allowed apartments to leave the stabilization system. After the HSTPA, that mechanism was eliminated. A landlord who claims deregulation based on a vacancy that occurred before the HSTPA may or may not be correct, depending on whether the deregulation was lawful at the time. A landlord who claims deregulation based on a post-HSTPA vacancy is wrong.

Each of these misclassifications can be investigated and challenged by the tenant. The tools for doing so are publicly available.

How Tenants Investigate Exemption Claims

Exemption claims leave records. Tenants who know where to look can often determine whether a landlord's claim is accurate before the dispute reaches court.

Check the certificate of occupancy. The CO shows the building's configuration, including the number of authorized residential units and the date of construction. You can search for the CO through the Department of Buildings' online portal.

Check the rent history. Request the apartment's rent history from DHCR (as described in Chapter 5). If the apartment was ever registered as rent-stabilized, the registration history will show it. If stabilization was claimed to have ended, the records will show when and on what basis.

Check HPD's building registration. Buildings with three or more residential units must be registered with HPD as multiple dwellings. If the building is registered, the registration will show the number of units, the owner's name and address, and the managing agent's contact information. If the building is not registered but appears to contain three or more units, the landlord may be operating an unregistered multiple dwelling, which creates its own set of legal consequences.

Check property records. The New York City Department of Finance maintains publicly searchable records that show building ownership, tax lot information, and building classification. The ACRIS (Automated City Register Information System) database allows you to search for deeds, mortgages, and ownership transfers. These records can help determine who actually owns the building, whether the ownership is through an LLC, and whether the owner's claimed residence matches public records.

Check the Department of Buildings for permits and construction history. If the landlord claims the building was constructed after 2009, the DOB records will show when the original certificate of occupancy was issued. If the landlord claims extensive renovations that justify some regulatory position, the permit history will show what work was actually authorized and performed.

Talk to other tenants in the building. Neighbors may have information about the building's history, the landlord's residence, and whether other tenants have been told the same or different things about their regulatory status.

These searches take time but not money. They are available to any tenant, and they often reveal that the landlord's exemption claim does not match the facts.

Does This Exemption Apply to My Apartment?

The following framework walks through the most common exemption claims and helps you determine whether the claim is likely valid. This is a simplified guide, not legal advice. If the stakes are high (an eviction, a major rent increase, or a dispute about your apartment's regulatory status), consult a tenant attorney.

Start with rent stabilization.

Was the building constructed before 1974? If yes, does it contain six or more residential units? If both answers are yes, the building is likely subject to rent stabilization unless a specific exemption applies (such as an expired tax benefit). Request the rent history to confirm.

If the building was constructed in 1974 or later, did it receive a 421-a, J-51, or other tax benefit that triggered stabilization? If yes, the apartments are stabilized for the duration of the benefit period (and possibly beyond, depending on the program). Check HPD and DOF records for tax benefit status.

If the building does not meet either criterion, it is likely not subject to rent stabilization.

Next, check Good Cause Eviction.

Is the apartment in New York City or a municipality that has opted into Good Cause? If yes, proceed. If no, Good Cause does not currently apply.

Was the building's certificate of occupancy issued on or after January 1, 2009? If yes, the apartment is exempt from Good Cause for 30 years from the date of the CO.

Is the building owner-occupied with 10 or fewer units? If yes, verify that the owner actually lives in the building as their primary residence. If they do, the apartment may be exempt from Good Cause.

Is the landlord a "small landlord" (a natural person who owns 10 or fewer residential units total in New York State)? If yes, verify the total unit count across all properties, including those held through LLCs. If the total exceeds 10, the exemption does not apply.

Is the rent above 245 percent of the Fair Market Rent for the unit size? If yes, the apartment is exempt from Good Cause. The threshold for a one-bedroom in New York City is currently above $6,000 per month.

Is the apartment already subject to rent stabilization, rent control, or another form of government rent or income restriction? If yes, it is exempt from Good Cause because it already has stronger protections.

If the apartment is not exempt under any of these criteria, Good Cause protections apply.

Finally, regardless of the answers above, confirm that baseline protections remain.

Even if the apartment is exempt from both rent stabilization and Good Cause, the tenant retains the security deposit cap (one month's rent), the warranty of habitability, the 30/60/90-day notice requirement for non-renewal or rent increases above 5 percent, protection against illegal eviction, protection against retaliation, protection against discrimination, and the right to file complaints with government agencies.

An exempt apartment is never an unprotected apartment. The question is which layers of protection apply, not whether any do.

Real-World Example: The Exemption That Didn't Exist

A tenant rented an apartment in a six-unit building in Flatbush. The landlord, an individual who also lived in the building, told the tenant the apartment was exempt from both rent stabilization and Good Cause because it was an "owner-occupied small building."

The tenant accepted this explanation for two years. During that time, the landlord raised the rent twice without following any formal process, once by $200 and once by $150. No written notice was provided for either increase. No Good Cause disclosure was ever given.

When the tenant questioned the second increase, the landlord repeated the exemption claim and said tenant protections "don't apply here."

The tenant investigated. She checked the Department of Buildings records and confirmed the building was constructed in 1962 and contained six residential units. She requested the rent history from DHCR. The records showed that the building had been registered as rent-stabilized for decades, and that her apartment had a rent history going back to the 1980s.

The building was rent-stabilized. It had always been rent-stabilized. The landlord's claim that it was exempt was wrong.

The six-unit threshold for stabilization was met. The owner-occupied exemption under Good Cause was irrelevant because the apartment was covered by rent stabilization, which provides stronger protections. And the rent increases the landlord had imposed without renewal leases were unlawful.

The tenant filed an overcharge complaint. DHCR confirmed the apartment's stabilized status. The rent was reduced to the correct legal amount. The tenant recovered the excess she had paid.

The landlord had not been lying in the sense of fabricating a claim from nothing. The landlord lived in the building. It was a relatively small building. But the landlord's understanding of what those facts meant legally was wrong, and the tenant's reliance on that understanding cost her hundreds of dollars per month for two years.

The exemption didn't exist. The tenant's rights did.

What to Take From This Chapter

Exemptions in New York tenant law are narrow, fact-specific, and must be proved by the landlord. An assertion of exemption is not proof of exemption.

Rent stabilization exemptions depend on building age, unit count, and tax benefit history. The HSTPA eliminated vacancy decontrol, making many pre-2019 deregulation claims subject to challenge.

Good Cause exemptions depend on building age, owner occupancy, landlord size, rent level, and existing regulatory status. Each criterion is defined specifically and must be verified.

Owner-occupied and small landlord exemptions apply only to Good Cause. They do not eliminate any other tenant protection.

Even fully exempt apartments retain baseline protections: security deposit caps, habitability, notice requirements, anti-retaliation, anti-discrimination, and the prohibition on illegal eviction.

Landlords frequently overstate exemptions. Tenants can investigate claims through public records: the certificate of occupancy, DHCR rent history, HPD building registration, and property ownership records.

If your landlord says the law doesn't apply to them, the right response is not "Oh, okay." It's "Show me how the statute actually says that."

In the next chapter, we'll move to the endgame: buyouts, cash-for-keys deals, and why many tenant waivers don't hold up when tested.

25

Buyouts, Cash-for-Keys and Tenant Waivers

When landlords can't raise the rent or evict easily, they often try something else: paying tenants to leave.

Buyouts, commonly called "cash for keys" deals, are legal in New York. They happen every day, in every borough, across every type of building. Some are genuinely fair. Some are life-changing opportunities that give tenants the financial flexibility to move on their own terms. And some are coercive, rushed, misleading, or structured to extract maximum value from the tenant's ignorance about what they're giving up.

The difference between a good buyout and a bad one is almost never the dollar amount on the first offer. It is whether the tenant understands the value of what they hold, whether the process was conducted lawfully, and whether the agreement protects the tenant as thoroughly as it protects the landlord.

This chapter explains when buyouts are regulated, what landlords are required to disclose, how to evaluate an offer using real financial analysis, when and how to counteroffer, what terms to insist on beyond the check, and why many tenant waivers collapse once they are examined closely.

What a Buyout Actually Is

A buyout is an agreement in which a tenant accepts money (or other consideration) in exchange for voluntarily vacating the apartment and surrendering their tenancy rights.

The landlord's motivation is straightforward. In rent-regulated apartments, the tenant's rent is often far below market. As long as the tenant stays, the landlord collects less than the apartment is worth on the open market. Eviction requires just cause, and the permissible grounds are narrow and difficult to prove. A buyout allows the landlord to achieve through negotiation what they cannot achieve through litigation: a vacant apartment that can be rented at a higher price or sold without an encumbrance.

For the tenant, the calculus is more complex. The apartment may be their most valuable financial asset, even though they don't own it. The below-market rent represents a benefit that can be worth tens of thousands of dollars per year. Giving it up permanently, in exchange for a lump sum, is a decision with long-term financial consequences that many tenants do not fully appreciate in the moment.

Buyouts can be opportunities. A tenant who is planning to move anyway, who has found better housing, who is aging out of a walk-up they can no longer manage, or who simply wants cash to start a new chapter may find a buyout genuinely beneficial. The key is that the decision must be informed, voluntary, and made with full understanding of what is being surrendered.

When Buyouts Are Regulated

Buyouts are not always informal, handshake deals. In many situations, they are regulated by law, and the landlord must follow specific procedures designed to protect tenants from coercion.

In New York City, Local Law 1 of 2015 established comprehensive buyout disclosure requirements for rent-regulated apartments. Under this law, any offer by a landlord to buy out a tenant in a rent-regulated apartment must comply with formal procedures.

The landlord must provide the offer in writing. Verbal offers, casual conversations, and informal suggestions do not satisfy the requirement. The written offer creates a record and gives the tenant time to evaluate it.

The written offer must include specific disclosures, including a statement that the tenant has the right to remain in the apartment, a statement that the tenant is not required to accept the buyout offer, a statement that the tenant may seek independent legal advice, a statement that the tenant may reject the offer without penalty or retaliation, and disclosure of the tenant's rent-regulated status and the protections that status provides.

These disclosures must be provided in the tenant's primary language if reasonably ascertainable.

The tenant must be given a minimum period to consider the offer. The law provides a cooling-off period, during which the tenant may review the offer, consult an attorney, and make an informed decision. The tenant may also rescind (cancel) the agreement within a specified period after signing.

If these procedures are not followed, the buyout agreement may be voidable. An agreement signed without the required disclosures, without adequate time for consideration, or under pressure that negated the tenant's ability to make a free choice may not hold up when challenged.

Outside of rent-regulated apartments, buyouts are less formally regulated. But even in unregulated or Good Cause-covered apartments, the principles of voluntary consent, freedom from coercion, and accuracy of information apply. A buyout obtained through misrepresentation or duress is vulnerable regardless of the regulatory framework.

The Disclosure Requirements in Detail

The disclosure requirements under Local Law 1 deserve careful attention, because their absence is one of the most common reasons buyout agreements fail.

The first required disclosure is that the tenant has the right to remain in the apartment. This sounds obvious, but many landlords present buyout offers in a way that implies the tenant must leave eventually, that the offer is a kindness rather than a negotiation, or that the alternative to accepting is something worse (eviction, harassment, litigation). The disclosure corrects this by reminding the tenant, in writing, that staying is an option.

The second required disclosure is that the tenant is not required to accept. Again, this seems obvious, but the framing of many buyout offers suggests otherwise. Landlords may say things like "this is your best option" or "we really need the apartment" or "this offer won't be available later." The disclosure ensures the tenant understands that "no" is a complete answer.

The third required disclosure is that the tenant may consult an attorney. Many tenants do not realize they can get legal advice about buyouts, or they assume legal advice is prohibitively expensive. The disclosure reminds them that the option exists. In many cases, tenant legal services organizations will review buyout offers for free.

The fourth required disclosure is that the tenant may reject the offer without retaliation. This addresses the fear described in Chapter 19: that saying no will lead to punishment. The disclosure makes explicit what the law already requires, that retaliation for rejecting a buyout is illegal.

The fifth required disclosure is a description of the tenant's rent-regulated status and the rights that status provides. This is the disclosure landlords are least likely to include and most likely to misstate. A tenant who does not understand what rent stabilization means, what renewal rights they have, and what their apartment is worth over time cannot make an informed decision about whether to give it up. The disclosure is designed to ensure the tenant has that understanding before they sign.

Agreements signed without these disclosures are vulnerable. The absence of even one required disclosure may be sufficient to void the agreement, depending on the circumstances and the court.

How to Evaluate a Buyout Offer: The Real Math

The most common mistake tenants make when evaluating a buyout offer is comparing the offer to their current financial situation rather than to the long-term value of what they are giving up.

A $50,000 buyout offer sounds like a lot of money. But if the tenant's rent-stabilized apartment saves them $1,500 per month compared to market-rate alternatives, that $50,000 represents roughly 33 months of the rent differential. After less than three years, the tenant would have been better off staying.

The right way to evaluate a buyout is to calculate the value of the tenancy over time and compare it to the offer. Here is how to think through that calculation.

Start with the rent differential. Determine the difference between your current rent and the market rent for a comparable apartment in the same neighborhood. If you pay $1,600 and comparable market-rate apartments rent for $3,200, the monthly differential is $1,600. Annualized, that is $19,200 per year.

Project the differential over time. Consider how long you expect to remain in the apartment. If you plan to stay for five more years, the total value of the rent differential is roughly $96,000 (before accounting for future rent increases, which would widen the gap further since RGB increases in stabilized apartments are typically much smaller than market-rate increases). If you plan to stay for ten years, the total exceeds $192,000.

Add the value of renewal rights. In a rent-stabilized apartment, you have the right to renew indefinitely. This right has value because it protects you from displacement and from market-rate rent for as long as you live there. Succession rights may also extend the value of the apartment to a qualifying family member. These are rights that, once surrendered, cannot be recovered.

Add relocation costs. Moving in New York is expensive. Calculate the costs of moving itself (movers, truck rental, packing materials), the broker fee for a new apartment (if applicable), the security deposit on the new apartment, any overlap in rent if you need to pay for both apartments simultaneously, and the time and productivity lost to the relocation process.

Consider the tax implications. Buyout payments may be taxable as ordinary income. A $100,000 buyout may net significantly less after federal, state, and city income taxes. Consult a tax professional before signing.

Consider the non-financial costs. Displacement from your neighborhood, disruption to children's schooling, loss of proximity to work or medical care, separation from a community you've built over years. These factors are real, even if they don't have a dollar value.

After doing this analysis, many tenants discover that the landlord's initial offer represents a fraction of what the tenancy is worth. This does not mean every buyout should be rejected. It means every buyout should be evaluated against the real numbers, not against the emotional impact of a large check.

When to Counteroffer

Most initial buyout offers are low. This is by design. Landlords start low because some tenants accept immediately, and because the initial offer establishes a floor for negotiation. Very few tenants who receive a first offer should accept it without negotiation.

Counteroffering makes sense when the rent differential analysis shows the tenancy is worth significantly more than the offer, when you are willing to move but want compensation that reflects the true value of what you are giving up, when you have time and are not under immediate pressure, and when you have consulted an attorney or tenant advocate who can help you assess the negotiation dynamics.

Counteroffering does not make sense when you have already decided to move regardless of the offer (in which case any buyout is a bonus), when the landlord's offer is genuinely fair based on your analysis, or when the negotiation has reached a point where further pushing is unlikely to yield meaningful improvement.

When you counteroffer, be specific. State a number. Explain the basis for the number (rent differential, relocation costs, length of tenancy, succession value). A counteroffer supported by reasoning is more credible than one that is simply higher.

Do not feel pressured by artificial deadlines. Landlords often present buyout offers as time-limited: "This offer expires on Friday" or "We can only hold this amount for two weeks." These deadlines are almost always negotiable. A landlord who wants your apartment will not withdraw a genuine offer because you took time to evaluate it. If they do withdraw, the offer was either not genuine or will be renewed later at a higher amount.

Do not feel pressured by threats. A landlord who combines a buyout offer with threats of eviction, suggestions of future harassment, or implications that your tenancy will become difficult is crossing a legal line. Coercive buyout practices are illegal, and documentation of these threats strengthens your position.

What to Negotiate Beyond the Dollar Amount

The check is not the only thing that matters in a buyout. The terms of the agreement determine whether the buyout works for you in practice, not just on paper.

The timeline for vacating should give you adequate time to find a new apartment, sign a lease, arrange movers, and transfer utilities. In New York's competitive rental market, this can take months. Insist on a timeline that is realistic, not one that suits the landlord's renovation schedule.

Moving costs should be covered separately from the buyout amount. Moving in New York can cost $1,000 to $5,000 or more depending on the distance and the amount of belongings. The landlord should bear this cost, either as a direct payment or as a reimbursement upon submission of receipts.

A neutral reference should be included. Some tenants worry that a landlord who wanted them out will provide negative references to future landlords. The agreement should include a clause stating that the landlord will provide a neutral or positive reference to any future landlord who inquires, confirming that the tenant was in good standing and left voluntarily.

A mutual release of claims protects both parties. The landlord releases any claims against the tenant (for back rent, alleged damages, lease violations). The tenant releases any claims against the landlord (for overcharges, harassment, deposit disputes). This mutual release prevents either side from using the buyout as a springboard for future litigation.

The agreement should specify the payment method and timing. A cashier's check or wire transfer at or before the time of vacating is standard. Avoid agreements where the payment is made after you leave, or where payment is conditioned on an inspection the landlord controls.

The agreement should be in writing, signed by both parties, and ideally reviewed by an attorney before signing. An oral buyout agreement is difficult to enforce and offers no protection if either side disputes the terms later.

Consider whether you want a confidentiality clause. Some landlords include clauses preventing the tenant from disclosing the buyout terms to other tenants. These clauses benefit the landlord (who does not want other tenants to know what they might get) and have limited value to the tenant. You may agree to confidentiality, but understand that doing so helps the landlord's negotiating position with your neighbors.

Pressure Tactics That Undermine Buyouts

Buyouts often fail not because of the amount offered but because of how they are obtained.

The most common pressure tactics include surprise offers with artificial deadlines designed to prevent the tenant from consulting an attorney or thinking clearly, statements that eviction is inevitable and the buyout is the tenant's only realistic option, threats of increased scrutiny, code enforcement, or nonrenewal if the tenant rejects the offer, discouraging the tenant from seeking legal advice by framing lawyers as expensive or unnecessary, misrepresenting the tenant's rights (telling a stabilized tenant they have no right to remain, or telling a Good Cause tenant that the law doesn't apply to their building), and repeated offers after the tenant has declined, particularly when combined with other harassing conduct.

Each of these tactics is a red flag. Some are independently illegal (retaliation, harassment, misrepresentation). Others undermine the voluntariness of the agreement, which is required for the buyout to be enforceable.

If you experience any of these tactics, document them. Save every communication. Note dates, times, and the identity of everyone present. This documentation serves dual purposes: it protects you if you ultimately reject the offer and face retaliation, and it creates grounds to challenge the agreement if you accept it and later discover you were misled.

Why Many Tenant Waivers Don't Hold Up

When a tenant signs a buyout agreement, they are waiving rights. The waiver is the core of the deal: in exchange for money, you give up the right to remain, the right to a renewal lease, the right to regulated rent, and potentially the right to bring future claims against the landlord.

But waivers are not unlimited, and courts scrutinize them carefully, particularly when the tenant is giving up rights they may not fully understand.

Waivers may fail when they contradict statutory protections that cannot be waived by agreement. Certain rights under the Rent Stabilization Code are non-waivable regardless of what the tenant signs. If the waiver purports to eliminate a right the tenant cannot legally give up, the waiver is unenforceable as to that right.

Waivers may fail when required disclosures were missing or misleading. If the landlord did not provide the disclosures required under Local Law 1, or if the disclosures contained inaccurate information about the tenant's rights, the agreement was not the product of informed consent.

Waivers may fail when the tenant was misinformed about their rights. A tenant who signed a buyout believing their apartment was not rent-stabilized (because the landlord said so) may challenge the waiver when they discover the apartment was stabilized all along. The waiver was based on a false premise.

Waivers may fail when the agreement violates public policy. Courts may refuse to enforce agreements that serve to perpetuate illegal conduct, such as a buyout designed to cover up an overcharge scheme or to circumvent anti-harassment protections.

Waivers may fail when they were signed under duress or coercion. A tenant who signed because the landlord threatened eviction, reduced services, or created an atmosphere of fear did not act voluntarily. Courts look at the totality of the circumstances surrounding the signing.

Signing an agreement does not end the analysis. Courts look at substance over form. The question is not just "Did the tenant sign?" but "Did the tenant understand what they were giving up, and was the decision genuinely voluntary?"

Timing Matters More Than Tenants Realize

Many tenants believe that once they move out and accept the money, everything is final. This is not always true.

If a buyout was improper, remedies may still exist after the tenant has vacated. The rescission period under Local Law 1 allows tenants to cancel the agreement within a specified time after signing. Even outside the formal rescission period, agreements obtained through fraud, misrepresentation, or coercion can be challenged.

Delay weakens claims. Evidence fades, witnesses become unavailable, and courts are less sympathetic to tenants who wait years to challenge an agreement. But improper buyouts do not become legal simply because time passes. A buyout based on missing disclosures or false representations about the tenant's rights carries those defects permanently.

If you signed a buyout agreement and later discovered that the process was improper, that your apartment was stabilized when you were told it wasn't, or that the landlord misrepresented your rights, consult an attorney. The claim may still be viable.

Real-World Example: The Offer That Became a Fair Deal

A tenant in a rent-stabilized apartment in the West Village received a buyout offer of $75,000. The landlord framed it as generous, noting that it was "more than a year's rent." The landlord's representative urged the tenant to accept quickly, suggesting the offer might not be available later.

The tenant consulted a tenant attorney through a legal services organization. The attorney helped the tenant analyze the offer.

The tenant's stabilized rent was $1,400 per month. Comparable market-rate apartments in the neighborhood rented for approximately $4,200. The monthly rent differential was $2,800, or $33,600 per year. The tenant was 45 years old, in good health, and planned to stay in New York indefinitely. Over ten years, the rent differential alone would exceed $336,000. Over twenty years, it would approach $700,000, not counting the compounding effect of smaller RGB increases versus larger market-rate increases.

The $75,000 offer represented roughly 27 months of the rent differential. After that period, the tenant would be paying market rent with no regulatory protection, and the financial advantage of the stabilized apartment would be gone.

The attorney helped the tenant prepare a counteroffer. The counteroffer was $350,000, supported by a written analysis of the rent differential, projected over the tenant's expected remaining tenancy. The counteroffer also included terms for moving costs (up to $5,000 reimbursed on receipts), a 90-day vacating timeline, a mutual release of claims, a neutral reference clause, and payment by cashier's check on the date of vacating.

The landlord countered at $200,000. After further negotiation, the parties agreed on $275,000, with all of the tenant's requested terms included in the written agreement. The agreement included the required Local Law 1 disclosures. The tenant had adequate time to find a new apartment and to plan the transition.

The tenant left on her own terms, with financial security, a reasonable timeline, and an agreement that protected her interests.

The initial offer was $75,000. The final deal was $275,000 with comprehensive terms. The difference was not luck. It was information.

What to Take From This Chapter

Buyouts are legal, but they are not unregulated. In New York City, buyout offers to rent-regulated tenants must comply with Local Law 1 disclosure requirements. Offers that do not comply may be voidable.

The required disclosures include the tenant's right to remain, the right to reject the offer without penalty, the right to consult an attorney, and a description of the tenant's rent-regulated status and protections.

Evaluate every buyout offer against the long-term financial value of the tenancy. Calculate the rent differential, project it over time, add relocation costs, and consider tax implications. Most initial offers represent a fraction of the tenancy's true value.

Counteroffer when the analysis supports a higher number. Be specific, be reasonable, and support your number with reasoning.

Negotiate terms beyond the dollar amount. Timeline, moving costs, neutral reference, mutual release, payment method, and timing all matter.

Pressure tactics, including artificial deadlines, threats, and misrepresentation of rights, are red flags that may undermine the enforceability of the agreement.

Waivers fail when disclosures are missing, when the tenant was misinformed, when the agreement violates public policy, or when the tenant acted under duress. Signing is not the end of the analysis.

If your landlord offers you money to leave, the key question is not "Is this a good deal?" It's "Was this offer made in full compliance with the law, and does the amount reflect the true value of what I'm being asked to give up?"

In the next chapter, we'll address a topic most tenant guides avoid: what happens when you're not perfectly in the right, and how to navigate disputes where you bear some responsibility.

26

When You're Not Perfectly in the Right

Every chapter in this book so far has focused on situations where the landlord is doing something wrong. Overcharging rent. Missing deadlines. Filing defective notices. Withholding deposits illegally. Retaliating against tenants who assert their rights.

Those situations are real, they are common, and they deserve the attention they received. But they represent a fraction of the disputes that New York tenants actually face. The majority of landlord-tenant conflicts are messier. The tenant is partially at fault. The landlord has a legitimate grievance. The violation is real, even if the response is disproportionate. And the tenant's strongest move is not righteous indignation but strategic damage control.

This is the chapter most tenant guides leave out, because acknowledging tenant imperfection feels like weakening the case. The opposite is true. Understanding how to navigate disputes where you bear some responsibility is what separates tenants who keep their housing from tenants who lose it unnecessarily. Partial fault is not the same as no defense. Being wrong about one thing does not mean you are wrong about everything. And a tenant who knows how to respond to a legitimate complaint is far harder to evict than one who pretends the complaint doesn't exist.

The Reality of Imperfect Disputes

Most landlord-tenant disputes are not clean. They involve a tenant who is behind on rent but also lives in an apartment with serious habitability problems. A tenant who has a roommate the landlord doesn't know about but who also has a lease full of unenforceable clauses. A tenant who made unauthorized alterations to the apartment but whose landlord is overcharging on rent. A tenant who is genuinely noisy but whose landlord is using the noise complaints as a pretext for an eviction motivated by something else entirely.

In these situations, the tenant's first instinct is often to focus on the landlord's misconduct and ignore their own. That instinct is understandable but dangerous. Courts evaluate the full picture. A judge who sees a tenant with legitimate defenses but who is also clearly violating the lease will weigh both sides. Pretending your side of the ledger is clean when it isn't undermines your credibility on the issues where you are right.

The better approach is to acknowledge what you can fix, fix it quickly, and focus your energy on the issues where the landlord's position is weak. Being imperfect does not mean being defenseless. It means being strategic about which battles to fight and which problems to solve.

Late Rent: When You Owe Money and Still Have Rights

Being behind on rent is the most common form of tenant imperfection, and it is the one that creates the most anxiety. Tenants who owe money often assume they have no leverage, no defenses, and no options other than paying immediately or being evicted.

That assumption is wrong, but it requires qualification. Owing rent is a real problem. Courts take it seriously. Landlords are entitled to be paid. And a tenant who ignores rent obligations without explanation or effort is in a weaker position than one who communicates, pays what they can, and addresses the arrears proactively.

That said, owing rent does not eliminate your other rights. A tenant who owes two months' rent but who lives in an apartment with serious habitability violations may be entitled to a rent abatement that reduces or eliminates the arrears. A tenant who owes rent but whose landlord served a defective rent demand still has a procedural defense that can delay or dismiss the case. A tenant who owes rent but whose legal rent is lower than what thc landlord is charging may actually owe less than the demand claims, or may not owe anything at all after the overcharge is corrected.

The strategic approach to late rent involves several steps.

Communicate with the landlord before a case is filed. A tenant who contacts the landlord, explains the situation, and proposes a specific payment plan (with dates and amounts) is in a meaningfully better position than a tenant who goes silent. Written communication creates a record of good faith that courts consider.

Pay what you can, when you can. Partial payments demonstrate effort and reduce the total arrears. They also affect how a judge views the case. A tenant who has been making regular partial payments is treated differently than a tenant who has paid nothing.

Set aside whatever you are unable to pay. If you cannot pay the full rent, put the shortfall in a separate account. If the case reaches court, showing the judge that you have the money available (even if you couldn't pay it on time) demonstrates good faith and may result in a more favorable settlement.

Check the rent demand carefully. As Chapter 20 explained, inflated demands are common and can be fatal to the landlord's case. Even when you owe money, the amount the landlord claims may be wrong. Late fees above the cap, charges during the grace period, non-rent charges, and amounts above the legal rent in stabilized apartments are all potential defects.

Raise habitability defenses if they exist. If you owe rent and your apartment has serious condition problems, these are not unrelated issues. The warranty of habitability reduces the value of the apartment during the period when conditions were substandard, which reduces the amount of rent you owed. You don't need to be a perfect tenant to assert a habitability defense. You need to have a documented condition that affected the livability of your home.

Apply for rental assistance. Programs change over time, but New York has historically maintained multiple emergency rental assistance programs for tenants facing arrears. Apply as early as possible. Processing takes time, and having an application pending can affect the dynamics of a court proceeding.

The central principle is that owing rent changes the conversation but does not end it. You still have procedural rights. You may still have substantive defenses. And you almost certainly have more options than you think.

Lease Violations: When the Landlord Has a Point

Sometimes the landlord's complaint is legitimate. You have a pet the lease prohibits. You installed a washing machine without permission. You painted the walls a color the landlord objects to. You have a roommate you never disclosed. You are using the apartment for a business the lease doesn't authorize.

The instinct in these situations is either to deny the violation (which rarely works if the evidence is clear) or to panic (which leads to poor decisions). The better approach is to evaluate the violation honestly, determine whether it can be cured, and act before the landlord escalates.

The first question is whether the violation is real. Not every landlord complaint corresponds to an actual lease provision. Sometimes the landlord is asserting a rule that doesn't exist in the lease, or is characterizing normal behavior as a violation. Read the lease. Identify the specific clause the landlord claims you are violating. If the clause doesn't exist, or if the conduct the landlord describes does not actually violate the clause, you have a defense.

The second question is whether the clause is enforceable. As Chapter 8 explained, many lease clauses are unenforceable under New York law. A no-pet clause may be waived under the three-month rule. A no-roommate clause may be overridden by the Roommate Law. A no-subletting clause may be superseded by statutory subletting rights. A clause requiring the tenant to waive habitability protections is void. Before conceding a violation, determine whether the rule the landlord is invoking is one the law actually supports.

The third question is whether you can cure the violation. If the violation is real and the clause is enforceable, the most powerful response is often the simplest: fix it. Remove the unauthorized alteration. Disclose the roommate. Obtain permission for the pet. Stop the prohibited activity. Curing the violation eliminates the landlord's ground for eviction and demonstrates good faith.

In rent-stabilized apartments, the HSTPA strengthened the tenant's right to cure. After a lease violation case is decided against the tenant, the tenant has 30 days to cure the violation. And even within that period, if the tenant is making substantial progress toward curing, the court may extend the opportunity. The right to cure is designed to prevent the loss of housing over correctable problems.

The fourth question is whether the violation is substantial. Not all lease violations support eviction. Courts evaluate whether the violation is serious enough to warrant the most extreme remedy available. A tenant who installed a towel rack without permission has technically violated an alterations clause. A court is unlikely to find that this violation justifies eviction. A tenant who demolished a wall and reconfigured the apartment layout is in a different position.

The fifth question is whether the landlord tolerated the violation. If the landlord knew about the condition for an extended period and took no action, the landlord may have waived the right to enforce the clause. A landlord who saw the pet every day for two years and never objected cannot suddenly claim the pet is grounds for eviction (especially under the three-month pet waiver rule in NYC). A landlord who observed the roommate, accepted rent, and said nothing for a year has a weak case for claiming the roommate was unauthorized.

Tolerance is not a blanket defense, but it is a powerful one when combined with the other factors. A violation that is minor, curable, and previously tolerated is very unlikely to support an eviction. A violation that is serious, ongoing, and flagged by the landlord at the time it occurred is harder to defend.

Noise Complaints: When Your Neighbors Have a Legitimate Grievance

Noise complaints occupy an uncomfortable space in tenant law because they involve subjective judgments about what constitutes reasonable behavior, and because they can be used both legitimately and pretextually.

If you have received noise complaints, the first step is honest self-assessment. Are you actually causing unreasonable noise? Late-night music, parties on weeknights, heavy footfall amplified by hard floors, barking dogs left alone for hours, these are genuine problems that affect your neighbors' quality of life. A tenant who is causing real disruption and refuses to address it is creating a ground for eviction that may eventually succeed, regardless of what other defenses exist.

If the noise complaints are legitimate, address them. Install rugs or carpet padding if you have hardwood floors above a downstairs neighbor. Reduce volume after 10 p.m. Address the barking issue with training or schedule adjustments. These practical steps often resolve the problem entirely and eliminate the landlord's leverage.

If the noise complaints are pretextual or exaggerated, the analysis changes. A landlord who receives a single complaint from one neighbor and immediately serves a notice to cure may be using the complaint as a pretext for an eviction motivated by something else (low rent, a desire for the apartment, retaliation for a complaint the tenant filed). Courts evaluate nuisance claims based on evidence of persistent, serious conduct that substantially affects others. A single incident, a subjective opinion, or a conflict between neighbors does not meet this standard.

Document your own behavior if you believe the complaints are unfounded. Keep a log of your activities and noise levels. Note the times you are home and what you are doing. If the landlord escalates to a court proceeding, this documentation helps you counter the landlord's characterization.

Consider whether the noise issue reflects a building problem rather than a tenant problem. Poor soundproofing, thin walls, inadequate insulation between floors, these are conditions the landlord is responsible for, not the tenant. A tenant who makes normal household noise that is transmitted through poorly constructed floors is not creating a nuisance. The landlord is failing to maintain adequate sound separation.

The goal with noise complaints is to be reasonable. If the complaint is legitimate, address it. If it is exaggerated or pretextual, document why. And in either case, do not give the landlord additional ammunition by being confrontational with the complaining neighbor.

Unauthorized Alterations: When You Changed Something You Shouldn't Have

Most leases prohibit alterations to the apartment without the landlord's written consent. Common unauthorized alterations include painting walls in non-standard colors, removing or modifying built-in fixtures, installing shelving, cabinetry, or appliances, adding or removing flooring (replacing carpet with hardwood, for example), modifying electrical or plumbing systems, and removing doors, walls, or other structural elements.

The severity of the issue depends on the nature and reversibility of the alteration.

Minor, easily reversible alterations (painting a wall, installing removable shelving, adding a curtain rod) are unlikely to support an eviction even if they technically violate the lease. Courts distinguish between substantial violations that affect the landlord's property interest and trivial modifications that are part of normal residential use.

Major, irreversible alterations (removing a wall, reconfiguring plumbing, installing a gas line) are more serious. These changes may create building code violations, may affect the structural integrity of the unit, and may require significant expense to undo. Courts are more likely to find these violations substantial.

If you have made unauthorized alterations and the landlord has raised the issue, your options depend on the situation.

If the alteration is easily reversible, offer to reverse it. Repainting walls, removing installed fixtures, and restoring the apartment to its original condition eliminates the violation and the ground for eviction. Do this promptly and document that you did it.

If the alteration is not easily reversible, assess whether you can negotiate with the landlord. Some landlords will accept the alteration in exchange for the tenant bearing the cost of restoration at move-out, or will agree to a lease amendment acknowledging the change. A landlord who is offered a reasonable solution and rejects it may be using the alteration as a pretext rather than a genuine concern.

If the alteration created a safety hazard, address the hazard immediately regardless of the legal implications. Unauthorized electrical or plumbing work that doesn't meet code can be dangerous. Your safety comes first.

In all cases, the key is to be proactive. A tenant who acknowledges the issue, takes steps to correct it, and communicates constructively with the landlord is in a fundamentally better position than a tenant who denies the alteration, argues about whether it's a violation, or ignores the landlord's complaints until they escalate to court.

How Partial Fault Affects Legal Strategy

When you bear partial responsibility for a dispute, your legal strategy must account for both your vulnerability and your strengths. The worst approach is to pretend you are entirely in the right when you are not. The second-worst approach is to assume you are entirely at fault when the landlord's case has problems too.

The strategic framework for imperfect positions involves several principles.

Fix what you can fix immediately. Curing a violation, paying down arrears, addressing a legitimate complaint: these actions reduce your exposure and strengthen your position on other issues. Every problem you solve is one fewer argument the landlord can make.

Separate the issues. A tenant who owes two months' rent and lives in an apartment with no heat has two separate issues. The rent issue does not eliminate the habitability issue, and the habitability issue does not eliminate the rent issue. Each should be addressed independently. Cure one while asserting the other.

Don't let one problem undermine unrelated defenses. If the landlord's rent demand is defective, that defect exists regardless of whether you actually owe money. If the landlord's notice was served improperly, that error exists regardless of whether you violated the lease. Procedural defenses are independent of the substantive dispute. Use them.

Maintain credibility. A tenant who acknowledges the things they did wrong and focuses their arguments on the things the landlord did wrong is more credible than a tenant who denies everything. Judges appreciate honesty and are skeptical of parties who claim perfection.

Document the landlord's conduct even when your own position is imperfect. If the landlord is retaliating, if the notice is defective, if the rent demand is inflated, if the eviction ground is pretextual, these issues exist independently of your own imperfections. The fact that you violated one lease clause does not give the landlord permission to violate the law in response.

Negotiate from an informed position. A tenant who says "I know I owe two months' rent, and I also know your rent demand includes $600 in illegal late fees, so let's talk about a payment plan based on the correct amount" is negotiating from a position of knowledge. A tenant who says "I don't owe you anything" when they clearly do has lost credibility before the conversation starts.

When to Get Help, Even When You're Not Perfect

One of the biggest reasons tenants in imperfect positions don't seek legal help is shame. They feel that because they did something wrong, an attorney will judge them, refuse to help, or tell them there's nothing to be done.

This is not how tenant law works. Tenant attorneys handle imperfect cases every day. The vast majority of cases involve tenants who bear some responsibility for the dispute. An experienced attorney knows how to separate the tenant's vulnerability from the tenant's defenses, how to negotiate from imperfect positions, and how to present a case that acknowledges reality without conceding everything.

Seek legal help when you receive any court papers, regardless of whether you believe you are at fault. The filing starts a clock, and missing deadlines can result in default judgments.

Seek legal help when the landlord's response seems disproportionate to the issue. A noise complaint that leads to an eviction filing. A minor lease violation that triggers a termination notice. A late rent payment that produces a demand for ten months of arrears. Disproportionate responses often indicate pretextual motives.

Seek legal help when multiple issues are entangled. Owing rent while also having a habitability claim, facing a lease violation allegation while also suspecting an overcharge, being behind on rent while also experiencing retaliation: these situations involve legal complexity that benefits from professional analysis.

Seek legal help before you sign anything. Settlement agreements, stipulations, and buyout offers all contain terms that may affect your rights permanently. Having an attorney review the document before you sign costs far less than trying to undo a bad agreement afterward.

The Right to Counsel program in New York City provides free legal representation to income-eligible tenants facing eviction, regardless of whether the tenant is at fault. Legal Aid Society, Legal Services NYC, and community-based legal organizations also represent tenants in imperfect situations. These organizations exist to help people navigate complex problems, not to judge them.

Real-World Example: The Tenant Who Was Right and Wrong

A tenant in a rent-stabilized apartment in Bed-Stuy fell two months behind on rent after an unexpected medical expense. Around the same time, her upstairs neighbor began complaining about noise. The noise complaints were partially legitimate. The tenant had a dog that barked when left alone during the day, and the tenant's work schedule had recently changed, leaving the dog alone for longer stretches.

The landlord served a rent demand for the two months of arrears plus $400 in late fees. Two weeks later, the landlord served a separate notice to cure for the noise violation. The tenant received both documents on the same day and felt overwhelmed.

Her instinct was to fight everything. She felt the landlord was piling on. But when she consulted an attorney through a legal services organization, the attorney helped her separate the issues.

On the rent demand: the late fees exceeded the statutory cap. The demand was inflated by $350 ($200 in fees charged before the grace period expired, plus $150 above the $50-per-incident cap). The demand was therefore defective. This was a strong procedural defense that could result in dismissal of a nonpayment case if filed.

On the noise violation: the complaint had some basis. The barking was real. But the tenant had already begun addressing it by adjusting the dog's schedule and arranging for a dog walker during working hours. The attorney advised the tenant to document the steps she was taking to cure the issue and to respond to the notice to cure in writing, explaining the corrective measures.

On the overall strategy: the attorney helped the tenant propose a payment plan for the legitimate arrears (two months of rent at the correct legal amount, without the illegal late fees) while simultaneously documenting the cure of the noise violation. The attorney also checked the rent history and discovered that the tenant's legal rent was $85 less than what she had been paying, suggesting a potential overcharge.

The tenant paid the arrears over two months. The barking issue was resolved. The overcharge claim was filed. And the landlord, who had served a defective demand and was collecting an illegal rent, decided not to pursue either case further.

The tenant was not perfectly in the right. She owed rent. Her dog was a problem. But she was not entirely wrong either. The late fees were illegal. The demand was defective. And the rent was too high.

She didn't win by claiming perfection. She won by being honest about her problems, strategic about her defenses, and proactive about fixing what she could fix.

What to Take From This Chapter

Most landlord-tenant disputes involve imperfect positions on both sides. Acknowledging your share of the responsibility does not eliminate your rights. It positions you to exercise them more effectively.

Fix what you can fix. Cure violations, pay down arrears, address legitimate complaints. Every problem you solve reduces the landlord's leverage and strengthens your credibility.

Separate the issues. Your fault on one issue does not waive your defenses on another. Procedural defects, overcharge claims, habitability defenses, and anti-retaliation protections exist independently of your own imperfections.

Maintain credibility. Acknowledge what you did wrong. Focus your arguments on what the landlord did wrong. Courts reward honesty and punish denial.

Negotiate from knowledge, not from fear. A tenant who understands both their vulnerability and their leverage is harder to push around than a tenant who knows only one side.

Seek legal help even when you're not perfect. Tenant attorneys handle imperfect cases every day. The Right to Counsel program and legal services organizations exist to help tenants in difficult situations, not to judge them.

If you're facing a housing problem and you're not entirely blameless, the most important thing to understand is this: being wrong about one thing does not mean you are powerless. It means you have to be smarter about how you respond.

In the next chapter, we'll bring everything together, helping you decide when to fight, when to negotiate, and when to bring in professional help.

27

When to Fight, When to Negotiate, When to Get Help

Knowing your rights is powerful. Knowing how far to push them is strategic.

Not every landlord dispute should become a court battle. Not every eviction threat should be ignored. And not every problem requires a lawyer, until it suddenly does. The hardest part for many renters isn't understanding the law. It's deciding what to do next, right now, with the specific problem in front of them, under real-world constraints of time, money, and emotional energy.

This book has given you the map. This chapter helps you decide which road to take.

The Three Questions That Guide Every Decision

Before taking action on any housing dispute, ask three questions.

What do I stand to gain? The answer might be a rent reduction, a refund of overcharges, the right to stay in your apartment, the return of your security deposit, the cessation of harassment, or simply the knowledge that you're being treated lawfully. Be specific about the outcome you want. "Making the landlord pay" is not a strategy. "Recovering $8,000 in overcharges and reducing my rent to the legal amount" is.

What do I risk? The answer might be retaliation (addressed by anti-retaliation protections, but still stressful), the time and energy of a legal proceeding, the cost of an attorney if you hire one privately, the emotional toll of conflict with someone who controls your housing, or the possibility of losing if your case is weaker than you believe.

What will this cost me, financially and emotionally? Fighting for your rights takes time. Court dates mean days off work. Documentation takes discipline. Prolonged disputes create stress that affects your daily life. These costs are real. They don't make fighting wrong, but they make fighting a choice that should be made with clear eyes.

The answers to these three questions will point you toward one of three paths: fight, negotiate, or get professional help. Sometimes the right answer is a combination of all three.

When Fighting Works Best

Asserting your rights directly, without negotiation or compromise, works best when the law is clearly on your side, the violation is documented, and the landlord's position is weak.

Strong situations for fighting include defective notices. If the landlord's rent demand is inflated, the termination notice was served late, or the predicate notice lacks required disclosures, the procedural defect may be fatal to the landlord's case regardless of the underlying facts. These defenses are powerful because they do not require you to prove anything about your own conduct. The landlord's error is the defense.

Strong situations also include clear overcharges. If the rent history shows your apartment is stabilized and your rent exceeds the legal amount, the numbers speak for themselves. Overcharge claims are among the most objective disputes in tenant law because they turn on math, not interpretation.

Missed deadlines are another strong basis for fighting. If the landlord missed the 14-day security deposit deadline, failed to offer a timely renewal lease, or filed a case before the notice period expired, the violation is measurable and usually dispositive. Calendars don't lie.

Illegal fees, whether application fees above the $20 cap, broker fees charged in violation of the FARE Act, or disguised deposits that exceed the one-month limit, are provable with receipts, bank records, and communications. The evidence is usually in your own files.

False eviction claims also warrant a direct fight. If the landlord claimed owner use but re-rented the apartment, or claimed demolition but never applied for permits, the falsity of the claim can be established through public records and is worth pursuing.

In all of these situations, fighting works because the tenant's position is strong on the facts or the procedure, and because the landlord's failure is objectively verifiable. These are cases where the tenant should not concede, should not rush to settle, and should not be intimidated by the landlord's confidence. Confidence is not evidence. Evidence is evidence.

When Negotiation Works Better

Negotiation is not surrender. It is the strategic use of leverage to achieve an outcome you control.

Negotiation makes more sense than fighting when the outcome is uncertain. If the case could go either way, a negotiated resolution eliminates the risk of losing and gives you control over the terms. Certainty has value, even when you might have won in court.

Negotiation also makes sense when time matters more than principle. A court proceeding can take months or longer. If you need resolution quickly (because you're planning to move, because the stress is affecting your health, because you need cash now rather than a judgment later), negotiation compresses the timeline.

Negotiation is often the right choice when the landlord also wants certainty. Landlords who face the risk of losing an eviction case, paying overcharge damages, or having their conduct scrutinized in court are often willing to offer terms that give the tenant something meaningful in exchange for avoiding that risk. A landlord who knows their notice is defective may offer a generous payment plan or withdraw the case entirely. A landlord facing an overcharge claim may offer a rent reduction and partial refund rather than risk treble damages.

Negotiation works well when you want control over the exit. If you've decided to move, a negotiated buyout or settlement gives you the ability to set the timeline, secure financial terms, and leave on your own terms rather than under the pressure of a court proceeding.

The key to effective negotiation is knowing your leverage before you start. A tenant who says "I'd like to work something out" without understanding their legal position is negotiating blind. A tenant who says "I'd like to work something out, and here's what happens if we don't" is negotiating from knowledge.

Smart negotiation involves using legal leverage quietly rather than as a threat. Focus on outcomes, not arguments. Propose specific terms rather than vague requests. Secure any agreement in writing, signed by both parties. And avoid unnecessary escalation that closes off options you might need later.

A good negotiated outcome often beats a righteous victory that takes a year to achieve.

Red Flags That Mean You Should Get Professional Help

Some situations warrant immediate legal advice, regardless of how confident you feel about your understanding of the law.

Eviction filings in Housing Court are the clearest red flag. Once a case is filed, deadlines begin. Missing your first court date can result in a default judgment. The answer to the petition must include all defenses or they may be waived. Having an attorney from the first appearance dramatically changes the trajectory of the case.

Owner-use or demolition claims require legal analysis because the defenses are fact-specific, the procedures are technical, and the consequences of losing are permanent displacement.

Allegations of lease violations that you are uncertain how to address benefit from legal review. An attorney can assess whether the violation is substantial, whether it was previously tolerated, whether the notice to cure is defective, and whether the landlord's response is proportionate.

Harassment or retaliation cases involve complex questions of evidence, timing, and burden of proof. An attorney can help you build the timeline, identify the strongest claims, and determine whether to proceed defensively or offensively.

Large overcharge claims justify professional involvement because the stakes are high, the lookback rules are complex, and treble damages may be available. An attorney can calculate the overcharge precisely, navigate the DHCR process, and maximize the recovery.

Buyout offers should always be reviewed by an attorney before signing. The long-term financial implications of surrendering a rent-stabilized tenancy are substantial, and the landlord's attorney drafted the agreement to protect the landlord's interests, not yours.

Succession disputes involve fact-intensive inquiries into co-residency, family member status, and primary residence documentation. An attorney experienced in succession cases can evaluate the strength of your claim and prepare the evidence.

Any situation involving court papers, legal deadlines, or a potential loss of housing warrants professional involvement. The cost of early legal help is almost always less than the cost of trying to fix a mistake made without it.

Preparing Before You Call an Attorney

You don't need to know the law to talk to a lawyer. But preparation saves time, improves the quality of the advice you receive, and shows the attorney that you are organized and serious.

Before your first consultation, gather the following materials.

Your current lease and any renewal leases. These documents establish the terms of the tenancy, the rent amount, the lease dates, and any provisions the landlord may be invoking.

Any notices you have received. Rent demands, termination notices, notices to cure, Golub Notices, Good Cause disclosures, and any other official communications from the landlord should be organized chronologically.

Rent payment records. Bank statements, canceled checks, money order receipts, and electronic payment confirmations showing what you paid and when. If there is a dispute about arrears, these records are essential.

The rent history, if you have requested it. If you haven't, tell the attorney and they can advise whether requesting it should be a priority.

Photographs and documentation of apartment conditions. If habitability is an issue, your photographs, videos, 311 complaint confirmations, and HPD violation records form the evidentiary foundation.

A written timeline of events. A simple chronological list of what happened and when, including when you moved in, when problems began, when you complained, when the landlord responded (or didn't), and when you received any notices or filings. This timeline helps the attorney understand the situation quickly and identify the critical issues.

Correspondence with the landlord. Emails, text messages, letters, and notes of phone conversations. These communications often contain admissions, threats, or representations that have legal significance.

Clear facts make advice sharper. An attorney who receives organized materials can focus on strategy rather than spending the first hour sorting through a pile of papers.

Free and Low-Cost Legal Resources

Many tenants assume they cannot afford legal help. In New York City, that assumption is often wrong.

The Right to Counsel program (also called Universal Access) provides free legal representation to tenants facing eviction in Housing Court, regardless of immigration status. The program now covers every zip code in New York City and is available for nonpayment cases, holdover cases, and NYCHA administrative proceedings. If you have a pending eviction case, attend your first court date and tell the court you would like an attorney. Right to Counsel legal service providers are present at Housing Court and will connect with you at your first conference. If you cannot reach a provider at court, call Housing Court Answers at 718-557-1379 or 212-962-4795, Monday through Friday, 9 a.m. to 5 p.m.

The Legal Aid Society is the largest provider of free legal services for tenants in New York City. Their housing practice handles eviction defense, harassment cases, HP actions, overcharge claims, NYCHA proceedings, and a wide range of other tenant issues. They have offices in every borough. Manhattan: 212-426-3000. Brooklyn: 718-722-3100. Bronx: 718-991-4600. Queens: 718-286-2450. Staten Island: 347-422-5333. If you have an upcoming eviction case, you do not need to contact Legal Aid directly. The Right to Counsel program will connect you with a provider at your first court date. For non-eviction housing issues, including tenant group advocacy, call the Housing Justice Unit at 212-577-7988, Monday through Friday, 10 a.m. to 4 p.m.

Legal Services NYC provides free legal representation to low-income tenants across the city. They handle eviction defense, harassment, disrepair, overcharges, and other housing issues. Call 917-661-4500, Monday through Friday, 10 a.m. to 4 p.m.

New York Legal Assistance Group (NYLAG) provides free legal services to tenants through their Tenants' Rights Unit, handling eviction defense, anti-harassment cases, and other housing matters. They serve tenants across the city and can be reached through their main intake line.

Mobilization for Justice offers anti-eviction programs for low-income tenants, seniors, and SRO residents. They also provide legal information through fact sheets in English, Spanish, and Chinese.

The Met Council on Housing Tenants' Rights Hotline provides free information and guidance to tenants, staffed by trained volunteers who are deeply knowledgeable about New York City housing law. They are not lawyers, but they can explain your rights, describe your options, suggest strategies, and refer you to legal services organizations when representation is needed. Call 212-979-0611 on Mondays and Wednesdays, 1:30 to 8:00 p.m., and Fridays, 1:30 to 5:00 p.m.

Housing Court Answers provides information and referrals for tenants with pending Housing Court cases. Call 718-557-1379 or 212-962-4795, Monday through Friday, 9 a.m. to 5 p.m., or email housingcourtanswers@clsny.org.

The HRA Office of Civil Justice coordinates Right to Counsel services and other tenant legal assistance. Call 311 and ask for the Tenant Helpline, or visit the HRA website for information about free legal services.

JustFix.nyc provides free online tools that help tenants document conditions, generate repair request letters, access building information, and connect with legal resources. Their tools are available at justfix.nyc and are designed to be used without an attorney.

The New York City Bar Association Legal Referral Service provides referrals to attorneys for tenants who do not qualify for free legal services. They also offer free legal advice one evening per week on specific issues, including landlord-tenant matters. Call 212-626-7373 for referrals, or 212-626-7383 for the free counseling line.

Law school legal clinics at NYU, Columbia, Fordham, Brooklyn Law School, CUNY School of Law, and other institutions provide free legal assistance to tenants through supervised clinical programs. These clinics handle a range of housing cases, and law students working under faculty supervision provide the representation. Availability varies by semester, and eligibility requirements may apply. Contact the law school's clinical programs office for current information.

Community-based organizations in every borough offer housing counseling, tenant organizing assistance, and referrals to legal services. Organizations like the Chinese-American Planning Council, Catholic Charities, University Settlement, and numerous others provide culturally and linguistically specific services. Call 311 for referrals to community-based organizations in your area.

The depth and breadth of available resources is greater than most tenants realize. Free legal representation is not limited to the most desperate cases. It covers a wide range of housing issues, is available regardless of immigration status, and can be accessed at multiple points in a dispute, from the first sign of trouble through a court proceeding.

The single biggest barrier to accessing these resources is not eligibility. It is awareness. Tenants who do not know these resources exist do not use them. Now you know.

Why Many Disputes Never Reach Court

Landlords prefer predictable outcomes, cost control, and vacancy certainty. Court proceedings deliver none of these. A Housing Court case involves legal fees, judicial scrutiny, time delays, and the risk of losing.

Tenants with knowledge change the calculus. When a landlord knows the tenant understands the law, the landlord's options narrow. Defective notices can't be relied on. Inflated demands will be challenged. Procedural shortcuts will be caught. And the cost of litigating against an informed tenant often exceeds the cost of resolving the dispute directly.

This is why many disputes resolve before a case is filed. A letter from a tenant that cites the correct statute, identifies the landlord's error, and proposes a reasonable resolution can accomplish more than months of litigation. The letter signals that the tenant knows the rules, is prepared to enforce them, and would prefer to resolve the matter without court involvement, but is willing to go to court if necessary.

Often, the strongest position is the credible willingness to fight. You don't have to file a case to benefit from the leverage that filing would create. You just have to demonstrate, clearly and specifically, that you know what filing would involve.

The Emotional Cost of Housing Disputes

This book has focused on law, strategy, and leverage. But housing disputes are not academic exercises. They involve your home, your stability, your family, and your sense of security.

The emotional cost of fighting is real. Court appearances mean time off work. Prolonged disputes create chronic stress. The power imbalance between a tenant and a landlord who controls the physical space you live in can feel overwhelming. And the fear that asserting your rights will make things worse is corrosive, even when the anti-retaliation protections described in Chapter 19 exist to address it.

These costs are worth acknowledging because they affect decision-making. A tenant who is emotionally exhausted may accept a bad settlement. A tenant who is consumed by anger may escalate a dispute past the point of productive resolution. A tenant who is paralyzed by fear may do nothing when action is warranted.

The goal is not to eliminate the emotional dimension. It is to make decisions that account for it. Ask yourself: is this fight worth the stress? Can I sustain the effort? Am I making decisions from a place of clarity or from a place of fear? Do I have support, whether from legal advocates, friends, family, or community organizations?

Sometimes the smartest move is to fight hard. Sometimes the smartest move is to negotiate firmly. Sometimes the smartest move is to take the deal, move on, and protect your energy for what comes next.

All of those can be the right choice. What makes them right is that they were made deliberately, with full information, and not by default.

Real-World Example: Winning Without Filing

A tenant in a rent-stabilized apartment in Prospect-Lefferts Gardens received a termination notice that appeared valid. The landlord claimed the tenant had violated the lease by having an unauthorized pet, a cat the tenant had kept for eight months.

The tenant researched the issue. She learned that under the three-month pet waiver rule (NYC Administrative Code Section 27-2009.1), the no-pet clause was waived because the landlord had known about the cat for more than three months without taking action. The building's superintendent had seen the cat repeatedly and had never raised an issue. Neighbors had seen the cat in the window. The landlord had visited the apartment for an inspection four months earlier and had observed the cat without comment.

Instead of waiting for a court case, the tenant sent the landlord a letter. The letter was three paragraphs long. It cited the pet waiver statute by name and section number. It described the evidence of the landlord's knowledge (the superintendent's observations, the neighbors, the inspection). It stated that the no-pet clause had been waived by operation of law and that the termination notice was therefore based on a ground that no longer existed.

The letter concluded by proposing that the landlord withdraw the notice and offer a standard renewal lease, and stated that if the notice was not withdrawn, the tenant would raise the waiver defense in court and would seek attorney's fees under the reciprocal fee provision in the lease.

The landlord withdrew the notice. A renewal lease was offered. The cat stayed.

The tenant didn't hire a lawyer. She didn't file a case. She didn't go to court. She spent an afternoon researching the law, an hour writing a letter, and $7 on certified mail.

She won because she knew the rule, cited it correctly, and made it clear that the landlord's case would not survive a challenge. The credible willingness to fight was enough.

What to Take From This Chapter

Before acting on any housing dispute, ask three questions: what do I gain, what do I risk, and what will this cost me financially and emotionally? The answers guide whether to fight, negotiate, or seek help.

Fighting works best when the law is clearly on your side, the violation is documented, and the landlord's position is objcctively weak. Procedural defenses, overcharge claims, and deadline violations are particularly strong grounds.

Negotiation is not surrender. It is the strategic use of leverage to achieve a controlled outcome. It works best when the result is uncertain, time is a factor, or you want control over the terms.

Professional help is most valuable early. Eviction filings, owner-use claims, large overcharge claims, buyout offers, and succession disputes all warrant legal assistance. Preparation before calling an attorney (gathering documents, creating a timeline) makes the consultation more productive.

Free and low-cost legal resources in New York City are extensive. The Right to Counsel program, Legal Aid Society, Legal Services NYC, NYLAG, Met Council on Housing, Housing Court Answers, JustFix.nyc, the NYC Bar Association, and law school clinics all provide assistance to tenants. The biggest barrier to accessing them is not eligibility but awareness.

Many disputes resolve before court because informed tenants change the landlord's calculus. A letter that correctly identifies the landlord's error and proposes a resolution can accomplish more than months of litigation.

The emotional cost of housing disputes is real and should be factored into your decisions. The goal is not to fight every battle but to make every decision deliberately, with full information, and not from fear.

If you're facing a housing problem, the smartest question isn't "What are my rights?" It's "What's the best move right now?"

The conclusion brings it all together: how to enforce New York tenant rights without burning out, and why informed renters change the market for everyone.

28

Using New York Tenant Rights Without Burning Out

Knowing your rights is only half the battle. The other half is knowing how to use them without letting the fight take over your life.

New York tenant law is powerful, but it is also dense, procedural, and emotionally demanding. The goal of this book was never to turn every renter into a full-time legal combatant. It was to give you enough clarity to choose your battles, protect your housing, and avoid being worn down by a system that often counts on exhaustion.

This conclusion is about sustainability: enforcing your rights effectively, preserving your energy, and knowing when the best move is to stop pushing.

Strategic Enforcement vs. Escalation

There is a difference between using the law and escalating conflict.

Strategic enforcement means understanding which law applies, identifying the landlord's weakest point, acting at the moment that gives you the most leverage, and stopping once the goal is reached. It is precise, targeted, and outcome-focused. It treats the legal system as a tool, not a weapon.

Escalation looks different. Reacting emotionally to every violation. Arguing instead of documenting. Threatening action you're not prepared to take. Turning every issue into a crisis. Sending long, angry emails at midnight that feel satisfying to write and are devastating to your case.

The most effective tenants are not the loudest. They are the most precise.

Sometimes the strongest move is a formal complaint filed with the correct agency at the correct time. Sometimes it's a quiet letter citing the right statute, sent by certified mail, with a copy kept for your records. Sometimes it's doing nothing, on purpose, while the landlord makes a mistake that hands you leverage you couldn't have created on your own.

Strategic enforcement requires discipline. It requires separating what you feel from what you do. It requires the patience to build a record when you'd rather scream. And it requires the judgment to know when you've achieved what you set out to achieve, even if justice feels incomplete.

Perfect outcomes are rare. Effective outcomes are not. The difference is usually not the law. It's the approach.

Protecting Your Housing and Your Sanity

Housing disputes are stressful because they're personal. Your home is not an abstract asset. It's where you sleep, work, recover, and raise your family. When that space is threatened, the response is visceral. Fear, anger, helplessness, and exhaustion arrive together and feed on each other.

Protecting your sanity while protecting your housing requires conscious effort.

Recognize when a fight is draining more than it's giving. Not every violation is worth pursuing. A $50 illegal late fee that has been charged once and will not recur may not justify the time and energy of a formal complaint. A $5,000 overcharge that has been compounding for three years justifies serious effort. The calculation is different for everyone, and it changes over time.

Use systems instead of personal confrontation. Courts, agencies, and documentation processes exist so that you don't have to resolve disputes through direct conflict with your landlord. Filing a 311 complaint is less stressful than arguing in the hallway. An HP action is less draining than a shouting match about the broken radiator. An overcharge complaint with DHCR is less exhausting than months of angry emails. Let the systems do the work.

Set boundaries on how much energy you spend. Decide in advance how much time per week you will devote to a housing dispute. Decide what tasks you will handle yourself and what tasks require professional help. Decide which communications you will respond to and which you will ignore. Boundaries are not weakness. They are resource management.

Build support. Talk to other tenants in your building. Contact tenant organizations like Met Council on Housing. Attend community meetings. Join a tenant association if one exists, or help start one if it doesn't. Housing disputes are isolating by design. Landlords benefit when tenants feel alone. Community dissolves that isolation.

Remember that winning doesn't always mean staying forever. Some tenants fight to keep their apartment and succeed. Some fight to negotiate a fair exit. Some fight to recover money they were overcharged, and then move on. All of these are victories. The goal is not to die in the apartment you were born in. The goal is to make every transition on your own terms, with full information and fair compensation for what you're giving up.

It's okay to enforce your rights and still decide to move. It's okay to negotiate even when you could win in court. It's okay to prioritize peace over principle, especially when the law gives you leverage to do so safely.

Burnout helps landlords. Clarity helps tenants.

Why Informed Renters Change the Market

Tenant law doesn't work because every tenant enforces it. It works because enough tenants do.

When renters request rent histories, landlords who have been overcharging get caught. When tenants challenge illegal increases, landlords who rely on tenant ignorance lose that advantage. When tenants enforce notice requirements, landlords who cut corners face consequences. When tenants refuse unlawful fees, landlords who treat fees as profit centers find the practice unprofitable. When tenants document harassment, landlords who harass face penalties.

Each of these actions affects more than the individual tenant. When a landlord loses an overcharge case, they are less likely to overcharge the next tenant. When a landlord's defective notice is dismissed, they are more likely to follow the rules next time. When a landlord pays treble damages on a security deposit, they are more likely to meet the 14-day deadline for the next tenant who moves out.

Most landlord misconduct survives on one assumption: this tenant won't push back. Every informed renter who does push back weakens that assumption. Not just for themselves, but for the next person who lives there.

This is why tenant knowledge has a multiplier effect that goes beyond any individual case. It changes landlord behavior. It changes market norms. It changes the cost-benefit analysis that landlords perform every time they consider cutting a corner. And it does so quietly, steadily, without requiring every tenant to become a housing activist.

You don't need to save the rental market. You just need to know your own rights well enough to exercise them when it matters. The market effect takes care of itself.

The Quiet Power of Knowing the Rules

You don't need to threaten lawsuits. You don't need to quote statutes in every email. You don't need to become an expert in housing court procedure. You don't need to read every DHCR fact sheet or memorize every RGB order.

Often, the power comes from not being surprised.

When you know that a notice might be defective, you read it carefully instead of panicking. When you know that a rent increase may be illegal, you check the math instead of paying automatically. When you know that a waiver may not hold up, you ask questions instead of signing. When you know that an exemption might not apply, you investigate instead of accepting.

That shift, from reactive to informed, changes how you move through every interaction with your landlord. Calm replaces panic. Options appear where you thought there were none. Conversations that used to feel like ultimatums start to feel like negotiations.

That shift, more than any single law or any single case, is what protects you.

Real-World Example: The Tenant Who Knew When to Stop

A tenant in a rent-stabilized apartment in Astoria had been paying $1,850 per month for four years. She had never questioned the rent. The landlord was responsive about repairs. The building was well-maintained. The relationship was cordial.

In her fifth year, she heard about rent stabilization from a coworker and, out of curiosity, requested her apartment's rent history from DHCR. The records arrived three weeks later.

The rent history showed that her apartment's legal rent was $1,575. The landlord had claimed IAI costs after the previous tenant moved out, but the claimed amounts exceeded the post-HSTPA caps. The difference between what she was paying and what she should have been paying was $275 per month. Over four years, the total overcharge was approximately $13,200 before any compounding or treble damages.

She consulted an attorney through Legal Aid's housing hotline. The attorney confirmed the overcharge and explained her options. She could file a complaint with DHCR, which would investigate, order a rent reduction, and potentially award treble damages. The total recovery, including treble damages for willfulness, could exceed $40,000.

She could also negotiate directly with the landlord.

She thought about it for a week. The landlord had been decent about repairs. She liked the apartment. She did not want a prolonged adversarial process. She also did not want to leave $40,000 on the table.

She chose a middle path. She wrote the landlord a letter, citing the rent history, identifying the IAI overcharge, and proposing a resolution: an immediate reduction in her rent to the correct legal amount, a refund of $13,200 (the base overcharge without treble damages), and a proper renewal lease reflecting the corrected rent.

The letter was factual, not angry. It cited the relevant provisions. It was sent by certified mail. And it concluded by stating that if the landlord agreed to these terms, she would not pursue the overcharge through DHCR, where treble damages could apply.

The landlord's attorney called within a week. After brief negotiation, the landlord agreed to reduce the rent to $1,575, to refund $10,000 (slightly less than the full overcharge, reflecting the negotiation), and to issue a proper renewal lease.

The tenant accepted. She stayed in the apartment. Her rent dropped by $275 per month. She received a check for $10,000. And she continued living in a building with a landlord who now understood that she knew the rules.

She did not file a complaint. She did not go to court. She did not retain an attorney beyond the initial consultation. She did not wage a campaign. She researched, she calculated, she wrote one letter, and she settled on terms that reflected the reality of her situation.

She left roughly $30,000 in potential treble damages on the table. She gained $10,000 in cash, $3,300 per year in rent savings going forward, and a resolution that took six weeks instead of the two years a DHCR proceeding might have required.

Was it the maximum recovery the law allowed? No. Was it a good outcome that reflected her priorities, her values, and her tolerance for conflict? Yes.

She knew when to push. She knew when to stop. And she moved on with her life intact.

Final Takeaway

New York tenant rights are not about winning every fight. They're about not losing by default.

The tenants who lose by default are the ones who never request the rent history. Who accept every landlord explanation without verification. Who sign whatever is put in front of them. Who move out when told to, without checking whether the notice was valid. Who pay illegal fees because they don't know the fees are illegal. Who surrender apartments they had every right to keep.

The tenants who don't lose by default are the ones who read this book.

Use the law strategically. Protect your energy as carefully as your rent. Document before you need to, and prepare before you have to. Know the resources that are available to you, and use them before a crisis forces you to.

And remember: the goal is not to live in permanent conflict. It's to live securely, on terms you understand, with the knowledge that if your landlord crosses a line, you know exactly where it is.

When renters know the rules, the market changes. Quietly. Steadily. And for the better.

Appendices

Appendix A

Glossary of Key Terms

This glossary defines the terms used throughout this book. Definitions are written in plain English and reflect how the terms are used in practice, not how they might appear in a legal dictionary. Where a term has a specific statutory definition that differs from its everyday meaning, the legal meaning is provided.

421-a Tax Exemption. A New York State tax benefit program that provided property tax reductions to developers of new residential buildings in exchange for including affordable housing units. Buildings that received 421-a benefits are generally required to keep their apartments rent-stabilized for the duration of the benefit period, which can extend for decades. The program has been modified and renamed multiple times. Buildings that received 421-a benefits may remain stabilized even though the building was constructed after 1974.

Adjournment. A postponement of a court date to a later date. Adjournments are common in Housing Court, particularly at the first appearance. An adjournment does not mean anything has been decided. It means the case will continue on the new date.

Affidavit of Service. A sworn written statement by the person who served a legal document, describing when, where, how, and to whom the document was delivered. Courts rely on affidavits of service to determine whether service was proper. Inaccuracies or inconsistencies in the affidavit can be grounds for dismissal.

Affirmative Defense. A legal argument raised by a tenant in response to a landlord's petition that, if proven, defeats the landlord's claim even if the landlord's underlying facts are true. Examples include breach of the warranty of habitability, retaliation, and waiver. Affirmative defenses must be raised in the tenant's answer to the petition or they may be waived.

Answer. The tenant's formal written response to a landlord's petition in Housing Court. The answer includes denials of the landlord's allegations and any affirmative defenses the tenant wishes to raise. Filing a timely answer is critical because defenses not included may be lost.

Basement. A story of a building that is partly below curb level but has at least one-half of its height above the curb level. Basements may be lawfully rented for residential use only if they meet specific requirements for ceiling height, light, ventilation, egress, and dampproofing, and if the certificate of occupancy authorizes residential use. Compare with cellar.

Buyout. An agreement in which a tenant accepts money or other consideration in exchange for voluntarily vacating the apartment and surrendering their tenancy rights. Buyouts of rent-regulated tenants in New York City are subject to disclosure requirements under Local Law 1 of 2015, including the tenant's right to remain, the right to reject the offer, and the right to consult an attorney.

Cellar. A story of a building that has less than one-half of its height above curb level. Cellars in one- and two family homes can never be lawfully rented for residential use in New York City. Compare with basement.

Certificate of Occupancy (CO). A document issued by the Department of Buildings that specifies how a building may legally be used, including the number of dwelling units, the permitted use of each floor, and the type of occupancy authorized. Buildings constructed after April 18, 1929 are required to have a certificate of occupancy. An apartment that does not appear on the CO, or that exists in a space designated for non-residential use, may be an illegal apartment.

Class A Violation. An HPD violation for a non-hazardous condition that must be corrected within 90 days.

Class B Violation. An HPD violation for a hazardous condition that must be corrected within 30 days.

Class C Violation. An HPD violation for an immediately hazardous condition that must be corrected within 24 hours. Examples include no heat during the heating season, lead paint hazards, and gas leaks.

Commingling. The practice of mixing a tenant's security deposit with the landlord's personal or operating funds. In buildings with six or more units, landlords are required to hold security deposits in separate interest-bearing accounts. Commingling is a violation of the law.

Conspicuous Place Service. A method of serving legal documents by affixing them to the door of the apartment and mailing a copy. Also called "nail and mail." This method may be used only after personal delivery and substituted service have been attempted and failed, and it requires documented prior attempts.

Co-Residency Requirement. The minimum period a family member must have lived in an apartment with the tenant of record to qualify for succession rights. The general requirement is two years. For senior citizens (62 and older) and disabled persons, the requirement is reduced to one year. Certain temporary absences (military duty, full-time student enrollment, hospitalization, temporary employment relocation) do not interrupt the period.

Cure. The act of correcting a lease violation within the time period allowed by law. In rent-stabilized apartments, the HSTPA provides tenants with 30 days to cure a violation after a court judgment, with possible extensions for substantial progress. A violation that is cured within the allowed period eliminates the ground for eviction.

Default Judgment. A judgment entered against a party who fails to appear in court or fails to file a required response. A tenant who does not appear at a Housing Court date may have a default judgment entered against them, potentially resulting in a warrant of eviction. Default judgments can sometimes be vacated (set aside) if the tenant shows a reasonable excuse for the absence and a meritorious defense.

DHCR (Division of Housing and Community Renewal). The state agency that administers rent regulation in New York. DHCR operates within Homes and Community Renewal (HCR). Its Office of Rent Administration handles rent stabilization matters, including overcharge complaints, registration, and lease complaints. DHCR and HCR are often used interchangeably in practice.

Discovery. The formal process of exchanging information and evidence between parties in a legal proceeding. Discovery can include document requests, interrogatories (written questions answered under oath), and depositions (oral questioning under oath). Discovery is less common in Housing Court than in other courts but can be important in complex cases.

FARE Act (Fairness in Apartment Rental Expenses Act). A New York City law, effective June 11, 2025, that prohibits landlord-hired brokers from charging fees to tenants. Under the FARE Act, whoever hires the broker pays the broker. The law creates a rebuttable presumption that any broker who publishes a listing does so with the landlord's permission and is therefore the landlord's agent.

Golub Notice. A written notice of non-renewal that a landlord must serve on a rent-stabilized tenant in New York City between 150 and 90 days before the current lease expires, when the landlord intends to pursue an owner-use eviction. Named after the court case that established the requirement. Failure to serve a timely and proper Golub Notice is a jurisdictional defect that can result in dismissal of the holdover proceeding.

Good Cause Eviction. A set of tenant protections, effective April 20, 2024, that limit when landlords can evict tenants or refuse to renew leases in covered apartments. Under Good Cause, the landlord must prove a legally recognized reason for eviction. The law also limits rent increases, creating a presumption that increases above a set threshold are unreasonable. Good Cause covers many previously unregulated apartments, with exemptions for certain building types, owner-occupied buildings, small landlords, and high-rent apartments.

Good Cause Notice. A written disclosure that landlords must include with every predicate notice, lease, and renewal since August 2024, stating whether the apartment is covered by the Good Cause Eviction Law and, if not, explaining the basis for the claimed exemption.

Grace Period. The period after rent is due during which the tenant cannot be penalized for late payment. For monthly rent in New York, the statutory grace period is generally five days. Late fees cannot be charged during the grace period, and nonpayment proceedings cannot be initiated until the grace period has expired.

HCR (Homes and Community Renewal). The New York State agency that oversees housing programs and rent regulation. HCR encompasses DHCR (the Division of Housing and Community Renewal), which administers rent stabilization and rent control. The terms HCR and DHCR are often used interchangeably.

Holdover Proceeding. A type of eviction case in which the landlord seeks to remove a tenant who remains in the apartment after the tenancy has allegedly ended. Unlike nonpayment proceedings, holdover cases are based on grounds other than unpaid rent, such as lease violations, owner use, or expiration of the tenancy. Holdover cases require a valid predicate notice.

HP Action. A court proceeding filed in Housing Court by a tenant (or by HPD or another interested party) to compel the landlord to make repairs or correct conditions that violate the housing code. HP stands for "Housing Part." HP actions do not involve rent withholding and do not create rent arrears. The court can order repairs, set deadlines, impose fines, and hold landlords in contempt for noncompliance.

HPD (Department of Housing Preservation and Development). The New York City agency responsible for enforcing the Housing Maintenance Code, conducting housing inspections, issuing violations, and overseeing building registration. HPD inspections can be triggered by tenant complaints filed through 311.

HSTPA (Housing Stability and Tenant Protection Act). A New York State law enacted on June 14, 2019, that constituted the most significant overhaul of tenant protections in a generation. Key provisions include the elimination of vacancy decontrol, limits on MCI and IAI rent increases (making them temporary rather than permanent), elimination of vacancy bonuses and longevity increases, a hard cap on security deposits at one month's rent, a $20 cap on application fees, strengthened overcharge lookback periods, and enhanced protections for senior, disabled, and long-term tenants facing owner-use evictions.

IAI (Individual Apartment Improvement). An improvement made to a specific rent-stabilized apartment (as opposed to the building as a whole) that the landlord may claim as a basis for increasing the legal rent. Under the HSTPA, IAI increases are capped in total amount, must be documented with proof of actual costs, and expire after 30 years. Before the HSTPA, IAI increases were permanent and were a primary mechanism for pushing rents toward the deregulation threshold.

Illegal Apartment. An apartment that is used for residential purposes in a manner that does not comply with the building's certificate of occupancy, the zoning code, or the housing maintenance code. Common examples include basement apartments, attic conversions, and commercial-to-residential conversions without proper permits. Tenants in illegal apartments retain certain protections (including protection against illegal eviction and security deposit rules) but may face complications with other protections.

Implied Warranty of Habitability. See Warranty of Habitability.

Itemized Statement. A written document that a landlord must provide to a tenant when withholding any portion of a security deposit. The statement must list each deduction, describe the specific condition justifying the charge, and state the cost. Vague or lump-sum descriptions do not satisfy the requirement. The statement must be provided within 14 days after the tenant vacates.

J-51 Tax Abatement. A New York City tax benefit program that provides property tax reductions and exemptions to building owners who perform qualifying rehabilitation and improvement work. Buildings that received J-51 benefits are generally required to keep their apartments rent-stabilized for the duration of the benefit period.

Judgment of Possession. A court order determining that the landlord is entitled to possession of the apartment. A judgment of possession is a prerequisite to the issuance of a warrant of eviction. The judgment does not mean the tenant is removed immediately; the warrant must still be executed by a marshal or sheriff.

Just Cause. The legal requirement that a landlord must have a recognized reason before evicting a tenant or refusing to renew a lease. In rent-stabilized apartments, just cause has been required for decades. The Good Cause Eviction Law extended similar protections to many previously unregulated apartments. Valid causes include nonpayment of rent, substantial lease violations, nuisance, owner occupancy, and withdrawal from the rental market.

Late Fee. A charge imposed by the landlord when rent is paid after the grace period expires. Late fees in New York are capped at the lesser of $50 or 5 percent of the monthly rent. Fees above the cap are unenforceable. Fees imposed during the grace period are illegal.

Legal Rent. The maximum rent a landlord is permitted to charge for a rent-stabilized apartment. Legal rent is created by a chain of documented, lawful steps: the prior legal rent plus RGB increases, approved MCI adjustments, documented IAI costs, and any other increase specifically authorized by law. Legal rent is not necessarily the same as the advertised rent, the lease rent, or the rent the previous tenant paid.

Lookback Period. The period of time that DHCR or a court may examine when investigating a rent overcharge complaint. For overcharges accruing after the HSTPA (June 14, 2019), the lookback is generally six years. For pre-HSTPA overcharges, the standard lookback is four years. A fraud exception may extend the lookback further in cases involving landlord misconduct.

MBR (Maximum Base Rent). The system used to calculate allowable rents in rent-controlled apartments. The MBR is recalculated periodically, and landlords may apply for increases based on the recalculation. This system is distinct from the RGB process used for rent-stabilized apartments.

MCI (Major Capital Improvement). A building-wide improvement (such as a new roof, boiler, or elevator) for which a landlord may apply to HCR for permission to increase the rent on all apartments in the building. Under the HSTPA, MCI increases are capped, are temporary (expiring after 30 years), and are subject to stricter documentation requirements than before 2019.

Motion to Dismiss. A formal written request asking the court to throw out a case for a legal deficiency, without the need for a trial. In Housing Court, common grounds for motions to dismiss include defective predicate notices, improper service, lack of standing, failure to include required disclosures, and failure to state a cause of action. If granted, the case is dismissed.

Multiple Dwelling. A building with three or more residential units. Multiple dwellings must be registered with HPD and are subject to the Housing Maintenance Code and the Multiple Dwelling Law. A building that contains illegal apartments bringing the total to three or more units may be an unregistered multiple dwelling, which carries legal consequences for the landlord.

Nonpayment Proceeding. A type of eviction case in which the landlord alleges that the tenant has failed to pay rent that is lawfully owed. Nonpayment cases require a valid rent demand served at least 14 days before the case is filed. The demand must state the correct amount, identify the specific periods covered, and exclude illegal charges.

Normal Wear and Tear. The natural, expected deterioration of an apartment that results from ordinary, reasonable living over time. Normal wear and tear includes faded paint, small nail holes, worn carpet, and minor scuffs. It does not include damage caused by the tenant's negligence, misuse, or abuse. Landlords cannot charge tenants for normal wear and tear when deducting from security deposits.

Notice to Cure. A written notice that a landlord must serve on a tenant before filing an eviction case based on a lease violation (other than nonpayment). The notice must identify the specific violation and give the tenant a specified period to correct it. If the tenant cures the violation within the allowed time, the ground for eviction is eliminated.

ORA (Office of Rent Administration). The division within DHCR/HCR that handles rent stabilization matters, including overcharge complaints, registration, lease complaints, and owner-use applications. ORA investigates complaints and issues orders that are enforceable through the courts.

Overcharge. The amount by which the rent a landlord collects exceeds the legal regulated rent for a rent-stabilized apartment. Overcharges can result from illegal rent increases, improper IAI or MCI claims, vacancy bonuses applied after the HSTPA eliminated them, or rents set after fraudulent deregulation. Tenants can file overcharge complaints with DHCR or pursue claims in court. Willful overcharges may result in treble (triple) damages.

Owner-Use Eviction. An eviction based on the landlord's claimed intent to use the apartment as a primary residence for themselves or an immediate family member. In rent-stabilized apartments, the HSTPA raised the standard from "good faith" to "immediate and compelling necessity." Owner-use evictions are limited to one unit per building, and senior, disabled, and long-term tenants receive additional protections. A Golub Notice is required.

Personal Delivery. The preferred method of serving legal documents, in which the notice or papers are handed directly to the person being served. Personal delivery is the most reliable form of service and the most difficult to dispute.

Petition. The formal legal document that initiates an eviction case in Housing Court. The two main types are nonpayment petitions and holdover petitions. The petition must correctly identify the parties, state the legal basis for the proceeding, and be supported by a valid predicate notice.

Predicate Notice. Any notice that must be served before a case can be filed in court. In nonpayment cases, the predicate notice is the rent demand. In holdover cases, the predicate notice is the termination notice, cure notice, or notice of non-renewal. Defects in the predicate notice can result in dismissal of the case.

Preferential Rent. A rent lower than the legal regulated maximum that a landlord voluntarily offers to a tenant in a rent-stabilized apartment. Under the HSTPA, landlords generally cannot jump from the preferential rent to the full legal rent during the tenancy. Future increases must generally be calculated on the preferential amount, not the legal rent.

Primary Residence. The place where a person lives most of the time and where their personal, legal, and financial life is centered. In rent-stabilized apartments, the tenant must maintain the apartment as their primary residence, generally occupying it for at least 183 days per year. Primary residence is established through the totality of evidence, including voter registration, tax filings, driver's license, utility accounts, and mail delivery.

Quiet Enjoyment. A tenant's legal right to use and occupy their apartment without unreasonable interference from the landlord. The right to quiet enjoyment is implied in every residential lease and encompasses privacy, peace, and freedom from intrusions, disruptions, or pressure that undermines the tenancy. Violations of quiet enjoyment may constitute harassment.

RA-23.5. A DHCR form that allows a tenant of record to formally notify the landlord of family members residing in the apartment who may be entitled to succession rights. Filing the form is optional and creates a contemporaneous record but does not prove succession rights and does not begin the succession process.

RA-54. A DHCR form used by landlords to apply for a certificate of eviction, required for owner-use evictions in rent-stabilized apartments outside New York City and for rent-controlled apartments statewide.

RA-89. The DHCR form used by tenants to file a rent overcharge complaint. The form requires the tenant's contact information, the building address, details of the lease, the rent being paid, and a description of the basis for the overcharge claim. The form is available on the HCR website and at DHCR borough rent offices.

RA-90. A DHCR form used by tenants to file a lease complaint when the landlord fails to offer a renewal lease or fails to provide a copy of the signed lease.

Rent Abatement. A court-ordered reduction in the rent owed for a period when the apartment was substandard due to the landlord's breach of the warranty of habitability. The abatement is calculated as a percentage of the rent, reflecting the degree to which conditions impaired the apartment's livability. Abatements can be awarded in HP actions, in nonpayment cases (as a defense), and in affirmative claims by the tenant.

Rent Control. The older and rarer of New York's two rent regulation systems. Rent-controlled apartments exist almost exclusively in New York City and apply only when the building was constructed before 1947, the tenant (or qualifying family member) has lived there continuously since before July 1, 1971, and the apartment has never been lawfully deregulated. As tenants move out or pass away, rent-controlled units disappear. No new rent-controlled apartments are being created.

Rent Demand. A written notice that a landlord must serve on a tenant before filing a nonpayment eviction case. The demand must state the correct amount of rent owed, identify the rental periods covered, exclude illegal charges, and give the tenant at least 14 days to pay or respond. A defective rent demand can result in dismissal of the nonpayment case.

Rent Guidelines Board (RGB). A nine-member panel appointed by the mayor of New York City that sets the maximum allowable percentage increases for renewal leases in rent-stabilized apartments each year. The RGB conducts research, holds public hearings, and votes annually. The approved increases set the ceiling for what landlords can charge at renewal.

Rent History. The official record maintained by DHCR of every rent that a landlord has registered for a specific apartment over the years. Rent history records show whether the apartment was registered as stabilized, the legal rent for each registration period, the type of lease (renewal or vacancy), and codes indicating the basis for rent changes. Tenants can request their rent history for free, without the landlord's permission, through DHCR's online portal, by email, by phone, by text, or in person.

Rent Stabilization. The modern and more common of New York's two rent regulation systems. Rent stabilization generally applies to buildings with six or more units constructed before 1974, or to buildings that received certain tax benefits. In stabilized apartments, rent increases are set by the RGB, tenants have the right to renewal leases, landlords must register annually with HCR, and overcharges carry penalties. Since the HSTPA eliminated vacancy decontrol, stabilized apartments remain stabilized regardless of rent level.

Rent Stabilization Lease Rider. A document that landlords are required to provide to rent-stabilized tenants at the time they sign a lease. The rider explains how the proposed rent was calculated, discloses the legal regulated rent, states whether a preferential rent is being charged, and describes the tenant's rights under rent stabilization. The absence of the rider is a serious red flag and may be evidence of willfulness in an overcharge claim.

Rescission. The cancellation of an agreement. Under Local Law 1 of 2015, tenants who sign buyout agreements for rent-regulated apartments have a cooling-off period during which they may rescind (cancel) the agreement.

Retaliation. Any adverse action by a landlord motivated by a tenant's exercise of a legal right. Retaliatory actions include eviction filings, rent increases, service reductions, harassment, and refusal to make repairs. New York Real Property Law Section 223-b creates a statutory presumption of retaliation when adverse action occurs within a protected window (generally six months) after a tenant engages in a protected activity.

Right to Counsel. A New York City program, also called Universal Access to Legal Services, that provides free legal representation to tenants facing eviction in Housing Court. The program covers every zip code in New York City and is available regardless of immigration status. Tenants with pending eviction cases should attend their first court date and request an attorney.

RTP-8. The DHCR form used for renewal lease offers in rent-stabilized apartments in New York City. A valid renewal must be offered on this form (or an approved equivalent) within the required time window.

Self-Help Eviction. Any attempt by a landlord to remove a tenant from an apartment without a court order. Self-help evictions include changing locks, removing belongings, shutting off utilities, and using physical force. Self-help eviction is illegal in New York regardless of the tenant's status, the apartment's legal classification, or whether the tenant owes rent.

Small Landlord. Under the Good Cause Eviction Law, a natural person who owns no more than 10 residential units total in New York State. The small landlord exemption applies only to Good Cause and does not exempt the landlord from any other tenant protection. If the building is owned by an LLC, the 10-unit threshold applies to any individual person with an ownership interest.

Stay. A court order that temporarily prevents an action from being carried out. In eviction cases, a stay of the warrant of eviction delays the physical removal of the tenant. Courts may grant stays for various reasons, including pending appeals, applications for rental assistance, or changed circumstances.

Stipulation of Settlement. A written agreement between the landlord and tenant that resolves a court case on negotiated terms. Stipulations are "so-ordered" by the judge, giving them the force of a court order. Both sides are bound by the terms. Stipulations may include payment plans, move-out dates, withdrawal of claims, or other provisions.

Substituted Service. A method of serving legal documents by delivering them to a person of suitable age and discretion at the recipient's residence or place of business, followed by mailing a copy to the recipient. Both steps are required. Substituted service may be used when personal delivery cannot be accomplished after reasonable attempts.

Succession Rights. The right of a qualifying family member to inherit a rent-regulated tenancy when the tenant of record dies or permanently vacates the apartment. The successor must have resided in the apartment with the tenant of record as a primary resident for the required co-residency period (generally two years, or one year for senior citizens and disabled persons). "Family member" is defined broadly to include both traditional family relationships and non-traditional relationships demonstrating emotional and financial interdependence.

Treble Damages. A penalty in which the amount of damages is tripled. In security deposit cases, courts may award treble damages when the landlord withheld the deposit in bad faith. In rent overcharge cases, treble damages may be imposed for willful overcharges. Treble damages exist to deter intentional misconduct and to level the power imbalance between landlords and tenants.

Vacate Order. An official directive from a city agency (usually HPD or the Department of Buildings) requiring all occupants to leave a space that is unsafe or illegal. Vacate orders are most commonly issued for illegal basement and cellar apartments, buildings with serious fire safety violations, or buildings with structural failures. Compliance is mandatory.

Vacancy Bonus. A percentage increase that landlords were previously entitled to apply to the legal rent when a rent-stabilized apartment became vacant. Vacancy bonuses were typically 20 percent for a two-year lease. The HSTPA eliminated vacancy bonuses entirely, effective June 14, 2019.

Vacancy Decontrol. The mechanism by which rent-stabilized apartments could be permanently removed from the stabilization system when the rent exceeded a specified threshold and the apartment became vacant. The HSTPA eliminated vacancy decontrol in 2019. Under current law, stabilized apartments remain stabilized regardless of rent level.

Warrant of Eviction. A court order authorizing a city marshal or county sheriff to carry out the physical removal of a tenant from an apartment. A warrant can only be issued after a judgment of possession. The marshal must serve the tenant with a notice of eviction providing at least 14 days' notice before executing the warrant.

Warranty of Habitability. A legal guarantee, implied in every residential lease in New York by operation of law (Real Property Law Section 235-b), that the landlord will maintain conditions that are safe, sanitary, and fit for human habitation. The warranty covers essentials such as heat, hot water, functioning plumbing, structural safety, and freedom from infestation. It cannot be waived, and any lease clause purporting to shift the habitability obligation to the tenant is unenforceable.

Appendix B

Sample Letters and Requests

This appendix provides template letters for five common tenant situations. Each letter is designed to be adapted to your specific circumstances, sent by the method described in the instructions, and kept as part of your documentation record.

These letters are not legal documents. They are practical tools for communicating clearly, creating written records, and invoking your rights in a manner that courts and agencies recognize. They are written in plain language because plain language is more effective than legal jargon in most tenant communications.

For every letter in this appendix, follow three rules. Send it by certified mail, return receipt requested, unless the instructions specify otherwise. Keep a copy of the letter and the certified mail receipt. And note the date you sent it in your personal log.

If you are facing an active court case, an imminent eviction, or a situation involving potential loss of your housing, consult an attorney before sending any letter. These templates are starting points, not substitutes for legal advice in urgent situations.

Letter 1: Rent History Request

When to use this letter. Use this letter when you want to obtain the official rent history for your apartment from the state housing agency (DHCR/HCR). As Chapter 5 explained, the rent history is the single most important document for determining whether your apartment is rent-stabilized, what the legal rent is, and whether you have been overcharged.

You do not need the landlord's permission to request your rent history. The landlord is not notified when you make the request. The process is free.

How to send it. You can make this request by email to RentInfo@hcr.ny.gov, through the HCR online portal, by phone at 833-499-0343, by text to (646) 783-0627, or by mailing a letter to the DHCR office serving your borough. The email method is recommended because it creates a written record of the request and is typically processed within two to four weeks.

If you prefer to mail a physical letter, send it to the DHCR office that covers your borough. For Queens and citywide general inquiries, the address is: DHCR Office of Rent Administration, 92-31 Union Hall Street, Queens, NY 11433.

[Your Name]
[Your Address, Apartment Number]
[City, State, Zip Code]
[Your Email Address]
[Your Phone Number]
[Date]

New York State Division of Housing and Community Renewal
Office of Rent Administration
92-31 Union Hall Street Queens, NY 11433

Re: Request for Rent History
Building Address: [Full building address]
Apartment Number: [Your apartment number]

To Whom It May Concern:

I am a current tenant at the above address. I am writing to request the complete rent history for my apartment.

Please send the rent history to me at the address listed above, or by email to [your email address].

My name is [your full name]. I have resided at this apartment since [approximate move-in date]. I am enclosing [or attaching] a copy of my current lease as proof of tenancy.

Thank you for your assistance.

Sincerely,

[Your Signature]
[Your Printed Name]

Notes. If sending by email, attach a scan or photograph of your lease. If you do not have a copy of your lease, include any document that confirms your tenancy at the address (a utility bill, a rent receipt, or a bank statement showing rent payments). If you are making the request by phone or text, note the date, time, and confirmation number (if provided) in your personal log.

Letter 2: Repair Notice to Landlord

When to use this letter. Use this letter when a condition in your apartment requires repair and you want to create a written record that the landlord was notified. As Chapter 17 explained, written notice is the foundation of every enforcement action related to repairs and habitability. Verbal requests are difficult to prove. Written requests create a timestamped record that establishes when the landlord knew about the problem.

Send this letter at the earliest opportunity after discovering the condition. If you have already made verbal requests that were ignored, this letter documents those prior requests as well.

How to send it. Send by certified mail, return receipt requested, to the landlord at the address listed in your lease for notices. Also send a copy by email if you have the landlord's email address. If the building has a managing agent, send copies to both the landlord and the managing agent. Keep copies of everything.

[Your Name]
[Your Address, Apartment Number]
[City, State, Zip Code]
[Your Email Address]
[Your Phone Number]
[Date]

[Landlord's Name or Management Company Name]
[Landlord's Address]
[City, State, Zip Code]

Re: Request for Repair
Building Address: [Full building address]
Apartment Number: [Your apartment number]

Dear [Landlord's Name or "Property Owner"]:

I am writing to notify you of the following condition in my apartment that requires repair:

[Describe the condition specifically. Include the location within the apartment, the nature of the problem, and when you first noticed it. Be factual and specific. For example: "There is a persistent water leak in the kitchen ceiling, directly above the sink. The leak began approximately three weeks ago and has worsened. There is now visible water damage to the ceiling plaster and what appears to be mold growth around the edges of the damaged area."]

[If you have previously reported this condition verbally, add: "I previously reported this condition verbally to [name of person you spoke with, such as the superintendent or property manager] on [date]. As of today, no repair has been made."]

This condition affects the habitability of my apartment. Under New York Real Property Law Section 235-b, you are required to maintain the apartment in a condition that is safe, sanitary, and fit for human habitation.

I request that you arrange for repair of this condition as soon as possible. Please contact me at [your phone number] or [your email address] to schedule access to the apartment for the repair.

I have documented the condition with photographs and will continue to document it until it is resolved.

Thank you for your prompt attention to this matter.

Sincerely,

[Your Signature]
[Your Printed Name]

Notes. After sending this letter, file a 311 complaint for the same condition. The 311 complaint will trigger an HPD inspection, which creates an official violation record that is independent of your letter. Both records together (your written notice and the HPD violation) create strong evidence of the landlord's knowledge and failure to act. If the condition is an emergency (no heat, gas leak, flooding, structural failure), do not wait for a letter. Call 311 immediately, and follow up with the letter afterward.

Letter 3: Security Deposit Demand Letter

When to use this letter. Use this letter when you have moved out of your apartment, the 14-day deadline for return of the security deposit has passed, and the landlord has either failed to return the deposit or has returned less than the full amount without a proper itemized statement.

As Chapters 14 and 15 explained, the landlord must return the full deposit or provide an itemized statement of lawful deductions within 14 days after the tenant vacates. Failure to meet this deadline may result in forfeiture of the right to claim deductions and may support an award of treble damages for bad-faith withholding.

How to send it. Send by certified mail, return receipt requested, to the landlord at the address listed in your lease. If you know the landlord's current address and it differs from the lease address, send to both. Keep a copy of the letter and the certified mail receipt. If the landlord does not respond within a reasonable period (14 to 30 days), consider filing a claim in small claims court.

[Your Name]
[Your Current Address]
[City, State, Zip Code]
[Your Email Address]
[Your Phone Number] [Date]

[Landlord's Name or Management Company Name]
[Landlord's Address]
[City, State, Zip Code]

Re: Demand for Return of Security Deposit
Former Address: [Your former apartment address, including apartment number]
Date of Vacatur: [The date you moved out]
Security Deposit Amount: $[Amount of deposit]

Dear [Landlord's Name or "Property Owner"]:

I am writing to demand the return of my security deposit in the amount of $[amount].

I vacated the apartment at the above address on [date you moved out]. I provided my forwarding address to you in writing on [date you provided forwarding address]. More than 14 days have passed since my departure.

[Choose the paragraph that applies to your situation:]

[If no deposit or statement was received:] As of the date of this letter, I have not received my security deposit or any itemized statement of deductions. Under New York General Obligations Law Section 7-108, you were required to return the full deposit or provide an itemized statement of lawful deductions within 14 days after I vacated. You have failed to comply with this requirement.

[If a partial deposit was received without proper itemization:] On [date], I received a check in the amount of $[amount returned], representing a partial return of my deposit. The accompanying statement listed the following deductions: [list the deductions as described by the landlord]. These deductions are improper for the following reasons: [briefly state why, such as "the repainting charge represents normal wear and tear after a [length]-year tenancy" or "the 'general repairs' charge is not sufficiently itemized to allow evaluation"]. Additionally, the statement was received [number] days after I vacated, which exceeds the 14-day deadline.

[If the full deposit was withheld with a statement:] On [date], I received an itemized statement indicating that you have retained the full deposit of $[amount]. The deductions listed are improper for the following reasons: [briefly state why]. Additionally, [if applicable] the statement was received after the 14-day deadline.

I demand the return of the full security deposit of $[amount] within 14 days of your receipt of this letter. If the deposit is not returned, I intend to pursue this matter in court, where I will seek the return of the deposit plus any additional damages available under the law, including treble damages for bad-faith withholding.

Sincerely,

[Your Signature]
[Your Printed Name]

Enclosures: [List any documents you are including, such as copies of move-out photographs, the forwarding address notification, or the key return confirmation]

Notes. This letter is designed to give the landlord one clear, final opportunity to return the deposit before you file a court case. The reference to treble damages is factual, not a threat. Courts can and do award treble damages for bad-faith withholding. If the landlord does not respond or does not return the full deposit, file a claim in small claims court. Bring copies of this letter, the certified mail receipt, your lease, your move-out photographs, your forwarding address notification, and any other relevant documentation.

Letter 4: Sublet Permission Request (Rent-Stabilized Apartment)

When to use this letter. Use this letter when you are a rent-stabilized tenant who wishes to sublet your apartment temporarily and needs to request the landlord's permission. As Chapter 21 explained, rent-stabilized tenants generally have the right to sublet, but the request must follow a specific written procedure. The landlord has 30 days after receiving all required information to respond. If the landlord does not respond within 30 days, consent is deemed granted.

How to send it. Send by certified mail, return receipt requested, to the landlord at the address listed in your lease. Keep a copy of everything. Note the date you sent the letter and calculate the 30-day response deadline.

[Your Name]
[Your Address, Apartment Number]
[City, State, Zip Code] [Your Email Address]
[Your Phone Number] [Date]

[Landlord's Name or Management Company Name]
[Landlord's Address]
[City, State, Zip Code]

Re: Request for Permission to Sublet Building Address: [Full building address]
Apartment Number: [Your apartment number]

Dear [Landlord's Name or "Property Owner"]:

I am writing to request your permission to sublet my apartment for a temporary period, in accordance with New York Real Property Law Section 226-b and the Rent Stabilization Code.

The details of the proposed sublet are as follows:

Term of proposed sublease: [Start date] through [End date]

Name of proposed subtenant: [Full legal name of subtenant]

Permanent home address of proposed subtenant: [Subtenant's current address]

Business address of proposed subtenant: [Subtenant's work address, or "Not applicable"]

Reason for subletting: [State your reason. For example: "I have accepted a temporary work assignment in [city] and intend to return to the apartment at the conclusion of the assignment." Or: "I will be traveling for [reason] and intend to return to the apartment at the end of the sublet period."]

My address during the sublet period: [The address where you will be staying]

I have enclosed the following documents with this request:

A copy of the proposed sublease between myself and the proposed subtenant

A copy of my current lease for the apartment [3. If applicable: Written consent of any cotenant or guarantor]

The proposed rent to be charged to the subtenant is $[amount], which is equal to my current rent of $[amount]. [If the apartment is furnished, add: "A surcharge of 10 percent ($[amount]) has been added for the furnishings, bringing the total to $[amount], in accordance with the Rent Stabilization Code."]

I understand that you have 30 days from your receipt of this letter and all required information to consent to or reasonably withhold consent for this sublet. If you require additional information reasonably related to this request, please notify me in writing within 10 days.

I intend to maintain the apartment as my primary residence and plan to return at the conclusion of the sublet period.

Thank you for your consideration.

Sincerely,

[Your Signature]
[Your Printed Name]

Enclosures:

1 - Copy of proposed sublease
2 - Copy of current lease
3 - Written consent of cotenant/guarantor, if applicable]

Notes. Mark your calendar for 30 days after the landlord receives the letter (use the return receipt date). If the landlord does not respond within 30 days, consent is deemed granted by operation of law. If the landlord responds with a request for additional information, provide it promptly. The 30-day clock restarts when the additional information is received. If the landlord unreasonably withholds consent, you may sublet anyway, but consult an attorney before proceeding if the landlord has explicitly refused. Do not charge the subtenant more than your stabilized rent (plus the 10 percent furnished surcharge, if applicable). Overcharging the subtenant can jeopardize your own tenancy.

Letter 5: Cease-and-Desist for Unauthorized Entry

When to use this letter. Use this letter when your landlord has entered your apartment without proper notice, without your consent, and without a genuine emergency. As Chapter 18 explained, landlords must provide reasonable advance notice (generally at least 24 hours) and have a legitimate purpose before entering. Repeated unauthorized entry may constitute harassment.

This letter serves two purposes. It puts the landlord on formal written notice that the entries are unauthorized and must stop. And it creates a dated record that can be used as evidence in a harassment complaint or HP action if the behavior continues.

How to send it. Send by certified mail, return receipt requested, to the landlord at the address listed in your lease. Also send a copy by email if you have the landlord's email address. Keep copies of everything. If the unauthorized entries continue after the landlord receives this letter, the letter becomes evidence that the landlord was warned and persisted, which strengthens a harassment claim.

[Your Name]
[Your Address, Apartment Number]
[City, State, Zip Code]
[Your Email Address]
[Your Phone Number] [Date]

[Landlord's Name or Management Company Name]
[Landlord's Address]
[City, State, Zip Code]

Re: Unauthorized Entry into My Apartment
Building Address: [Full building address]
Apartment Number: [Your apartment number]

Dear [Landlord's Name or "Property Owner"]:

I am writing to inform you that you [or your agent, employee, or representative] have entered my apartment without proper notice and without my consent on the following occasions:

[List each incident with as much detail as possible. For each, include the date, the approximate time, the circumstances (whether you were home or not, how you learned of the entry), and the stated reason (if any). For example:]

[Date]: I returned home at approximately [time] and found evidence that someone had entered my apartment while I was at work. [Describe the evidence: items moved, lights left on, smell of cleaning products, tools left behind, etc.] I had not received any prior notice of entry. No emergency existed.

[Date]: [Landlord's name or "the superintendent"] entered my apartment at approximately [time] without prior notice. When I asked the reason, I was told [state the reason given, such as "to check on the pipes" or "to look at something"]. No advance notice had been provided, and no emergency existed.

[Date]: [Describe the incident.]

Under New York law, you are required to provide reasonable advance notice (generally at least 24 hours) and to have a legitimate purpose before entering my apartment. The only exception is a genuine emergency involving an immediate threat to life or property, such as a fire, flood, or gas leak. None of the entries described above involved such an emergency.

I hereby demand that you cease all unauthorized entries into my apartment immediately. Any future entry must be preceded by reasonable written notice stating the date, approximate time, and purpose of the visit. I reserve the right to be present during any non-emergency entry.

If unauthorized entries continue, I will file a harassment complaint in Housing Court and will seek all remedies available under the law, including a court order restricting your access and civil penalties for harassment.

I am documenting all entries and attempted entries, and I will continue to do so.

Sincerely,

[Your Signature]
[Your Printed Name]

Notes. After sending this letter, continue documenting every entry and attempted entry. Keep a log with dates, times, circumstances, and evidence. Take photographs of anything that suggests unauthorized entry (items moved, evidence of work done without your knowledge, locks or doors in different positions than you left them). If the landlord installs cameras directed at your apartment or changes your locks without providing a key, document these actions immediately. They may constitute separate violations.

If the unauthorized entries continue after the landlord receives this letter, you have several options. File a complaint through 311 if the entries involve disruption of services or interference with your tenancy. File an HP action in Housing Court that includes a harassment claim. Contact a tenant legal services organization for assistance with a standalone harassment petition. The cease-and-desist letter is not the end of the process. It is the beginning of the documented record that makes enforcement possible.

Appendix C

Eviction Notice Checklist

Use this checklist within the first 24 hours of receiving any notice related to eviction, non-renewal, or nonpayment of rent. Work through each section in order. A "no" answer to any question may indicate a defect that could invalidate the notice or the case built on it.

This checklist is not legal advice. It is a diagnostic tool designed to help you identify potential problems quickly so you can bring them to an attorney's attention. If you answer "no" to any question, do not assume the notice is automatically invalid. Consult a tenant attorney or legal services organization as soon as possible.

Do not move out, stop paying rent, or sign anything based on a notice you have received without first working through this checklist and, if possible, speaking with an attorney.

Section 1: What Kind of Notice Is This?

Before evaluating the notice, identify what it is. The type of notice determines which requirements apply.

Is this a rent demand (a written demand for unpaid rent)? If yes, this is the predicate to a nonpayment case. Proceed to Section 2 and evaluate under the rent demand requirements.

Is this a notice to cure (a notice identifying a lease violation and giving you time to correct it)? If yes, this is a preliminary step in a holdover case based on a lease violation. Proceed to Section 3.

Is this a notice of termination or non-renewal (a notice stating that your tenancy is being terminated or your lease will not be renewed)? If yes, this is the predicate to a holdover case. Proceed to Section 4.

Is this a Golub Notice (a notice served 150 to 90 days before lease expiration in a rent-stabilized apartment, stating the landlord's intention not to renew based on a specific ground such as owner use)? If yes, this is the predicate to a rent-stabilized holdover case. Proceed to Section 5.

Is this a court petition and notice of petition (formal court papers stating that a case has been filed against you)? If yes, you have a court date. Skip to Section 6. Do not miss the court date.

If you are unsure what type of notice you received, bring it to an attorney, a legal services organization, or the Housing Court Help Center immediately.

Section 2: Rent Demand Checklist

Does the demand state a specific dollar amount owed?

Does the amount match what you actually owe based on the legal rent? In a rent-stabilized apartment, compare the demanded amount to the legal regulated rent, not the amount the landlord has been charging if you suspect an overcharge.

Does the demand identify the specific months or rental periods covered? A demand that states a total without specifying periods is potentially defective.

Does the demand exclude late fees? If late fees are included, are they within the legal cap (the lesser of $50 or 5 percent of monthly rent per incident)?

Were any late fees charged during the grace period (the first five days after rent was due)? Fees charged during the grace period are illegal.

Does the demand exclude non-rent charges such as attorney's fees, utility charges, repair costs, or administrative fees? These are generally not collectible through a rent demand.

Does the demand include the Good Cause Eviction notice (required since August 2024), stating whether the apartment is covered by Good Cause and, if not, explaining the basis for the claimed exemption?

Was the demand served at least 14 days before any court case was filed? If a petition was filed before the 14-day period elapsed, the case may be premature.

Note the date you received the demand and mark your calendar for the 14th day after service. You have until that date to pay the amount owed (if the demand is accurate) before the landlord can file a case.

Section 3: Notice to Cure Checklist

Does the notice identify a specific lease provision that you allegedly violated?

Does the notice describe the specific conduct or condition that constitutes the violation? A vague notice that says "you are in violation of your lease" without identifying the violation is potentially defective.

Is the alleged violation real? Read the lease clause cited in the notice. Does your conduct actually violate that clause?

Is the lease clause enforceable? Some clauses are overridden by law (such as no-pet clauses waived under the three-month rule, no-roommate clauses overridden by the Roommate Law, or habitability waivers that are void under RPL 235-b).

Does the notice give you a reasonable cure period? Determine how long you have to correct the violation.

Can you actually cure the violation? If yes, cure it immediately and document that you did so (with photographs, written confirmation, or other evidence).

Has the landlord previously tolerated the same condition without objection? If the landlord has known about the condition for an extended period and never raised it, the sudden enforcement may indicate retaliation or pretext.

Did the notice arrive shortly after you exercised a legal right (filed a complaint, requested repairs, organized with neighbors, asserted your rent-stabilized rights)? If yes, the timing may support a retaliation defense.

Section 4: Termination or Non-Renewal Notice Checklist

Does the notice state a reason for the termination? In rent-stabilized apartments and Good Cause-covered apartments, the landlord must state a legally recognized reason. In other apartments, the notice must still comply with notice period requirements.

Is the stated reason a valid ground under the applicable legal framework? Review Chapter 10 (just cause) and Chapter 11 (owner use, demolition) to determine whether the stated ground is legally recognized.

Does the notice provide the correct notice period based on your length of tenancy? For tenants who have lived in the apartment less than one year: 30 days. For one to two years: 60 days. For two years or more: 90 days. For rent-stabilized tenants receiving a Golub Notice: 150 to 90 days before lease expiration. Count the days from the date of service, not the date printed on the notice.

Does the notice correctly identify you by name? Does it correctly identify the landlord or building owner?

Does the notice include the Good Cause Eviction notice (required since August 2024)?

If you are in a rent-stabilized apartment, was this notice served on the proper form and within the required window? If the landlord is declining to renew your lease, a Golub Notice is required (see Section 5).

Is the notice addressed to the correct apartment? Errors in unit number or address can create jurisdictional problems.

Section 5: Golub Notice Checklist (Rent-Stabilized Apartments Only)

Was the notice served between 150 and 90 days before your current lease expires? Calculate the dates precisely. A notice served on day 89 or day 151 is outside the window.

Does the notice state the specific ground for non-renewal? In owner-use cases, it must identify the owner or family member who intends to occupy the unit.

If the ground is owner use, does the notice identify the specific unit being sought? Owner-use evictions are generally limited to one unit per building.

Are you a senior citizen (62 or older), a person with a disability, or a tenant who has lived in the apartment for 15 or more years? If yes, you have additional protections, including the landlord's obligation to provide equivalent or superior alternative housing.

Does the notice include the Good Cause Eviction notice?

Was the notice served by someone other than the landlord? Was it served by an approved method (personal delivery, substituted service, or conspicuous place service with proper documentation)?

Section 6: Service Checklist (Applies to All Notices)

This section evaluates how the notice was delivered. Service defects are independent grounds for dismissal, regardless of the content of the notice.

How did you receive the notice? Note the exact method: handed to you in person, left with another person at your apartment, taped to your door, slipped under your door, mailed, emailed, or some other method.

If it was handed to you personally, who handed it to you? Was it the landlord, a building employee, or a third-party process server? In many situations, the landlord cannot serve the notice personally.

If it was left with another person, was that person of suitable age and discretion? Was a copy also mailed to you? Both steps are required for substituted service.

If it was taped to your door (conspicuous place service), were prior attempts made to deliver it personally? How many attempts? Were those attempts documented in the affidavit of service? Was a copy also mailed to you? All of these steps are required.

If it was mailed only, was mailing alone sufficient for this type of notice? Some notices require personal delivery or substituted service before mailing alone is acceptable.

If it was emailed only, is email an approved method of service for this type of notice? For most predicate notices and court papers, email alone is not sufficient.

Does the affidavit of service (if you have seen one) accurately describe what actually happened? If the affidavit claims three attempts at personal delivery but you were home all three days and no one knocked, the affidavit may be inaccurate.

Section 7: Immediate Next Steps

After working through this checklist, take the following steps regardless of your answers.

Do not move out based on a notice alone. A notice is not a court order. You are not required to leave until a court issues a judgment of possession and a marshal serves a warrant of eviction.

Do not stop paying rent unless you have consulted an attorney and made a deliberate strategic decision to withhold. Nonpayment creates a separate legal issue that can complicate your position.

Do not sign anything the landlord presents to you in connection with the notice without consulting an attorney first.

Make copies of the notice and all documents that accompanied it. Store the originals in a safe place.

Photograph or scan the envelope or packaging the notice arrived in, including any postmarks, certified mail stickers, or delivery confirmation labels.

Write down everything you remember about how the notice was delivered: the date, the time, who delivered it, what they said, and whether anyone else was present.

Contact an attorney or legal services organization as soon as possible. If you have a pending eviction case, call Housing Court Answers at 718-557-1379 or 212-962-4795, Monday through Friday, 9 a.m. to 5 p.m. If you are eligible for the Right to Counsel program, attend your first court date and request an attorney. If you are not facing an active court case but have received a predicate notice, contact the Met Council on Housing hotline at 212-979-0611, Legal Aid Society, Legal Services NYC at 917-661-4500, or another legal services organization in your borough.

If your court date is within the next few days and you do not have an attorney, go to court. Do not miss the court date. Ask the clerk or court attorney about the Right to Counsel program. Tell the judge you need time to obtain counsel. Request an adjournment.

Time matters. The sooner you evaluate the notice and seek help, the more options you have.

Appendix D

Agency and Resource Directory

This directory lists the government agencies, legal services organizations, tenant hotlines, and advocacy groups that New York City tenants are most likely to need. Each entry explains what the organization does, when you should contact them, and how to reach them.

Contact information is current as of the date of publication. Agencies and organizations change phone numbers, addresses, and hours periodically. If a number listed here is not working, call 311 for updated contact information.

STATE AGENCIES

DHCR/HCR (Division of Housing and Community Renewal / Homes and Community Renewal)

What they do. DHCR is the state agency that administers rent regulation in New York. Through its Office of Rent Administration (ORA), DHCR handles rent stabilization and rent control matters, including overcharge complaints, registration of rent-stabilized apartments, lease renewal complaints, owner-use eviction applications, and the maintenance of rent history records. DHCR investigates complaints, issues orders, and calculates legal rents.

When to contact them. Contact DHCR when you want to request your apartment's rent history, when you believe you are being overcharged on rent in a stabilized apartment, when your landlord has failed to offer a renewal lease, when you need to file a complaint about any rent stabilization violation, when you want to verify whether your apartment is registered as stabilized, or when you are responding to an owner-use eviction and the landlord must file for a certificate of eviction.

How to reach them.

Rent Info Line (for rent history requests and general rent regulation questions): 833-499-0343.

Email for rent history requests: RentInfo@hcr.ny.gov.

Text for rent history requests: (646) 783-0627 (text "RENT HISTORY").

Online inquiry portal: Available through the HCR website at hcr.ny.gov.

Rent Regulated Building Search (to check whether a building has filed rent regulation records): apps.hcr.ny.gov/BuildingSearch.

Borough offices (in-person visits by appointment only):

Bronx: 2400 Halsey Street, 1st Floor. Brooklyn: 55 Hanson Place, 6th Floor. Lower Manhattan: 25 Beaver Street, 2nd Floor. Upper Manhattan: 163 West 125th Street, 5th Floor. Queens: 92-31 Union Hall Street, 6th Floor.

Mailing address for complaints and filings: DHCR Office of Rent Administration, 92-31 Union Hall Street, Queens, NY 11433.

CITY AGENCIES

HPD (Department of Housing Preservation and Development)

What they do. HPD is the New York City agency responsible for enforcing the Housing Maintenance Code. HPD conducts inspections of residential buildings, issues violations for substandard conditions, monitors landlord compliance with repair orders, oversees building registration for multiple dwellings, administers housing programs including lead paint compliance, and provides information about tenant rights and fair housing services.

When to contact them. Contact HPD (through 311) when your apartment has conditions that violate the housing code (no heat, no hot water, leaks, mold, infestation, broken locks, peeling paint, structural problems), when your landlord has failed to make repairs after you have provided written notice, when you want to trigger an official inspection that creates a violation record, or when you need information about your building's registration, violations, or complaint history.

How to reach them.

To file a complaint or request an inspection: Call 311, visit nyc.gov/311, use the NYC 311 mobile app, or text 311-692.

HPD Building Information Search (to look up building registrations, violations, and complaints): hpdonline.nyc.gov.

HPD general information: nyc.gov/hpd.

For information about fair housing counselors and tenant rights legal assistance: Visit the HPD website or call 311 and ask for HPD Tenant Resources.

311 (New York City Services)

What they do. 311 is New York City's central service line for non-emergency government services and information. For tenants, 311 is the primary channel for filing housing complaints, requesting inspections, and accessing city services related to housing conditions.

When to contact them. Contact 311 when you need to file a complaint about apartment conditions (heat, hot water, pests, leaks, mold, lead paint, broken locks, elevator outages, or any other housing maintenance issue), when you want to trigger an HPD inspection, when you need to report an illegal apartment or an illegal conversion, when you need information about city services, tenant resources, or emergency housing assistance, when you need to be connected to the HRA Tenant Helpline, or when you need referrals to legal services, community organizations, or government agencies.

How to reach them.

Phone: Call 311 from any phone in New York City, or 212-NEW-YORK (212-639-9675) from outside the city.

Online: nyc.gov/311.

Mobile app: NYC 311 (available for iOS and Android).

Text: 311-692.

311 is available 24 hours a day, 7 days a week, with translation services available in over 175 languages.

DOB (Department of Buildings)

What they do. The Department of Buildings regulates construction, alteration, and demolition of buildings in New York City. DOB issues building permits, certificates of occupancy, and violations for unauthorized construction or use. For tenants, DOB is relevant when questions arise about whether an apartment is legal, whether construction work is permitted, or whether the building's use matches its certificate of occupancy.

When to contact them. Contact DOB when you want to look up your building's certificate of occupancy (to determine whether your apartment is a legal residential unit), when you believe construction work in your building is unauthorized or unsafe, when you want to verify whether the landlord has obtained permits for claimed renovation or demolition work, or when you need to report an unsafe building condition (structural failure, facade hazard, or construction-related danger).

How to reach them.

Online tools (including certificate of occupancy search, permit search, and complaint filing): nyc.gov/buildings.

BIS (Building Information System) for building records: a810-bisweb.nyc.gov.

To file a complaint: Call 311 or file online through DOB NOW at nyc.gov/dobNOW.

DCWP (Department of Consumer and Worker Protection)

What they do. DCWP enforces consumer protection laws in New York City, including the FARE Act (which governs broker fees), regulations on tenant-facing fees, and other consumer-related housing provisions.

When to contact them. Contact DCWP when you believe a broker charged you a fee in violation of the FARE Act, when you were charged illegal application fees, move-in fees, or other unlawful charges, or when a landlord or broker engaged in deceptive practices in connection with renting an apartment.

How to reach them.

To file a complaint: Visit nyc.gov/dcwp or call 311 and ask for DCWP.

DCWP handles complaints, investigates violations, and can impose fines and penalties through OATH (the Office of Administrative Trials and Hearings).

COURTS AND COURT RESOURCES

Housing Court

What they do. New York City Housing Court handles residential landlord-tenant disputes, including nonpayment and holdover eviction cases, HP actions (tenant-initiated cases to compel repairs), harassment claims, and other housing-related matters. Housing Court has locations in each borough.

When to contact them. Contact Housing Court (or appear in person) when you have been served with court papers (a petition and notice of petition), when you need to file an HP action to compel repairs, when you need to file an Order to Show Cause for emergency relief, when you need to check the status of a pending case, or when you need information about the Right to Counsel program.

How to reach them.

Bronx: 1118 Grand Concourse, Bronx, NY 10456. Brooklyn: 141 Livingston Street, Brooklyn, NY 11201. Manhattan: 111 Centre Street, New York, NY 10013. Queens: 89-17 Sutphin Boulevard, Jamaica, NY 11435. Staten Island: 927 Castleton Avenue, Staten Island, NY 10310.

Housing Court information: nycourts.gov/courts/nyc/housing.

Housing Court Help Centers

What they do. Housing Court Help Centers provide free information and assistance to tenants appearing in Housing Court without an attorney. Staff and volunteers can help you understand court procedures, fill out forms, identify legal issues, and connect with legal services organizations. Help Centers are located in each borough courthouse.

When to contact them. Visit the Help Center when you have received court papers and do not have an attorney, when you need to fill out an answer to a petition, when you need information about the Right to Counsel program, when you need to file an HP action and want assistance with the forms, or when you need referrals to legal services organizations.

How to reach them. Help Centers are located within the Housing Court buildings listed above. Walk in during court hours. No appointment is necessary.

Housing Court Answers

What they do. Housing Court Answers is a nonprofit organization that provides free information, referrals, and assistance to tenants navigating Housing Court. They operate a telephone hotline and provide in-court assistance.

When to contact them. Contact Housing Court Answers when you have a pending eviction case and need information about the process, when you need to be connected with a Right to Counsel attorney, when you have questions about court procedures, deadlines, or forms, or when you need referrals to legal services organizations.

How to reach them.

Phone: 718-557-1379 or 212-962-4795, Monday through Friday, 9 a.m. to 5 p.m.

Email: housingcourtanswers@clsny.org.

FREE LEGAL SERVICES ORGANIZATIONS

Right to Counsel / Universal Access

What they do. New York City's Right to Counsel program provides free legal representation to tenants facing eviction in Housing Court, including nonpayment cases, holdover cases, and NYCHA administrative proceedings. The program covers every zip code in New York City and is available regardless of immigration status. Right to Counsel providers are present at Housing Court and connect with tenants at their first court conference.

When to contact them. If you have a pending eviction case, attend your first court date and tell the judge or court attorney that you would like an attorney. Right to Counsel providers will connect with you at court. If you cannot reach a provider at court, call Housing Court Answers at the numbers listed above, or call 311 and ask for the Tenant Helpline.

The Legal Aid Society

What they do. The Legal Aid Society is the largest provider of free legal services for tenants in New York City. Their housing practice handles eviction defense, harassment cases, HP actions, overcharge claims, NYCHA proceedings, tenant group advocacy, and a wide range of other housing issues.

When to contact them. Contact Legal Aid when you are facing eviction, when you need help with an overcharge claim, when you are experiencing harassment, when you need assistance with NYCHA housing issues, or when you want to organize a tenant association.

How to reach them.

Manhattan: 212-426-3000. Brooklyn: 718-722-3100. Bronx: 718-991-4600. Queens: 718-286-2450. Staten Island: 347-422-5333.

Homeless Rights Project: 800-649-9125, Monday through Friday, 10 a.m. to 3 p.m.

Housing Justice Unit (tenant group advocacy): 212-577-7988, Monday through Friday, 10 a.m. to 4 p.m. Email: HousingGrpAdv@legal-aid.org.

NYCHA Unit: 212-298-3450. Email: publichousingunit@legal-aid.org.

Note: If you have an upcoming eviction case in Housing Court, you do not need to contact Legal Aid directly. The Right to Counsel program will connect you with a provider at your first court date. Contact the numbers above for non-eviction housing issues.

Legal Services NYC

What they do. Legal Services NYC provides free legal representation to low-income tenants across New York City. They handle eviction defense, harassment, disrepair, overcharges, and other housing issues.

When to contact them. Contact Legal Services NYC when you need free legal representation for a housing issue, when you are facing eviction, when you are experiencing landlord harassment or disrepair, or when you need help with an overcharge claim.

How to reach them.

Phone: 917-661-4500, Monday through Friday, 10 a.m. to 4 p.m.

Website: legalservicesnyc.org.

New York Legal Assistance Group (NYLAG)

What they do. NYLAG provides free legal services to tenants through their Tenants' Rights Unit, handling eviction defense, anti-harassment cases, and other housing matters.

When to contact them. Contact NYLAG when you need free legal representation for a housing issue, when you are facing eviction or harassment, or when you need assistance with other tenant rights matters.

How to reach them.

Phone: 212-613-5000.

Website: nylag.org.

Mobilization for Justice

What they do. Mobilization for Justice offers anti-eviction programs for low-income tenants, seniors, and SRO (single room occupancy) residents. They provide legal representation, information, and advocacy.

When to contact them. Contact Mobilization for Justice when you are a senior tenant facing eviction or harassment, when you live in an SRO and need legal assistance, or when you need information about tenant rights (fact sheets available in English, Spanish, and Chinese).

How to reach them.

Phone: 212-417-3700.

Website: mobilizationforjustice.org.

HRA Office of Civil Justice

What they do. The Human Resources Administration's Office of Civil Justice coordinates Right to Counsel services and other tenant legal assistance programs. They fund free legal representation for tenants facing eviction, harassment, disrepair, and other housing-related issues.

When to contact them. Contact HRA when you need to be connected with a Right to Counsel attorney, when you need information about free legal services for housing issues, or when you need referrals to tenant assistance programs including rental assistance.

How to reach them.

Phone: Call 311 and ask for the Tenant Helpline.

Website: nyc.gov/hra.

TENANT HOTLINES AND INFORMATION SERVICES

Met Council on Housing Tenants' Rights Hotline

What they do. Met Council on Housing operates a free telephone hotline staffed by trained volunteers who are deeply knowledgeable about New York City housing law. They explain tenant rights, describe options for solving housing problems, suggest strategies for asserting rights, and refer tenants to legal services organizations when representation is needed. Hotline volunteers are not lawyers and cannot provide legal advice, but they are among the most knowledgeable people on tenant rights issues in the city.

When to contact them. Contact Met Council when you have a question about your rights as a tenant, when you need to understand your options before deciding whether to take action, when you need a referral to a legal services organization, when you want information about tenant organizing, or when you need practical guidance on a housing issue that does not yet require a lawyer.

How to reach them.

Phone: 212-979-0611.

Hours: Mondays and Wednesdays, 1:30 p.m. to 8:00 p.m. Fridays, 1:30 p.m. to 5:00 p.m.

Note: The hotline is heavily used and it may take several attempts to get through. Be patient and try during different time slots.

NYC Tenant Resource Portal

What they do. The city's online Tenant Resource Portal offers an Eviction Prevention Tool that takes tenants through a series of questions and directs them to the most useful public and private resources based on their responses.

When to contact them. Visit the portal when you need help identifying which resources apply to your situation, when you are at risk of eviction and want to explore all available options, or when you need information about rental assistance programs.

How to reach them.

Website: Available through nyc.gov (search "Tenant Resource Portal").

JustFix.nyc

What they do. JustFix is a nonprofit that provides free online tools to help tenants document conditions, generate repair request letters, access building information, research landlord ownership, and connect with legal resources. Their tools are designed to be used without an attorney and are available in multiple languages.

When to contact them. Visit JustFix when you need to send a repair request letter to your landlord, when you want to look up your building's violations, ownership, and complaint history, when you want to generate documentation for an HP action or overcharge complaint, or when you need to research your landlord's portfolio across multiple buildings.

How to reach them.

Website: justfix.nyc.

REFERRAL SERVICES AND BAR ASSOCIATIONS

New York City Bar Association Legal Referral Service

What they do. The NYC Bar Legal Referral Service provides referrals to private attorneys for tenants who do not qualify for free legal services or who need representation beyond what free providers can offer. They also offer free legal advice one evening per week on specific issues, including landlord-tenant matters, and operate a free counseling hotline for low-income NYC residents.

When to contact them. Contact the NYC Bar when you need a referral to a private tenant attorney, when you do not qualify for free legal services but need legal representation, when you want a brief free consultation on a landlord-tenant issue, or when you need help identifying the right type of attorney for your situation.

How to reach them.

Referral Service: 212-626-7373.

Free counseling line: 212-626-7383.

LAW SCHOOL LEGAL CLINICS

What they do. Several New York City law schools operate clinical programs that provide free legal representation to tenants under the supervision of licensed faculty attorneys. Law students handle cases as part of their legal training, with oversight from experienced practitioners.

When to contact them. Contact a law school clinic when you need free legal representation and are unable to obtain it through the organizations listed above, when your issue involves a complex legal question that benefits from in-depth analysis, or when you are willing to work with a student attorney supervised by a faculty member. Availability varies by semester, and not all clinics handle all types of housing cases.

Schools with housing-related clinical programs include NYU School of Law, Columbia Law School, Fordham University School of Law, Brooklyn Law School, CUNY School of Law, and Cardozo School of Law. Contact each school's clinical programs office for current availability, eligibility requirements, and intake procedures.

TENANT ORGANIZING GROUPS

Tenants and Neighbors

What they do. Tenants and Neighbors is a statewide tenant organizing and advocacy organization that helps tenants understand their rights, organize in their buildings, and advocate for stronger tenant protections.

When to contact them. Contact Tenants and Neighbors when you want to organize a tenant association in your building, when you need training on tenant rights and advocacy, or when you want to get involved in housing policy advocacy.

How to reach them.

Phone: 212-608-4320.

Right to Counsel NYC Coalition

What they do. The Right to Counsel NYC Coalition is the advocacy organization that led the campaign to establish New York City's Right to Counsel program. They provide resources on how to respond to eviction notices, connect with available legal services, and advocate for expanded tenant protections.

When to contact them. Visit their website when you need information about the Right to Counsel program, when you want resources on responding to an eviction, or when you want to get involved in advocacy for tenant legal protections.

How to reach them.

Website: righttocounselnyc.org.

ELECTED OFFICIALS

Your City Council Member's Office

What they do. New York City Council members represent constituents in their districts and often have staff dedicated to housing issues. Council members' offices can intervene with city agencies on your behalf, help escalate complaints about building conditions, connect you with legal services and tenant resources, and advocate for enforcement actions against non-compliant landlords.

When to contact them. Contact your Council member's office when you have filed complaints with city agencies and have not received a response, when building conditions are dangerous and enforcement has been slow, when you need help navigating the city bureaucracy, or when you want to report a pattern of landlord misconduct affecting multiple tenants in your building.

How to reach them.

To find your Council member: Visit council.nyc.gov and enter your address.

Your State Legislators (State Senator and Assembly Member)

What they do. Your State Senator and Assembly member represent you in Albany and can intervene with state agencies, including DHCR/HCR, on your behalf. They can help escalate stalled complaints, facilitate communication with state agencies, and connect you with resources.

When to contact them. Contact your state legislators when you have a pending complaint with DHCR that has been delayed, when you need help with a state-level housing issue, or when you want to advocate for changes to state tenant law.

How to reach them.

To find your State Senator: nysenate.gov.

To find your Assembly member: nyassembly.gov.

NEW YORK STATE ATTORNEY GENERAL

What they do. The Attorney General's office handles consumer protection matters, including complaints about security deposit violations, illegal fees, tenant harassment, and fraud. The AG's office investigates complaints, mediates disputes, and can take enforcement action against landlords who engage in widespread or systematic violations.

When to contact them. Contact the Attorney General when your landlord has failed to return your security deposit and you want to file a formal complaint, when you have been charged illegal fees, when you believe your landlord is engaged in a pattern of fraudulent or deceptive conduct, or when other enforcement channels have not resolved the issue.

How to reach them.

Phone: 800-771-7755.

Online complaint form: ag.ny.gov (search "File a Complaint").

A NOTE ON USING THESE RESOURCES

Many of these organizations experience high call volumes and limited capacity. You may not reach someone on your first attempt. Be persistent. Try during different hours. Try multiple organizations. If you leave a message, include your name, phone number, a brief description of your issue, and whether you have a court date approaching.

When you call, have the following information ready: your name, your address and apartment number, the name of your landlord or management company, a brief description of your issue, whether you have received any legal notices or court papers, and whether you have a court date (and if so, when).

The sooner you contact these resources, the more options you will have. Do not wait until you are in crisis if you can help it. Early engagement with legal services, tenant hotlines, and city agencies consistently produces better outcomes than last-minute intervention.

Appendix E

Decision Trees

The following decision trees walk you through four common tenant scenarios using simple yes-or-no questions. They are designed to be used under stress, when you need a quick assessment of your situation before seeking professional help.

These decision trees are diagnostic tools, not legal conclusions. A "yes" or "no" at the end of a flowchart tells you the likely direction of your situation, but specific facts can change the outcome. Use these trees to orient yourself, then consult an attorney or tenant hotline for confirmation.

Each tree ends with a recommended next step and a reference to the chapter that covers the topic in detail.

Decision Tree 1: Is My Apartment Rent-Stabilized?

Start here.

Was your building constructed before 1974?

If no, proceed to the next question. If yes, does your building contain six or more residential units? If yes, your apartment is likely rent-stabilized unless it was lawfully deregulated before the HSTPA (June 2019). Request your rent history from DHCR to confirm. Even if the landlord says it was deregulated, verify the claim. Many pre-HSTPA deregulations are being successfully challenged. See Chapter 5 for the request process and Chapter 4 for how stabilization works. If the building has fewer than six units, proceed to the next question.

Did your building receive a 421-a, J-51, or other tax benefit at any time?

If yes, your apartment may be rent-stabilized for the duration of the benefit period, regardless of when the building was constructed or how many units it has. Check HPD and Department of Finance records for tax benefit status. If the benefit has expired, consult an attorney about whether stabilization continues. If no, proceed to the next question.

Has your landlord told you the apartment is not stabilized?

If yes, do not rely on that statement alone. Landlords frequently misrepresent stabilization status, sometimes intentionally and sometimes through ignorance. Request your rent history from DHCR regardless of what the landlord says. If DHCR records show the apartment was registered as stabilized at any point, investigate further. See Chapter 5. If no (the landlord has not addressed the question, or you have never asked), request your rent history. The records will answer the question definitively.

Did you receive a Rent Stabilization Lease Rider when you signed your lease?

If yes, your apartment is stabilized. The rider confirms the landlord's acknowledgment of the apartment's regulatory status. Keep the rider in a safe place. If no, the absence of the rider does not prove the apartment is unregulated. It may indicate that the landlord failed to provide a required document, which is itself a violation. Request your rent history from DHCR. See Chapter 8 for why the rider matters.

Does the rent seem unusually round or market-like for a building that appears old enough to be stabilized?

If your rent is a round number (like $2,000 or $2,500) in a prewar building with six or more units, the rent may have been set by the landlord rather than calculated through the regulatory process. Regulated rents are often irregular amounts (like $1,847.23) because they result from RGB percentage increases applied to prior rents. A round number is not proof of a problem, but it is worth investigating.

Bottom line. The only reliable way to determine whether your apartment is rent-stabilized is to request the rent history from DHCR. The process is free, takes two to four weeks, and does not require the landlord's permission. Do not rely on what the landlord says, what the lease says, what the listing said, or what the rent amount suggests. Check the records. See Chapter 5 for step-by-step instructions.

Decision Tree 2: Is This Eviction Notice Valid?

Start here. You have received a document from your landlord that appears to be related to eviction. Before evaluating the content, determine what type of document it is.

Is this a rent demand (a written demand for unpaid rent)?

If yes, proceed through the following questions.

Does the demand state the correct amount of rent you owe? Compare the demanded amount to the legal rent (in a stabilized apartment) or the lease rent (in an unregulated apartment). If the amount is higher than what you actually owe, the demand may be inflated and therefore defective. See Chapter 20.

Does the demand include late fees? If yes, are the late fees within the legal cap (the lesser of $50 or 5 percent of monthly rent)? Were any late fees charged during the five-day grace period after rent was due? Fees above the cap or fees charged during the grace period are illegal. If they are included in the demand, the demand is inflated and potentially defective.

Does the demand include non-rent charges (attorney's fees, utility charges, repair costs, administrative fees)? If yes, these charges generally do not belong in a rent demand. Their inclusion may make the demand defective.

Does the demand identify the specific months or periods covered? A demand that states only a total without specifying periods may be defective.

Was the demand served at least 14 days before a court case was filed? If the landlord filed a petition before the 14-day period elapsed, the case is premature and may be dismissed.

Does the demand include the Good Cause Eviction notice (required since August 2024)? If not, the omission may be raised as a defect.

If you answered "no" to any of these questions, the demand may be defective. Consult an attorney. See Chapters 12 and 20.

Is this a notice to cure (identifying a lease violation and giving you time to fix it)?

If yes, proceed through the following questions.

Does the notice identify a specific lease provision you allegedly violated? If it is vague ("you are in violation of your lease" without specifying the clause or the conduct), it may be defective.

Is the alleged violation real? Read the lease clause cited. Does your conduct actually violate it?

Is the clause enforceable? Some clauses are overridden by law. No-pet clauses may be waived under the three-month rule. No-roommate clauses may be overridden by the Roommate Law. See Chapter 8.

Can you cure the violation? If yes, cure it immediately and document that you did so.

Has the landlord previously tolerated this same condition without objection? If yes, the sudden enforcement may support a retaliation or waiver defense. See Chapters 19 and 26.

If you answered "no" to any of the first three questions, or "yes" to the last question, the notice may be defective or the landlord's case may be weak. Consult an attorney. See Chapter 12.

Is this a termination notice or notice of non-renewal?

If yes, proceed through the following questions.

Does the notice state a reason for termination? If your apartment is rent-stabilized or covered by Good Cause, a reason is required. If no reason is stated, the notice may be defective.

Is the stated reason a legally recognized ground for eviction? Valid grounds include nonpayment, substantial lease violations, nuisance, owner use, and withdrawal from the rental market. "I want a higher-paying tenant" and "your lease expired" are not valid grounds in covered apartments. See Chapter 10.

Does the notice provide the correct notice period? For tenants with less than one year of occupancy: at least 30 days. One to two years: at least 60 days. Two years or more: at least 90 days. For rent-stabilized Golub Notices: 150 to 90 days before lease expiration. Count from the date of service, not the date on the notice.

Does the notice correctly identify you and the landlord? Errors in party names can create jurisdictional problems.

Does the notice include the Good Cause Eviction notice? If not, the omission may be a defect.

If you answered "no" to any of these questions, the notice may be defective. Consult an attorney. See Chapters 10, 11, and 12.

Is this court papers (a petition and notice of petition)?

If yes, you have a court date. Do not miss it. Attend the court date, request an attorney through the Right to Counsel program, and bring all documents related to your tenancy (your lease, all notices received, rent payment records, and any photographs or correspondence). See Chapter 13 and Appendix C.

For all notice types, check service.

How was the notice delivered? Was it handed to you personally, left with someone else, or taped to your door?

If it was left with someone or taped to your door, was a copy also mailed? Both steps are required for substituted and conspicuous place service.

If it was taped to your door, were prior personal delivery attempts made and documented? Conspicuous place service without documented prior attempts is defective.

Was the server someone other than the landlord? In many situations, the landlord cannot serve the notice personally.

If you answered "no" to any of these service questions, the service may be defective, which is an independent ground for dismissal regardless of the notice's content. See Chapter 12.

Bottom line. Do not move out based on a notice alone. A notice is not a court order. You are not required to leave until a court issues a judgment of possession and a marshal serves a warrant of eviction. Evaluate the notice using the questions above, and consult an attorney as soon as possible. See Chapter 12 for a complete analysis of notice requirements and Appendix C for the detailed eviction notice checklist.

Decision Tree 3: Can My Landlord Keep My Security Deposit?

Start here. You have moved out of your apartment and your landlord has either kept your security deposit, returned only a partial amount, or has not communicated at all.

Has it been more than 14 days since you vacated?

If yes and the landlord has not returned the deposit or provided an itemized statement, the landlord has missed the statutory deadline. This is a significant violation. The landlord may have forfeited the right to claim any deductions at all, regardless of whether actual damage existed. Proceed to the demand letter step below. See Chapter 14.

If no (it has been fewer than 14 days), wait for the deadline to pass. The landlord has the full 14 days to act. Mark your calendar for day 15.

Did the landlord provide an itemized statement of deductions?

If no statement was provided and the full deposit was kept or a partial refund was sent with no explanation, the landlord has failed to meet the itemization requirement. This failure, combined with missing the 14-day deadline, severely weakens the landlord's position. Proceed to the demand letter step.

If a statement was provided, evaluate each deduction using the questions below.

For each deduction on the statement, ask the following.

Is the deduction for routine repainting? If yes, was the repainting necessitated by specific tenant-caused damage (not normal fading, discoloration, or nail holes)? If the repainting was routine turnover maintenance, the charge is almost certainly illegal. See Chapter 15.

Is the deduction for cleaning? If yes, was the apartment left in a condition significantly worse than normal end-of-tenancy condition? Would the landlord have hired cleaners anyway before the next tenant moved in? If the cleaning was routine turnover cleaning, the charge is likely illegal.

Is the deduction for repairs? If yes, does the statement describe the specific damage and the specific repair? Vague descriptions like "general repairs" or "maintenance" do not satisfy the itemization requirement. Is the claimed damage something that existed before you moved in? Do you have move-in photographs that show the condition was pre-existing? Is the cost reasonable, or does it appear inflated?

Is the deduction for normal wear and tear (faded paint, worn carpet, minor scuffs, aging fixtures)? If yes, the deduction is illegal. Normal wear and tear is the landlord's responsibility.

Was the original deposit more than one month's rent? If yes, the excess was illegally collected and is recoverable regardless of the deduction analysis.

If any deductions are improper, take the following steps.

Send a demand letter requesting the return of the full deposit (or the improperly withheld portion) within 14 days. See Appendix B, Letter 3, for the template.

If the landlord does not respond to the demand letter, file a claim in small claims court. Bring your lease, your move-out photographs, the landlord's itemized statement (or documentation that none was received), your demand letter and the certified mail receipt, and any other relevant evidence.

If the deductions were improper and the withholding appears to be in bad faith (obviously illegitimate charges, no documentation, missed deadline, pattern of similar conduct), request treble damages in your court filing. See Chapter 15 for what constitutes bad faith and how treble damages work.

Bottom line. The landlord's right to keep any portion of your deposit depends on three things: whether the deductions are for actual tenant-caused damage beyond normal wear and tear, whether the deductions are properly itemized, and whether the landlord acted within the 14-day deadline. Failure on any of these points shifts leverage to the tenant. See Chapters 14 and 15 for the complete analysis.

Decision Tree 4: Do I Have a Retaliation Claim?

Start here. Your landlord has taken an adverse action against you, and you believe it may be connected to something you did to assert your legal rights.

Did you recently engage in a protected activity?

Protected activities include filing a complaint with a government agency (HPD, DHCR, 311, DOB, the Attorney General's office, or any other governmental body), requesting repairs from the landlord (in writing or verbally), reporting code violations or unsafe conditions, organizing with other tenants or participating in a tenant association, filing a legal proceeding (HP action, overcharge complaint, or any other case), exercising any legal right (requesting a renewal lease, demanding a rent stabilization rider, asserting Good Cause protections, declining a buyout, or requesting your rent history).

If you did not engage in any protected activity before the landlord's adverse action, retaliation is unlikely to apply (though other defenses may exist). If you did engage in a protected activity, proceed to the next question.

Did the landlord take an adverse action after your protected activity?

Adverse actions include commencing eviction proceedings (nonpayment or holdover), refusing to renew your lease, increasing your rent (in situations where the increase is discretionary), reducing or eliminating services (heat, hot water, repairs, building amenities), entering your apartment without authorization or increasing surveillance, filing baseless court proceedings, refusing to make repairs that were previously handled routinely, or engaging in harassment.

If the landlord took no adverse action, you do not currently have a retaliation claim (though you may want to document the protected activity in case the landlord acts later). If the landlord did take an adverse action, proceed to the next question.

How much time passed between your protected activity and the landlord's adverse action?

If the adverse action occurred within six months of the protected activity, the statutory presumption of retaliation applies. The burden shifts to the landlord to prove that the action was taken for a legitimate, non-retaliatory reason. This is a strong position for the tenant. See Chapter 19.

If the adverse action occurred more than six months after the protected activity, the statutory presumption does not apply automatically. You can still prove retaliation, but you bear the full burden of showing retaliatory motive through circumstantial evidence (timing, the landlord's pattern of conduct, statements by the landlord, the absence of any legitimate reason for the action, and similar evidence). The claim is harder but not impossible. Consult an attorney to evaluate the strength of the evidence.

Did the landlord have a legitimate, non-retaliatory reason for the action?

This is the question the court will ultimately evaluate. Consider the following.

Had the landlord previously tolerated the condition that is now the basis for the adverse action? If the landlord never enforced a lease clause before your protected activity and suddenly began enforcing it afterward, the timing suggests retaliation.

Is the landlord treating you differently from other tenants in the same building? If other tenants have the same condition (a pet, a roommate, a minor lease variation) and only you are being targeted, the selective enforcement suggests retaliation.

Did the landlord's behavior change in any other way after your protected activity? Increased scrutiny, more frequent visits, hostile communications, reduced responsiveness to repair requests, all of these changes in pattern can support a retaliation inference.

Has the landlord made any statements suggesting retaliatory intent? Comments like "you shouldn't have called the city" or "this is what happens when tenants complain" are direct evidence of motive.

If the landlord has no credible non-retaliatory explanation and the timing supports an inference of retaliation, you likely have a viable claim.

What should you do?

Document the timeline. Create a written chronology showing the date of your protected activity, the date of the landlord's adverse action, and the time between them. Preserve all evidence of both events.

Document the change in the landlord's behavior. Note any differences between how the landlord treated you before and after the protected activity. Save all communications.

If the retaliation takes the form of an eviction case, raise retaliation as an affirmative defense in your answer to the petition. The defense must be pleaded or it may be waived. See Chapter 19.

If the retaliation takes the form of conduct other than an eviction filing (service reductions, harassment, rent increases), consider filing an affirmative claim seeking damages, injunctive relief, and attorney's fees. See Chapter 19.

Consult a tenant attorney as soon as possible. Retaliation claims involve nuanced questions of timing, evidence, and strategy.

Bottom line. Retaliation is any adverse action motivated by your exercise of a legal right. If the action occurred within six months of a protected activity, the law presumes retaliation and the landlord must justify their conduct. The stronger your documentation of the timeline and the change in the landlord's behavior, the stronger your claim. See Chapter 19 for the complete analysis.

About the Author

Ngozi E. Bolin, Esq. has spent more than three decades in courtrooms, negotiation rooms, and the spaces in between where legal knowledge determines whether people keep what belongs to them or lose it by default.

Her career began under the British Commonwealth legal system, where she was admitted as a Barrister and Solicitor of the Supreme Court of Nigeria in 1989. She later relocated to the United States and was admitted to the New York State Bar in 1991, followed by admission to the United States Court of Appeals for the Second Circuit and the California State Bar in 2013. She has also studied at the Harvard Extension School, bringing an international and interdisciplinary perspective to her practice.

As a trial attorney, Ms. Bolin has worked across a wide range of legal areas, including consumer protection, real estate, contract disputes, employment law, unfair business practices, personal injury, bankruptcy, probate, and insurance litigation. Her professional record includes participation in significant cases addressing corporate misconduct, fiduciary duties, employee benefits, and unjust enrichment, including Louis Capital Markets, LP v. Refco Group Ltd., LLC, et al. (9 Misc.3d 283, 801 N.Y.S.2d 490, N.Y. Co. 2005), Giordano v. Thomson, et al. (438 F. Supp. 2d 35, E.D.N.Y. 2005), and Davis v. Commercial Bank of New York (275 F. Supp. 2d 418, S.D.N.Y. 2003).

Throughout her career, Ms. Bolin has been a consistent advocate for making the law accessible to the people who need it most. She has championed unbundled legal services, an approach that empowers consumers to understand and navigate the legal system without bearing the full cost of traditional representation. That philosophy is the foundation of this book.

Tenant Power: New York - A Renter's Plain-English Guide grew out of a conviction Ms. Bolin has carried through three decades of practice: that most people don't lose legal disputes because the law is against them. They lose because they don't know the law exists. The tenant who pays an illegal rent increase, the renter who moves out on a defective notice, the family that surrenders a rent-stabilized apartment without understanding what they're giving up, these outcomes happen not because the legal system failed, but because no one translated it into language that real people could use at the moment it mattered.

This book is that translation.

Ms. Bolin writes from the intersection of legal authority and practical experience, drawing on decades of litigation, negotiation, and client advocacy to produce a guide that respects the reader's intelligence without assuming legal training. The strategies in these pages are grounded in real courtrooms, real disputes, and real outcomes, not in theory.

She continues to practice law, to write, and to bridge the gap between what the law provides and what people actually know about it.

www.ingramcontent.com/pod-product-compliance
Lightning Source LLC
LaVergne TN
LVHW052027200926
848481LV00005B/1605
9798950322037